THE CAMBRIDGE COMPANION ͭ ͦ
# MONTAIGNE

Michel de Montaigne (1533–1592) is the author of a rich and varied philosophical and literary output which was influential in his lifetime and has continued to capture the attention of thinkers up to the present day. He made important philosophical contributions to ethics and skepticism, and his *Essays* had a significant impact on literary form. This volume brings together newly commissioned chapters on the full range of his work, and considers his relationship to his time and his lasting influence on other thinkers. New readers will find this the most convenient and accessible guide to Montaigne currently available. Advanced students and specialists will find a conspectus of recent developments in the interpretation of Montaigne.

ULLRICH LANGER is Professor of French and Senior Fellow, Institute for Research in the Humanities at the University of Wisconsin, Madison.

OTHER VOLUMES IN THE SERIES OF CAMBRIDGE COMPANIONS

ABELARD *Edited by* JEFFREY E. BROWER *and* KEVIN
   GUILFOY
ADORNO *Edited by* THOMAS HUHN
ANSELM *Edited by* BRIAN DAVIES *and* BRIAN LEFTOW
AQUINAS *Edited by* NORMAN KRETZMANN *and*
   ELENORE STUMP
ARABIC PHILOSOPHY *Edited by* PETER ADAMSON
   *and* RICHARD TAYLOR
HANNAH ARENDT *Edited by* DANA VILLA
ARISTOTLE *Edited by* JONATHAN BARNES
AUGUSTINE *Edited by* ELENORE STUMP *and*
   NORMAN KRETZMANN
BACON *Edited by* MARKKU PELTONEN
BRENTANO *Edited by* DALE JACQUETTE
CRITICAL THEORY *Edited by* FRED RUSH
SIMONE DE BEAUVOIR *Edited by* CLAUDIA CARD
DARWIN *Edited by* JONATHAN HODGE *and*
   GREGORY RADICK
DESCARTES *Edited by* JOHN COTTINGHAM
DUNS SCOTUS *Edited by* THOMAS WILLIAMS
EARLY GREEK PHILOSOPHY *Edited by* A. A. LONG
FEMINISM IN PHILOSOPHY *Edited by* MIRANDA
   FRICKER *and* JENNIFER HORNSBY
FOUCAULT *Edited by* GARY GUTTING
FREUD *Edited by* JEROME NEU
GALILEO *Edited by* PETER MACHAMER
GERMAN IDEALISM *Edited by* KARL AMERIKS
GREEK AND ROMAN PHILOSOPHY *Edited by*
   DAVID SEDLEY
HABERMAS *Edited by* STEPHEN K. WHITE
HEGEL *Edited by* FREDERICK BEISER
HEIDEGGER *Edited by* CHARLES GUIGNON
HOBBES *Edited by* TOM SORELL
HUME *Edited by* DAVID FATE NORTON
HUSSERL *Edited by* BARRY SMITH *and* DAVID
   WOODRUFF SMITH
WILLIAM JAMES *Edited by* RUTH ANNA PUTNAM
KANT *Edited by* PAUL GUYER

KIERKEGAARD *Edited by* ALASTAIR HANNAY *and* GORDON MARINO

LEIBNIZ *Edited by* NICHOLAS JOLLEY

LEVINAS *Edited by* SIMON CRITCHLEY *and* ROBERT BERNASCONI

LOCKE *Edited by* VERE CHAPPELL

MALEBRANCHE *Edited by* STEVEN NADLER

MARX *Edited by* TERRELL CARVER

MEDIEVAL JEWISH PHILOSOPHY *Edited by* DANIEL H. FRANK *and* OLIVER LEAMAN

MEDIEVAL PHILOSOPHY *Edited by* A. S. MCGRADE

MERLEAU-PONTY *Edited by* TAYLOR CARMAN *and* MARK HANSEN

MILL *Edited by* JOHN SKORUPSKI

NEWTON *Edited by* I. BERNARD COHEN *and* GEORGE E. SMITH

NIETZSCHE *Edited by* BERND MAGNUS *and* KATHLEEN HIGGINS

OCKHAM *Edited by* PAUL VINCENT SPADE

PASCAL *Edited by* NICHOLAS HAMMOND

PEIRCE *Edited by* CHERYL MISAK

PLATO *Edited by* RICHARD KRAUT

PLOTINUS *Edited by* LLOYD P. GERSON

QUINE *Edited by* ROGER F. GIBSON

RAWLS *Edited by* SAMUEL FREEMAN

THOMAS REID *Edited by* TERENCE CUNED *and* RENÈ VAN WOUDENBERG

ROUSSEAU *Edited by* PATRICK RILEY

BERTRAND RUSSELL *Edited by* NICHOLAS GRIFFIN

SARTRE *Edited by* CHRISTINA HOWELLS

SCHOPENHAUER *Edited by* CHRISTOPHER JANAWAY

THE SCOTTISH ENLIGHTENMENT *Edited by* ALEXANDER BROADIE

SPINOZA *Edited by* DON GARRETT

THE STOICS *Edited by* BRAD INWOOD

WITTGENSTEIN *Edited by* HANS SLUGA *and* DAVID STERN

*The Cambridge Companion to*
# MONTAIGNE

Edited by Ullrich Langer
*The University of Wisconsin, Madison*

CAMBRIDGE
UNIVERSITY PRESS

CAMBRIDGE UNIVERSITY PRESS
Cambridge, New York, Melbourne, Madrid, Cape Town, Singapore, São Paulo

Cambridge University Press
The Edinburgh Building, Cambridge CB2 2RU, UK

Published in the United States of America by Cambridge University Press, New York

www.cambridge.org
Information on this title: www.cambridge.org/9780521819534

First published 2005

Printed in the United Kingdom at the University Press, Cambridge

*A catalogue record for this book is available from the British Library*

*Library of Congress Cataloguing in Publication data*
The Cambridge companion to Montaigne / ed. Ullrich Langer.
    p. cm. – (Cambridge companions to philosophy)
Includes bibliographical references (p. ) and index.
ISBN 0-521-81953-9 – ISBN 0-521-52556-X (pb.)
    1. Montaigne, Michel de, 1533–1592.  I. Langer, Ullrich.   II. Series.
B785.M74C36   2005
194–dc22    2004062841

ISBN-13 978-0-521-81953-4 hardback
ISBN-10 0-521-81953-9 hardback
ISBN-13 978-0-521-52556-5 paperback
ISBN-10 0-521-52556-X paperback

What I chiefly portray is my cogitations, a shapeless subject that does not lend itself to expression in actions. It is all I can do to couch my thoughts in this airy medium of words. Some of the wisest and most devout men have lived avoiding all noticeable actions. My actions would tell more about [chance] than about me. They bear witness to their own part, not to mine, unless it be by conjecture and without certainty: they are samples which display only details. I expose myself entire: my portrait is a cadaver on which the veins, the muscles, and the tendons appear at a glance, each part in its place. One part of what I am was produced by a cough, another by a pallor or a palpitation of the heart – in any case dubiously. It is not my deeds that I write down; it is myself, it is my essence.

"Of Practice" (Montaigne, *Essays*, II.6, F274, V379)

# CONTENTS

*List of contributors*                                          page xi

*Acknowledgments*                                                    xiv

*Note on the text*                                                   xv

*Chronology*                                                         xvi

1   Introduction                                                      1
    ULLRICH LANGER

2   Montaigne's political and religious context                       9
    ULLRICH LANGER

3   Montaigne's legacy                                               27
    WARREN BOUTCHER

4   Montaigne and antiquity: fancies and grotesques                 53
    JOHN O'BRIEN

5   The *Essays* and the New World                                   74
    TOM CONLEY

6   Justice and the law: on the reverse side of
    the *Essays*                                                     96
    ANDRÉ TOURNON

7   Montaigne and the notion of prudence                            118
    FRANCIS GOYET

8   Montaigne and the truth of the schools                          142
    IAN MACLEAN

ix

x    Contents

9    The investigation of nature                           163
     GEORGE HOFFMANN

10   Montaigne and skepticism                              183
     ANN HARTLE

11   Montaigne on moral philosophy and the good life       207
     J. B. SCHNEEWIND

     *Bibliography*                                        229
     *Index*                                               238

# CONTRIBUTORS

WARREN BOUTCHER is Senior Lecturer in Renaissance Studies at the School of English and Drama, and Senior Visiting Scholar at the AHRB Centre of Editing Lives and Letters, both Queen Mary, University of London. His forthcoming publications include chapters on the early English reception of the *Essays* in *Montaigne et Shakespeare* (forthcoming, 2004) and on the modern reception in *Early Modern France*, volume 9. These are part of a book project entitled *The School of Montaigne: Essays and Agency in Early Modern Europe*.

TOM CONLEY is Professor in Romance Languages and in Visual and Environmental Studies at Harvard University. Author of *The Self-Made Map: Cartographic Writing in Early Modern France* (1996) and *L'Inconscient graphique* (2000), he is completing a study of topography and displacement in sixteenth-century France.

FRANCIS GOYET is Professor of French Literature at the Université Stendhal (Grenoble, France). He is a specialist in the history of rhetorics and poetics, with current research on the rhetorical practice of Jesuits and barristers (www.u-grenoble3.fr/rare/). His publications include *Traités de poétique et de rhétorique de la Renaissance* (1990, reissued 2000), *Le sublime du "lieu commun"* (1996), and a comprehensive commentary on Du Bellay's *Deffence et illustration de la langue françoyse* (2003). In the area of political theory, he is editor of *Devenir roi* (2001) and *L'éloge du prince* (2003).

ANN HARTLE is Professor of Philosophy at Emory University. Recent publications include *Michel de Montaigne: Accidental Philosopher* (2003), and articles on Montaigne in *Montaigne Studies, Philosophy and Literature, Faith and Philosophy*. She is currently writing a book on Montaigne and modern rationalism.

GEORGE HOFFMANN is Associate Professor in the Department of Romance Languages and Literatures at the University of Michigan. He is the author of *Montaigne's Career* (1998), editor of *New Biographical Criticism: The Making of Young of an Old Discipline* (2004), and has recently published "Anatomy of the Mass: Montaigne's 'Of cannibals,'" *Proceedings of the Modern Language Association of America* 117: 2 (2002), as well as contributing to the *Dictionnaire Montaigne* (2004).

ULLRICH LANGER is Professor of French at the University of Wisconsin, Madison. His publications include *Vertu du discours, discours de la vertu: Littérature et philosophie morale au XVIe siècle en France* (1999), *Perfect Friendship: Studies in Literature and Moral Philosophy from Boccaccio to Corneille* (1994); he is editor of *Au-delà de la* Poétique: *Aristote et la littérature de la Renaissance / Beyond the* Poetics: *Aristotle and Early Modern Literature* (2002). His current research centers on the notion of pleasure in Renaissance philosophy and literature.

IAN MACLEAN is Professor of Renaissance Studies in the University of Oxford and a Senior Research Fellow of All Souls College. Among his publications are *The Renaissance Notion of Woman* (1980, frequently reprinted), *Meaning and Interpretation in the Renaissance: The Case of Law* (1992), *Montaigne philosophe* (1996), *Logic, Signs and Nature in the Renaissance: The Case of Learned Medicine* (2001), and an edition of Cardano's *De libris propriis* (2004).

JOHN O'BRIEN is Professor of French at Royal Holloway College, University of London. Recent publications include: *Anacreon Redivivus* (1995), *Les Odes d'Anacréon de Remy Belleau* (1995), *Distant Voices Still Heard* (2000) and *La familia de Montaigne* (2001). He is currently working on the notion of the imagination in French Renaissance thought and literature.

J. B. SCHNEEWIND is Professor Emeritus in the Philosophy Department at Johns Hopkins University, where he has taught for more than twenty years. He has written numerous articles and is author of

*Sidgwick's Ethics and Victorian Moral Philosophy* (1977), and *The Invention of Autonomy: A History of Modern Moral Philosophy* (1998).

ANDRÉ TOURNON in Professor Emeritus at the University of Provence (Aix–Marseille I), where he taught French literature of the Renaissance. Editor since 1994 of the *Bulletin de la Société des Amis de Montaigne*, his publications include *Montaigne: la glose et l'essai* (1983, 2nd edn., 2000), *"En sens agile": Les acrobaties de l'Esprit selon Rabelais* (1995). He is editor of Montaigne's *Essais* (3 vols., Paris: Imprimerie Nationale, 1998, repr. 2003), in which the text divisions and punctuation of the last edition annotated by Montaigne are restored, and, with Hélène Moreau, of Béroalde de Verville, *Le Moyen de parvenir* (1984, 2nd edn., 2004). His current research includes a forthcoming study of the *Essays*, entitled *Route par ailleurs*, and another of Rabelais, entitled *Rire pour comprendre*.

# ACKNOWLEDGMENTS

I would like to express my gratitude to Noel Carroll, Philippe Desan, and Jan Miernowski for their help in the realization of this volume, and Peter Vantine for his translation of the essay by Francis Goyet. Hilary Gaskin of Cambridge University Press has been an exemplary editor.

Ullrich Langer

# NOTE ON THE TEXT

All references to Montaigne's *Essays* in this volume are to the page number in the translation by Donald M. Frame, *The Complete Essays of Montaigne* (Stanford: Stanford University Press, 1958), designated as *F*, and to the page number in the French edition by Pierre Villey, revised by Verdun-L. Saulnier (Paris: Presses Universitaires de France, 1965, and reprinted in the series "Quadrige"), designated as *V*. Occasionally the chronological "layer" of the text is indicated, as follows: A (the first edition of 1580, the first two books); B (the edition of 1588, in three books); C (Montaigne's handwritten annotations after 1588, on all three books). Square brackets indicate emendations of the Frame translation by the authors of the chapters.

# CHRONOLOGY

1533        Birth of Michel, son of Pierre Eyquem and Antoinette de Louppes, at the castle of Montaigne, on a noble estate bought by his great-grandfather Ramon, a wealthy merchant. The child learns Latin with a German tutor.

1539–48     Humanistic studies at the *Collège de Guyenne* in Bordeaux.

1556–57     Works at the *Cour des Aides* in Périgueux.

1557–70     Counselor at the *Chambre des Enquêtes* of the *Parlement* of Bordeaux.

1558        Encounters fellow jurist and future friend Etienne de La Boétie (see *Essays*, 1.28) at the *Parlement* of Bordeaux.

1563        Death of La Boétie.

1565        Marries Françoise de la Chassaigne, daughter of a wealthy bourgeois and parliamentarian Bordeaux family.

1568        Death of his father, Pierre. Michel is heir to the title and the estate of Montaigne. Throughout his life, he refers to himself as Michel de Montaigne.

1569        Montaigne publishes his translation of Raymond Sebond's *Liber creaturarum* (otherwise known as the *Natural Theology*) (see *Essays*, II.12).

1570        Publishes his edition of the works of Etienne de La Boétie.

1571        In February, he "retires" to his estate, to devote his time to its management and to his writings. His daughter Léonor is born in September. In October, he is received in the Order of Saint Michel.

| | |
|---|---|
| ca. 1572–3 | Begins composition of the *Essays*. |
| 1574 | Charged with a diplomatic mission to the royal army. |
| 1577 | Montaigne becomes *gentilhomme de la chambre* of Henri de Navarre. |
| 1578 | Begins to suffer from kidney stones. |
| 1580 | Publication of the first two books of the *Essays*. Referred to as [A]. |
| 1580–81 | Travels to Switzerland, Germany, Austria, and Italy (his travel journal will be published under the title *Journal de voyage de Montaigne* in 1774). |
| 1581 | Elected mayor of Bordeaux for a two-year term; he will be re-elected for another two-year term in 1583. |
| 1582 | Second edition of the *Essays*, with minor additions. |
| 1583 | Montaigne is involved in negotiations between the king and the leader of the Protestants, Henri de Navarre. |
| 1584 | Henri de Navarre visits Montaigne in his castle and spends two nights. |
| 1585 | First the civil wars, then the plague ravage the Périgord region. |
| 1588 | Publishes a further edition of the *Essays*, with the substantial addition of the third book, and various additions to the chapters of the first two books. Referred to as [B]. Montaigne travels to Paris to have his book printed; on the way he is robbed by bandits. He is briefly imprisoned in the Bastille by the ultra-Catholic *Ligueurs*. He meets Marie de Gournay, who becomes a friend and will act as editor of a posthumous edition of the *Essays*. |
| 1588 | Return to his estate in December. He demonstrates his loyalty to the crown in the civil conflicts. |
| 1592 | Death of Montaigne. He leaves behind a copy of the 1588 edition of the *Essays*, covered with marginal and intra-linear annotations, called the *Exemplaire de Bordeaux*. Referred to as [C]. A copy of this annotated book is edited and published in 1595 by Marie de Gournay. The *Exemplaire de Bordeaux* serves as the basis for modern editions. |

# 1 Introduction

"I am no philosopher" (III.9, F725, V950). Michel de Montaigne is no philosopher, on several counts, and proudly says so. Montaigne understands "philosopher" as someone indifferent to pain and pleasure, inhumanly (and sometimes comically) persistent in his convictions,[1] just like Pyrrho who finished saying what he had to say even when his interlocutors had left the room (II.29, F533, V705). In a different context, Montaigne imagines a philosopher suspended from the towers of the cathedral of Notre Dame in Paris, in a cage made of thin wire: although his reason tells him he will not fall, the philosopher will not be able to keep himself from being terrified by the sight of the space below him (II.12, F449, V594). Not only does Montaigne criticize philosophers for their inattentiveness to their own humanity, but he intentionally fashions his own writings to be unlike philosophy. Indeed, a reader who samples almost any one of the chapters of his *Essays* will be struck by several unsettling features of Montaigne's thought and writing:

1. Montaigne distrusts universal statements, and seems enamored of the exception, of the particular case ("but there are some who . . ."). We move from a general rule to an exception, then to an exception to the exception, until we seem to be left hanging. The impression of open-endedness that many chapters of the *Essays* convey[2] is linked to the author's willingness to indulge any sort of particular case.
2. Montaigne is also noted for his attention to the influence of the human body, and what we like to call the "human" element, on behavior and thought. The suspended philosopher can't avoid being terrified by the sight below his feet.

Montaigne's kidney stones figure prominently in his portrait of himself. The body has its beneficial ways, too. The emperor Otho resolves to kill himself one night: having made arrangements for the distribution of his wealth, having sharpened his sword, waiting for all his servants to go to bed he falls asleep, and sleeps so soundly that his servants are awakened by his snoring (1.44, F198, V271; the essay is aptly called "Of Sleep").

3. Finally, Montaigne "himself" is always present, also: rules, statements, observations undergo a sort of personal vetting. "As for me," Montaigne will write, and what is right for himself, he readily concedes, is not necessarily right for anyone else (although it could be . . .). The *Essays* are definitely the recordings of the thoughts of a particular man living a particular life, and Montaigne is rather cocky in insisting on just that.

Given these features of his writing, Montaigne is certainly *not* a philosopher in the way in which the sixteenth century understood the practice of contemporary philosophy. His *Essays* are not written in the form of a treatise: that is, there is no attempt at systematic coverage of a topic, according to the questions or categories inherited from the tradition. The closest we come to this is the "Apology for Raymond Sebond," but this chapter is set in the context of chapters quite evidently not systematic at all. He has not written a commentary, say, on Aristotle's *Nicomachean Ethics*. Nor has he engaged in a scholastic dispute, defending his conclusions on questions set up in the schools, such as the relationship between God's will and creation. Nor has he written a dialogue, another form practiced in the sixteenth century in rather inaccurate imitation of Plato's dialogues. The philosophical writing he comes closest to is Plutarch's *Moralia*, essays (or what we call essays today) on different topics loosely organized, and not always covering what today we would call strictly ethical questions. What distinguishes Montaigne, though, is his persistently personal perspective, the "study" of himself as the goal of his enterprise. Yet the *Essays* are not an autobiography, in the sense of a chronological account of his experiences, and he does not give his writings an encompassing providential perspective: Montaigne is not the Christian wayfarer, and he is not the former sinner set on the right path. Montaigne practices "inwardness," an unabashed attentiveness to one's self, but without any obvious sense of exemplarity, refusing explicitly to be a lesson to anyone else. This often disarming, unsystematic revealing of Montaigne's own judgments, tastes, bodily functions constitutes the ground of what can be called the modern "self," the recentering of esthetic, epistemological, and social reflection in the subject.[3]

Although it has become customary to refer to the individual chapters of the *Essays* as "essays," Montaigne himself never refers to a single chapter as an "essay." He does refer to the entire book as his "essays," and he does speak of his "essays" in a non-specific way. That is because the term *essai* in sixteenth-century French does not refer to a delineated segment of text, but instead retains the senses of "attempt," "trying-out," "test," "practice," "assay" that are still present in the French verb *essayer* (to try, to attempt, to taste) today. His book is full of all sorts of "attempts." He tries out all sorts of judgments, of observations, of reflections, and of arguments. But these judgments, observations, reflections, arguments are all as it were suspended: they are not meant to be the final word on the matter. They are usually juxtaposed – sometimes directly, sometimes at a certain remove – with statements saying the contrary. In most cases Montaigne does not claim universal validity for his statements; he insists on the fact that they are the product of his own judgment, and that another might judge differently. This skeptical meaning underlies Montaigne's use of the word "essay." Each individual chapter might contain, then, several "essays," several instances in which Montaigne "tries out" his judgment. Although arguably this skeptical tenor of the essay connects to ancient skepticism, in particular the philosophy of Pyrrho as transmitted by Sextus Empiricus,[4] Montaigne distinguishes himself above all from the sort of philosophy practiced during his lifetime. From this perspective, too, he is not a "philosopher."

Yet Montaigne was a philosopher, in a way, and several chapters in this volume are meant to bring out the philosophical elements of Montaigne's writings, whether they arise from the skeptical tradition, from Epicurean concerns, or from the Greek and Roman moral tradition. Others place Montaigne into an intellectual context that is his own, a context which inflects the philosophical arguments and ideas that form the main body of his philosophical thought.

Montaigne's legal training and thought, his (or the Renaissance's) conception of authorship, his position as a "modern" vis-à-vis the classical tradition as a whole, and his reaction to the New World all influence the philosophical thought we would like to glean from the *Essays*. For more so than any other philosopher before him, this philosophical writer is inseparably, indelibly linked as a particular person with his "message."

That particular person was part of a society that experienced at times catastrophic changes. The initial chapter is meant to convey an understanding of the social, political, and religious context in which Montaigne lived and wrote his essays.

Warren Boutcher's chapter analyzes the meaning that writing, owning, and giving a book had in the aristocratic culture of the sixteenth century. The book was largely composed and used for social purposes that had no necessary link to the author's own existential relationship to his text. Montaigne's innovation consists in a freedom of judgment judiciously displayed, a sense of personal attention if not adherence to what he composes, making the book less a transmitter of social and cultural authority than a record of self-knowledge. This opens the way for a new kind of philosophizing, where a Descartes, for example, will feel free to test and reject philosophical tradition.

John O'Brien tackles a feature of Montaigne's writing that strikes any modern reader: the omnipresence of classical antiquity in the *Essays*. Classical allusions, examples, quotations, and themes abound. O'Brien focuses on three questions within this area: the use of quotations, the choice of a philosophy, and the choice of models of conduct. Montaigne often reaches to antiquity to illustrate a point he is making, and it is worthwhile checking the quotation in its original context, for the Renaissance writer as often distorts the meaning as not. This is a productive distortion, shedding light on Montaigne's deeper concerns. Pyrrhonism is for Montaigne a rather attractive philosophy, but not only because of its propositions (or lack thereof), but also because it relates to the type of writing that the *Essays* represent. Finally, O'Brien indicates an ethical use of antiquity, as Montaigne chooses models of conduct among the numerous lives of famous men that the Renaissance so eagerly read.

Montaigne's *Essays* are one of the first documents in European culture to weigh the cultural and epistemological consequences of the discovery and exploration of the New World. There are several travel accounts available to the European reader before Montaigne, and there is an ardent defense of the Indians, coupled with an indictment of the Spanish, before Montaigne as well.[5] But the essayist is the first to explore with sensitivity and sophistication the challenge of the New World to Europe's sense of itself. Tom Conley's chapter investigates the two main discussions of the New World in the *Essays*, "Of Cannibals" and "Of Coaches," relating them to the themes of Otherness and friendship, both of which are fundamental to the *Essays* as a whole.

One of the salient themes of the *Essays* is the condemnation of laws, lawyers, and legal thinking. In spite of his avowed conservatism and resistance to social and theological reforms, Montaigne persistently attacked the French legal system. Montaigne himself received a legal education and had an essentially legal career in Périgueux and as counselor to the *Parlement* of Bordeaux. André Tournon argues that this legal experience is essential to understanding both Montaigne's rejection of dogmatism and the sort of philosophical writing that the essay represents. In concluding Tournon demonstrates the ultimate importance of subjective judgment, and thus of the self, for the conception in the *Essays* of what is just.

In a rather different perspective, one that goes beyond the Pyrrhonism present in the *Essays*, Francis Goyet argues that the *Essays* are the record of judgments, and specifically judgments of someone who styles himself as a "prudent" man, someone who, like Machiavelli, has an understanding of the art of statecraft and what is necessary to practice it. The classical notion of prudence is the key to this understanding. This means that Montaigne, on Goyet's count, is indeed fashioning a product, a book that is meant to have an "ethical" impact on the prince or on the noble elite in whose circle Montaigne moved. In this Goyet demonstrates that, in contrast to some current views, the *Essays* do not undermine any attempt at action in the world through their self-destructive skepticism and subjectivism.

Ian Maclean situates Montaigne's philosophical thought within the logic and epistemology of his time. Whereas his writing is notoriously unsystematic and hardly conforms to the formats through which philosophical argumentation was conducted, Montaigne does consider – and usually critiques – the language, criteria, and definitions of university philosophy. His skepticism towards "the epistemological virtues of objectivity, certainty and universality" is withering, but in the end the essayist is more pragmatic, more focused on action within the contingent and highly diverse world than his skepticism seems to entail. This is particularly true of his use of something like the notion of equity, of his praise (and apparently practice) of discussion, and true of his self-presentation in all its diverse details.

Although Montaigne does not call himself a "skeptic," he does call himself a "naturalist." George Hoffmann examines this term within the empirical investigation of nature as it was practiced in the sixteenth century. A naturalist is someone interested in natural causes, not divine ones, and for Montaigne this meant the study of cause and effects, as opposed to the analysis of means and ends. However, Montaigne submits such a study to skeptical examination, and according to Hoffmann found instead inspiration in Lucretius' *De rerum natura* which he annotated and whose physics of "accident" and "fortune" he used to explain natural *mental* phenomena, such as the process of judgment and even the meeting of Montaigne and his idealized friend Etienne de La Boétie.

Ann Hartle examines Montaigne's skepticism. Hartle surveys classical skepticism and summarizes the skeptical arguments in the "Apology for Raymond Sebond," undoubtedly the most traditionally philosophical of Montaigne's chapters. But Hartle also details several ways in which Montaigne cannot be understood to be a skeptic: his credulity, the fact that indeed he advances judgments, his project of self-knowledge, his rejection of the ideal of imperturbability, and his insistence on his Catholic faith. These features of his thought are an element in the dialectic characteristic of Montaigne's "accidental" philosophy, according to Hartle, a dialectic that is open to the accidental and the strange, that finds the unfamiliar in the familiar, then returns better to grasp the familiar.

The important subject of Montaigne's moral philosophy is treated by Jerome B. Schneewind. The models that Montaigne was dealing with were Raymond Sebond's natural theology and the different moral philosophies of antiquity, most notably Senecan Stoicism. Montaigne rejects the confident derivation of moral laws from humans' place in the hierarchy of beings that characterizes Sebond, as he demonstrates how similar we are to creatures inferior to us in that hierarchy. Montaigne also insists that we practice a moral life,

not simply theorize it. He rejects the Senecan, and generally classical, proposing of rules or ideals so difficult to attain that few human
beings can live a moral life. Schneewind sees Montaigne as sketching
out an alternative, an acknowledgment that desires and their satisfaction are limitlessly diverse, but that each human being can arrive
at a critical judgment of what is good, within him or herself. This
points the way to more modern, and especially Kantian notions of
morality. It also ties in with the conclusion of Tournon's chapter,
and illuminates a fundamental aspect of Montaigne's composition
of the "self."

Whether we focus on Montaigne's skepticism, on his notions of
the good life, of the virtues of justice and prudence, on his concept
of authorship, or on his empirical curiosity, we are struck by the
charm, the seductiveness of his inquiries and of his self-presentation.
In part, this charm derives from the reader's *impression*, justified or
not, that in most chapters of the *Essays* Montaigne is not writing
in order to convince us of a particular thesis, that he is not trying
to put forth an argument. He is not the school-master type. This
very style of philosophizing endeared him to many, philosophers and
non-philosophers alike, such that Nietzsche could say: "That such a
human being has written, truly increases one's desire to live on this
earth."[6]

NOTES

1.  He goes on to say: "Evils [*maux*] crush me according to their weight,
    and their weight depends on their form as much as on their matter, and
    often more." Unlike the Stoics and the Epicureans, not only can he not
    claim to have attained a true tranquility of the soul, impervious to pain
    and (excessive) pleasure, but he also isn't sure that this tranquility is
    worth attaining for himself.
2.  In fact, Montaigne was a highly careful writer who edited his own writ-
    ings extensively and was even involved in details such as punctuation
    (which for much of the sixteenth century was often haphazard).
3.  See Charles Taylor, *Sources of the Self: The Making of the Modern Iden-
    tity* (Cambridge, MA: Harvard University Press, 1989), and his pages on
    Montaigne, pp. 177–84.
4.  See the work of Emmanuel Naya, in particular *"La loy de pure
    obeïssance": le pyrrhonisme à l'essai chez Montaigne* (Paris: Champion,
    2004).

5. See Bartolomé de Las Casas, *In Defense of the Indians*, trans. Stafford Poole, C. M. (DeKalb: Northern Illinois University Press, 1992).

6. Nietzsche is comparing Montaigne to Schopenhauer (in "Schopenhauer als Erzieher," *Unzeitgemässe Betrachtungen* [1874], in *Werke in sechs Bände*, ed. K. Schlechta, Munich, Carl Hanser, 1980, vol. 1, p. 296).

# 2 Montaigne's political and religious context

Montaigne was born in 1533, during the reign of François I
(1515–47), but he did not begin writing his *Essays* until after his
"retirement" to his estate in 1571, as a mature man. France seemed
then a country very different from the heady days of François I. For
much of the second half of the sixteenth century, and especially so
in the southwest, it was a "disturbed and sick state," as Montaigne
himself remarked (III.8, F719, V941).[1] Many factors contributed to
this experience and to this perception, most obviously the wars
of religion (1562–98), which were fought intermittently, with varying intensity and with varying geographical extension.[2] However,
the religious conflict between Huguenots and Catholics was only
one of the factors inducing a sense of fragility and contingency in
French society. The sixteenth century witnessed a remarkable set of
political and religious changes, fuelled by an early economic expansion which produced exceptional social mobility at the upper levels
(from which Montaigne's own family benefited). On the political
level, the religious conflict enabled a critique and a corresponding
defence of the monarchy which in theory at least became a guarantor of order in a troubled society. Montaigne's political functions
as magistrate, mayor of Bordeaux for two successive terms (1581–5),
and administrator of his domain,[3] and his involvement in mediation attempts between the warring factions and in diplomatic mis-
sions at the highest level,[4] exposed him both to the local consequences of conflict and to the issues relevant to the direction of the
ship of state.

9

## THE RELIGIOUS CONFLICT AND ITS POLITICAL REPERCUSSIONS

The wars of religion in France had roots in the religious reform movement that spread across Europe in the early sixteenth century.[5] The French version originally encouraged reform (rather than rejection) of the Catholic Church by emphasizing the unadulterated teachings of the New Testament, and by proclaiming salvation by faith as opposed to good works channelled through church-sponsored practices. The impetus of this reform movement was provided by the new availability of a French translation of the New Testament (by Jacques Lefèvre d'Etaples, 1523), by preaching and lay Bible study, by the sympathy, initially at least, of the king François I, and by the enduring support of his sister, Marguerite de Navarre. However, Luther's virulent writings against the Roman Catholic Church were available in France from 1519 onwards, and in 1521 they were condemned by the Faculty of Theology of the University of Paris. The imprudent actions of reformist preachers (most notably during the "Affaire des placards" [1534], an attempt to spread anti-Catholic teachings through public posters in French cities), hardened royal policy towards the early reform movement. Their leaders within the Church, such as the bishop of Meaux, Guillaume Briçonnet, had in fact rejoined the fold earlier. However the seeds had been sown. In the following years the combination of a more radical spirit of reform, fostered by the publications of John Calvin (1509–1564), especially his *Institution de la religion chrétienne*,[6] and aided politically by the support of some of the French nobility to the reform movement, made it clear that the reformers were unwilling simply to ameliorate this or that practice of the Catholic Church. Their doctrinal positions, in any event, were drastically opposed to ecclesiastical tradition: they believed in the absolute priority of God's grace over human good works, predestination of the elect and even reprobation of the damned, universal priesthood (all Christians have equal status in the view of God in relation to the practice of their faith), and the modification of the Catholic view of the Eucharist, whereby the bread is transformed into the spiritual – not the physical – body of Christ not by the formula of consecration but by the sole grace of God at the moment of communion with the faithful. Calvin, mostly from his outpost in Geneva, was also able to organize a political party which operated in France and provided a structure to the French "Protestants." After 1560 they came to be called "Huguenots": the name is probably a phonetic imitation of the Swiss German "Eidgenossen," which denoted confederates sworn to an alliance, originally to defend the city of Geneva against the duke of Savoy.

The violent conflicts of the second half of the sixteenth century were motivated primarily by the differences in religious faith, but the military aspect of the conflict was often more complicated, as clientele arrangements and "friendships" between noble families traversed confessional differences. For example, during the battle of Coutras, alongside the Huguenots Henri de Navarre and Henri de Condé one finds Catholic nobles (Frédéric de Foix, François de Conti, and Charles de Soissons); Montaigne's younger brother, Bertrand de Mattecoulon, who, like Montaigne himself, remained Catholic, also fought in Henri de Navarre's army. Thus, although the troops might have believed themselves to be defending the faith first and foremost (indeed, Huguenot troops often marched into battle singing the Psalms, recently translated into French), in fact the wars came to be as much civil as religious wars. Foreign support (from England, the United Provinces, Spain, and German Protestant princes) increased the scale of violence and the suffering of the local populations, who were exposed to pillaging and devastation by foreign soldiers forced to live off the land.

Another complicating factor was the heterogeneity of the Catholic camp. From the beginning of the reign of Charles IX (1561–74), certain Catholics were horrified by the Protestants' iconoclasm, by their profanation of the Eucharistic host, and by their ridiculing of Catholic rituals. They began forming associations (ligues) in defence of the Catholic faith and in obeisance to the king (although only if he was faithful to the religion of his forefathers). The most important of these was created in 1584 by the Guise family, who in addition formed an alliance with the Spanish to ensure that royal succession would never pass to a Huguenot. The leader of the Huguenots Henri de Navarre (later Henri IV), according to interpretations of the Salic law of male primogeniture, was next in line to the throne after Henri III (1574–89), who like his brothers remained without male offspring. Parallel to this "aristocratic" Ligue there was a popular one, founded in Paris in the same year, which was more radical and more strictly religious (whereas some of the aristocratic Ligue's impetus was purely political, in reaction to threats to their members' privileges). The Parisian *Ligue*'s discontent with royal concessions to the Huguenots and their admiration for Henri de Guise led to open revolt against the king. On May 12–13, 1588, *Ligueurs* and sympathizers barricaded the streets of the city, forcing the king to negotiate the freedom of the troops he had sent to pacify Paris.[7] This act of treason in turn provoked Henri III's revenge, and he ordered the murder of the duke of Guise and his brother in December of the same year. Henri III's subsequent assassination in August 1589 by the Dominican monk Jacques Clément was felt by the *Ligue* to be an act of God.

Whereas the Catholic *Ligues* constituted the gravest challenge to royal authority, outside of the Huguenots themselves, the conflicts spawned other political factions, most notably the *Malcontents*, who were aristocrats literally "disappointed" by the monarchy's lack of respect for their positions, their service, and the "ancient laws of France." They were a loosely connected group, led by François d'Alençon, Henri de Condé, and other important nobles, and they forged a temporary alliance with the Huguenots during the fifth war of religion (1574–6). But the troubled monarchy also found defenders after 1568, and increasingly during the final decades of conflict, who preferred peace to an eradication of the Huguenots. Their name – the *Politiques* – was not complimentary, since it meant someone willing to compromise his principles, and the name implied that they were inspired by the infamous Machiavelli. They were a group of moderate Catholics, some highly educated and often of bourgeois background, who initially enjoyed the protection of Catherine de' Medici's chancellor Michel de l'Hospital (ca. 1505–1573). Many famous men of erudition, including the historiographer Estienne Pasquier and Montaigne himself, were associated with this movement.

According to *Politique* thinkers, only a strong monarchy could ensure order in these troubled times. During these decades there emerged what was later called absolutist political theory: sixteenth-century theorists use the term "absolute monarchy."[8] The most notable exposition is found in Jean Bodin's *Six livres de la république* (1576).[9] The sovereign, by virtue of the functioning of true sovereignty itself and of the power given to him by God, cannot be bound by the laws he lays down, but only by divine and natural law. Theories of sovereignty connect with justifications of extraordinary measures necessary to save the state ("raison d'état," a superior political calculation based on knowledge not available to ordinary subjects), and only the king by a sublime act of prudence can take these measures. On the other side, political thinkers who opposed the unbridled government of the realm by a single person, characterized later as the *monarchomaques* (a term coined in 1600 by William Barclay), believed in the sovereignty of the people, organized and represented by the assemblies of the estates. They thought that the people should decide on war and peace and hold power of legislation. The people had delegated its power to the king and in the event that the king did not hold to his promises (to respect the lives, possessions and liberties of his subjects, and to defend traditional laws and customs of the realm), the people had the right to resist, and in extreme cases to kill, the tyrannical king. Montaigne's friend Etienne de La Boétie (1530–1563) wrote a brief treatise in this spirit, *De la servitude volontaire*, that was later used by Protestant political thinkers during the religious conflicts. The first *monarchomaques* were Huguenots,[10] but as ultra-Catholic hostility to Henri III increased and the succession of the Protestant Henri de Navarre to the throne became a real possibility, this contractual thinking was found among Catholics as well.[11]

## VIOLENCE AND MASSACRES

Even if they were sporadic, the wars of religion were above all an incredibly wrenching experience. The intensity of the violence is reflected in literature and historiography of the period. One of the most striking examples is the Huguenot Agrippa d'Aubigné's epic of the wars of religion, *Les Tragiques* (published in 1616, but probably composed starting in 1572): the poet provides detailed descriptions of the horrors inflicted upon the population by marauding soldiers, including scenes of half-dead peasant families begging d'Aubigné for a *coup de grâce* (the poet figure, a combatant himself, is witness). The rivers of France are described as choked with maimed corpses. Even more sober historical accounts comprise the most graphic violence, such as Jean de Léry's account of the famine provoked by the siege of Sancerre (1573), whose population was reduced to acts of cannibalism. Fanatical polemics were conducted on both sides.[12] Descriptions and images of the massacres spread through the new medium of printing, in pamphlet literature, and through woodcuts and engravings, such as the prints of Jacques Tortorel and Jean Perissin (collected and published around 1570). Parallel to the violence caused by the religious conflict, France in the sixteenth and seventeenth centuries witnessed a marked increase in the persecution of witches, spawning literature on their identification and punishment, and cases of mass hysteria.[13]

Foremost among the atrocities connected with the religious conflict was the St. Bartholomew's massacre (August 24, 1572).[14] As a culmination of her efforts at reconciling the warring factions, Catherine de' Medici had invited Huguenot leaders to Paris to celebrate the wedding of Marguerite de Valois (Charles IX's sister) and Henri de Navarre. After the wedding ceremonies had taken place, during the night of August 23-4, the king arrived at the decision to execute a limited number of Huguenot nobles, undoubtedly believing them to be seditious. The royal troops surrounding the noblemen proceeded to do so, but the news of the executions reached the Parisian populace, inflamed by anti-Protestant preaching, and a general massacre ensued, devastating the Huguenot community of Paris. Bodies were stripped naked, mutilated, and thrown into the Seine. The massacres continued throughout France into the fall of 1572, spreading as far as Bordeaux, Toulouse, and Albi. Estimates of the total number of deaths vary widely; modern historians tend to accept the approximate number of 10,000. The St. Bartholomew's massacre marked the mentality of French Protestantism profoundly; the religious persecution produced vast numbers of martyrs, recorded and celebrated by the faithful. Huguenots were not entirely innocent of massacres themselves. The most famous occurred in the city of Nîmes at the beginning of the second war of religion (September 30 – October 1, 1567), when Catholics were killed and thrown into wells by the Huguenot majority. The scale of the "Michelade," as this massacre was called, was however not comparable (according to contemporary accounts there were up to 200 victims, but according to modern scholarship possibly as few as two dozen).

It is not until well after Montaigne's death in 1592 that a lasting peace was achieved. The newly Catholic king Henri IV (he converted in 1593 and was crowned in 1594) was able to subdue the final *Ligue* military resistance, make peace with Spain, and arrive at a settlement between Catholics and Huguenots. The

Edict of Nantes (1598), while stopping short of equal status for the Huguenots and intending an eventual reintegration of Protestantism into the Catholic Church, gave them many rights, places of worship, and protection.

## MONTAIGNE THE "BOURGEOIS GENTLEMAN"

Michel de Montaigne was a nobleman, owned a castle on noble land, and never hesitated to proclaim the validity of his noble ancestry.[15] Yet he was of very "recent" nobility. His great-grandfather Ramon Eyquem, having enriched himself in commerce, bought the noble domain of Montaigne in 1477. While Ramon's son Grimon continued his father's commerce, he also made sure that his children married honourably and undertook respectable careers, such as the law or the Church. His son Pierre Eyquem had a mainly military career and was able to establish himself on the domain of Montaigne, which he managed, and live in the château which he restored. Michel was born in the château, received a very respectable humanist education and legal training, and began calling himself not Eyquem but Montaigne, after the land. He lived "nobly," especially after his "retirement" to his domain, managing the vineyards, writing, travelling, and serving as mayor of Bordeaux for a four-year stretch. He was no longer directly involved in commerce, and he accumulated noble "honours": knight of the Order of Saint Michel (1571), "gentilhomme de la chambre" of Henri de Navarre (1577). The social trajectory of the Eyquem family is that of many wealthy bourgeois in the sixteenth century, who enriched themselves in banking, commerce, judicial or royal administration, bought noble lands and lived off the proceeds of their lands, sometimes occupying high-level posts in the kingdom, and ensuring for their children non-commercial careers.[16] They often had a legal education, and were well-educated in classical letters, mastering Latin and sometimes Greek. After three generations of possession of noble land and gradual withdrawal from commerce, these bourgeois considered themselves and were considered to be noble, and could enjoy the substantial social and especially fiscal privileges that nobility conferred. The aristocracy was granted an exemption from much royal direct taxation (with considerable regional variations concerning land, since nobles in the south were obliged to pay taxes on non-noble land), and had access to the highest civil, military, and ecclesiastical positions in the kingdom. It was not until the seventeenth century that this swelling of the "modern" nobility was inhibited. The "bourgeois gentilshommes" were not immune from resentment by the older, more strictly military aristocracy, both "grand" and poor. Some of the impoverished provincial noblemen turned to highway banditry to survive: indeed, Montaigne himself was robbed and held for ransom in a forest by "fifteen or twenty masked [noblemen]" during an uneasy truce (see III.12, F 813, V1061).

## THE NEW ECONOMY AND THE OLD ARISTOCRACY

One reason for the success of the bourgeoisie in moving into the ranks of the nobility was economic. From the mid-fifteenth century until the mid-sixteenth century France experienced a demographic and economic expansion that allowed it to recuperate from the disasters of the preceding century (the Black Death and the Hundred Years' War). Urban populations increased dramatically, and rural populations, less subject than before to malnourishment and famines, followed. Coupled with this demographic improvement, however, prices began to rise as well. The reasons for the inflation of the early Renaissance are not entirely clear. Thanks to American gold and silver more precious metal currency began to be available in Europe, and the Spanish were able to buy manufactured goods and simply give money to their allies. However, this does not account completely for the sharp rise in prices especially after the first two decades of the sixteenth century. The royal French currency, the *livre*, continued to be devalued during the century, which might also have contributed to the price rises. In any event, prosperous times for commerce, in conjunction with inflation, meant difficulties for small to medium landowners who depended upon (fixed) monetary income from their lands or who had large expenses associated with their status (as was the case for the nobility who needed to maintain horses, servants, armour, and weaponry, and might be called upon to travel or follow the court). This conjunction of circumstances also meant that wealthy bourgeois were in a good position to acquire land, including noble land. In addition to burgeoning commerce, during the reign of François I royal administration expanded, especially in the area of finances and taxation, opening career possibilities for educated nobles and non-nobles alike.

The changing composition of France's elites is reflected in the changing theoretical definition of nobility.[17] Conceptually at least, the aristocracy originated in the medieval theocratic partition of society into three "orders" or "estates." At the top of the hierarchy was the clergy, those who prayed and preached the Word. Next came the aristocracy or nobility, those who fought (to protect the Church and the community of faithful, and the weakest in society: women, orphans, and the poor). Finally, the third estate ("tiers état") comprised those who worked, that is, mainly the peasants but also all who engaged in manufacturing or commerce. The members of the third estate nourished the other two orders, for the first order provided their spiritual salvation and the second order their physical protection. The old nobility liked to trace its roots back to Charlemagne and the thirty-odd warrior families who constituted the backbone of his army and his court.

A nobleman's horse and sword were the symbols of his status and his responsibilities. His material survival was guaranteed by his "fief" (from Vulgar Latin *feudum* or *feodum*, which is the root for "feudal"), the goods or land given to him by his lord in exchange for his military services. The fief originally took various forms, but eventually came to mean land that he was expected to pass on to his eldest son who would continue to serve his lord. A nobleman was expected to provide *auxilium* and *consilium*, aid and counsel: military service, in response to the call from his lord (the king had "ban et arrière-ban" called out in the event of war, assembling, through the hierarchy of his vassals, the knights who were obliged to him). But the nobleman also furnished financial help (for example, to ransom his lord or to provide a dowry for his daughter), administrative and judicial assistance, and political counsel. The privileges he enjoyed as a compensation were first of all fiscal, but also honorific (hunting on his domain, carrying the sword, special seating in the church, burial rights, etc.). He needed above all to ensure his succession, that is, have a male heir, and he was obliged to maintain a "noble life," not working "with his hands" by personal field labour or commerce. In the event that he could not avoid engaging in work, he risked *dérogeance*, losing his title as nobleman. Certain remunerative activities were allowed, however, such as glass-making, mining, and iron-works, medicine and the law. Even though the nobility never constituted more than 1.5 percent of the population, they owned a considerable part of the land (approximately one-third of

French land was originally "noble," although by the sixteenth century much noble land was no longer owned by the aristocracy, who also owned non-noble lands) and occupied the highest posts in the military, the Church, and often in royal, provincial and municipal administration.

The common element of the old nobility was, ideally at least, the sword. One should emphasize "ideally," since by the sixteenth century in fact most members of the nobility practiced only intermittent military service if any at all. In addition, the conditions of warfare were evolving.[18] The impact of artillery, larger armies of infantry, and long sieges might only have been gradual, but the idea of the armoured knight had already been vulnerable for some time, and its anachronistic nature was becoming more and more apparent. It was already possible in the Middle Ages to receive a noble title as a reward for administrative talent, even if the noble ethos remained that of the warrior.

It was also in the Middle Ages that nobility began to be defined as "virtue," that is, as the exercise of several distinct virtues. The most commonly cited ones were piety and fidelity to the king, magnanimity (greatness of the soul, manifested in courage on the battlefield), liberality (an indifference to material wealth, manifested in generous gifts), loyalty or faithfulness to one's word, and *courtoisie* (a civil and peaceful demeanour when not on the battlefield). The increasing presence of virtues of temperance and prudence attested to the turning away of cultural ideals from raw warrior qualities to the more "civilized" ones which were essential to the courtier and servant of the state. Humanist discussions of nobility included the possibility that virtue might be all that is necessary for nobility. In the end, birth, that is lineage, "blood" or "race," did not alone suffice to constitute true nobility. Noble birth could provide a man with "seeds" of virtue, since he would be called upon to emulate the examples of his ancestors.[19] Although Montaigne openly admired the military life, in his personal conduct and in his discussions of various behaviour and virtues it is implied that the purely war-like qualities of the old nobility were not only insufficient but actually dangerous to the polity.[20] One sign of the increasing irrelevance of old warrior virtues was the frequency of duels "de point d'honneur" (on a point of honour) among aristocrats in the sixteenth century, a practice condemned by Montaigne.[21] Nobles risked decapitation (in defiance of the king's justice) and excommunication (since they were committing either intentional homicide or suicide, according to the Council of Trent), but in spite of the threat of harsh legal punishment if they were caught they fought duel after duel. Thousands of nobles lost their lives over questions of "honour," most spectacularly so during the reigns of Henri III and Henri IV.[22]

### INTEREST AND INFLATION IN THE NEW ECONOMY

If the status of the aristocracy was symbolically most invested, the development of commerce in the expanding economy accompanied changes no less significant in sixteenth-century culture. Montaigne's family's wealth derived from commerce. The "capitalist" energies of the period were aided by a loosening of the strictures put on interest. The Old as well as the New Testament seemed to banish the demanding of interest,[23] and medieval theology condemned usury, that is, excessive interest. In practice, however, the Church allowed payment for *damnum emergens* (damages occurring to the lender because of the loan) and *lucrum cessans* (the absence of profits he would have made with the lent money). Sixteenth-century economic thinkers expanded the possibilities for interest (and thus credit), even if they ended up giving theological justifications for their ideas.[24] The rise of prices in France occasioned debates on its causes by highly placed officials and historians, such as Malestroit (a pseudonym?), *Paradoxes sur le faict des monnoyes* (1566, "Paradoxes on Money"), Jean Bodin, *La Response . . . au paradoxe de monsieur de Malestroit* (1568), and Alexandre de la Tourette, *Response . . . aux paradoxes du sieur de Malestroict* (1567). Malestroit contended that the devaluation of the currency (in terms of the "real" value of the money) explained the apparent rise in prices, whereas Bodin identified as principal reason the greater abundance of gold and silver in the kingdom and the international scene, and for Tourette it was a question of the vicissitudes of the time. The growing importance of the merchant economy is also reflected in publications enabling better accounting and calculating procedures, such as the double-entry ledger (listing simultaneously credits and debits). The internationalization of the market increased the wealth of cities at commercial crossroads, such as Lyons, in the first half of the sixteenth century.

That being said, it is no doubt premature to speak of an economic "policy" in the sixteenth century, or of a true science of economics.[25] Economic terms, however, were often found in literature and the dynamics of the book trade influenced the composition and revision of material. Montaigne himself was financially involved in the publication of his *Essays*, which sold well, and their revision and expansion corresponded to the rhythm of the royal "privilege" system which gave printers publication rights that needed to be renewed regularly.

### THE RURAL LIFE

Montaigne's explicit pride in his noble pedigree on the one hand, and the actual merchant origins of his family on the other, conceal the fact that after 1570 the essayist was in touch on a daily basis with the peasants working his lands and the people employed on his estate. Montaigne spoke Gascon with ease and readily identified himself as a Gascon.[26] As a provincial nobleman with a solid but not spectacular income he and his wife managed the castle and the vineyards themselves. Peasants and other rural inhabitants (artisans, millers, tavern-owners, smiths, etc.) accounted for over 85 percent of the French population, and the rhythm of life was essentially bound to the seasons. Living "nobly" entailed for Montaigne, as well as for many provincial nobles, a thorough knowledge of agriculture. The sixteenth century witnessed publications designed precisely for the rural gentleman, such as Olivier de Serres' *Théâtre d'agriculture et mesnage des champs* (1600). But in spite of the attention which was being brought to agricultural techniques, peasant life in fact changed little in substance before the eighteenth century.[27] The "eternal village" comprised its social hierarchy, from *laboureurs* at the top to artisans and day-workers at the bottom. French agriculture remained heavily based on grains; the lack of diversity exposed rural populations to famine when weather or disease diminished the crop. The consequences of particularly the later wars of religion, coupled with a resurgence of the plague and colder weather, increased the suffering of the peasants, some of whom turned to open revolt in the 1590s. Montaigne admired the constancy of peasants stricken with the plague:

In this place the best part of my revenue is from manual labor; the land that a hundred men worked for me has lain idle for a long time. Now, what example of resoluteness did we not see then in the simplicity of this whole people? Each man universally gave up caring for his life. The grapes remained hanging on the vines, the principal produce of the country, as all prepared themselves indifferently, and awaited death that evening or the next day with face and voice so little frightened that it seemed that they had made their peace with this necessity . . . (III.12, F 802, V1048–9)

### STOICISM AND SURVIVAL

The relative tenuousness of social bonds and political life in France in the last third of the sixteenth century contributed to the revival of Stoicism among the elites.[28] Although the most influential neo-Stoical works postdate the *Essays*, clearly Montaigne's jurist milieu was attracted to a philosophy of internal constancy and freedom in the face of uncertainty and change. Justus Lipsius' *De constantia libri duo* ("Two books on Constancy," 1585), Guillaume du Vair's *Philosophie morale des stoïques* ("Moral Philosophy of the Stoics," privilege 1585, 2nd edn., 1599) and his *De la constance et consolation és calamitez publiques* ("On Constancy and Consolation during Public Calamities," 1594) provided a synthesis of stoicism and Christian theology.[29] Du Vair (1556–1621), a *Politique* parliamentarian and Ciceronian humanist, drew on Epictetus' *Manual* (which he had translated into French) and Seneca's epistles and their lessons for troubled times. The reliance on reason, the control of the passions, and the reflection on death are combined with Christian spirituality: Du Vair had written a meditation on the Psalms and an attempt at synthesizing Christianity and classical ethics, *De la saincte philosophie* (before 1585). Du Vair's publications enjoyed great success around the turn of the century. Montaigne referred admiringly in the *Essays* to the work of Lipsius (1547–1606) and corresponded with the scholar. Some of Montaigne's early essays took up Stoicism's themes, especially the contemplation of death, but he clearly rejected Stoic insistence on indifference to joy and suffering and the complete denigration of the passions. However, responding to the social and political context became an imperative for the educated, and Montaigne's generally pessimistic view of contemporary France was shared by many well into the reign of Henri IV.

Montaigne's reaction to the "disturbed and sick state" of France is, on the surface at least, a deep distrust of all social, legal, and religious reform (see in particular 1.23, "Of Custom, and not Easily Changing an Accepted Law"), and a corresponding willingness to obey the customs and laws which are in place, however bad they may be. While this attitude is consonant with his profound skepticism toward human reason and its ability to control the consequences of changes it foists upon the polity, Montaigne's "conservatism" is also produced by the necessity of surviving in a dangerous period of conflict and of making choices among the options of which each was more unpleasant than the others:

We may regret better times, but not escape the present; we may wish for different magistrates, but we must nevertheless obey those that are here. And perhaps there is more merit in obeying the bad than the good. As long as the image of the ancient and accepted laws of the monarchy shines in some corner, there will I be planted. If by bad fortune they come to contradict and interfere with each other, and produce two sides dubious and difficult to choose between, my choice is likely to be to steal away and escape from that tempest; in the meantime nature may lend me a hand, or the hazards of war. Between Caesar and Pompey I [would] have declared myself openly. But among those three robbers [Antony, Octavius, Lepidus] who came after, I should have had either to hide, or to follow with the wind, which I consider permissible when reason no longer guides. (III.9, F 760, V994)[30]

NOTES

1.  For an excellent overview of the connection between Montaigne's *Essays* and contemporary social and political issues, see Géralde Nakam, *Les Essais de Montaigne miroir et procès de leur temps: Témoignage historique et création littéraire* (Paris: Nizet, 1984). In this chapter I mainly discuss the social and political contexts to the period during which Montaigne composed and revised his work. Other chapters in the present volume deal specifically with other aspects of French culture of the sixteenth century (law, philosophy, humanism, etc.).

2.  During the eight distinct wars of religion, the areas around Montaigne's estate east of Bordeaux were affected, although his own castle escaped looting, at least once only through his personal intervention (see III.12, F812, V1060). On the two sides of the valley of the Garonne there were considerable Huguenot populations or sympathizers, and during the first and second wars (March–April 1562 – March 1563, September

1567 – March 1568), they organized armed resistance. During the third war (August 1568 – August 1570), royal armies marched south and north of Montaigne; after the St. Bartholomew's massacre in Paris (August 24, 1572), a similar massacre of Huguenots took place in Bordeaux (October 3, 1572); during the seventh war (November 1579 – November 1580), the Huguenot army marched toward Cahors from Nérac, and during the eighth war (April 1585 – March 1598), in 1586, the duke of Mayenne's troops pillaged the province of Guyenne. Henri de Navarre's forces traversed the area, preceding the battle of Coutras (October 20, 1587) against the royal and Catholic *Ligue* army. Henri de Navarre himself visited Montaigne's château on two occasions, and dined with him after Coutras.

3. See George Hoffmann, *Montaigne's Career* (Oxford: Oxford University Press, 1998), pp. 8–38. On the Eyquem family and on Montaigne's childhood and education, see Roger Trinquet, *La jeunesse de Montaigne: Ses origines familiales, son enfance et ses études* (Paris: Nizet, 1972). See also Trinquet's research on Montaigne's life and career, published in many articles mostly in the *Bulletin de la Société des Amis de Montaigne* in the 1960s and 1970s.

4. See Daniel Ménager, "Montaigne et la philosophie de l'ambassade," *Bulletin de la Société des Amis de Montaigne*, VIII, 17–18 (2000), pp. 55–67.

5. The intellectual and theological variety of the medieval Catholic Church, as well as the principal issues motivating the reformers, are described by Steven Ozment, *The Age of Reform 1250–1550. An Intellectual and Religious History of Late Medieval and Reformation Europe* (New Haven: Yale University Press, 1980). For succinct accounts of the political and religious aspects of the French Reformation, see Arlette Jouanna, *La France du XVIe siècle 1483–1598* (Paris: Presses Universitaires de France, 1996); also Gaston Zeller, *La Réforme* (Paris: SEDES, 1973), Mack P. Holt, *The French Wars of Religion, 1562–1629* (Cambridge: Cambridge University Press, 1995) and J. H. M. Salmon, *Society in Crisis. France in the Sixteenth Century* (London: Benn, 1975). A good reference work on the wars of religion is Arlette Jouanna, Jacqueline Boucher, Dominique Biloghi, and Guy Le Thiec, *Histoire et dictionnaire des guerres de religion* (Paris: Robert Laffont, 1998).

6. Calvin's treatise was published first in Latin in 1536, and then in French (1541). On Calvin, see William J. Bouwsma, *John Calvin. A Sixteenth Century Portrait* (Oxford: Oxford University Press, 1988).

7. Montaigne himself was imprisoned in the Bastille by the *Ligueurs* in July 1588, but was quickly released through intervention of Catherine de' Medici.

8. The term was based on the maxim derived from Roman law, *princeps legibus solutus est* ("the prince is absolved of the laws"), found in the *Corpus iuris civilis* (*Digest* 1.3.31).

9. See in particular book 1, ch. 8 ("De la Souveraineté").

10. Such as the jurist François Hotman, known for his *Francogallia* (1573).

11. Such as Jean Boucher, *De justa Henrici tertii abdicatione* (1589) ("On the Just Abdication of Henri III"). A sample of the political treatises of the time is provided in Julian H. Franklin, *Constitutionalism and Resistance in the Sixteenth Century: Three Treatises by Hotman, Beza, and Mornay* (New York: Pegasus, 1969).

12. On the emergence of "propaganda" in the polemics of the sixteenth century, see Donald R. Kelley, *The Beginning of Ideology: Consciousness and Society in the French Reformation* (Cambridge: Cambridge University Press, 1981).

13. See Robert Muchembled, *Sorcières, justice et société aux XVIe et XVIIe siècles* (Paris: Imago, 1987). While not excluding the possibility of their existence, Montaigne is skeptical of procedures for identifying witches (III.11, *F*788, *V*1031).

14. On the effect of this massacre on the Huguenot community, see Robert M. Kingdon, *Myths about the St. Bartholomew's Day Massacres 1572–1576* (Cambridge, MA: Harvard University Press, 1988). To this day the precise details of the decision-making leading to the massacre are unclear, and accounts of the number of victims vary greatly. For a reading of the religious violence in general as primarily inspired by notions of sacred "cleansing," see Denis Crouzet, *Les guerriers de Dieu. La violence au temps des troubles de religion vers 1525–vers 1610* (Seyssel: Champ Vallon, 1990).

15. For a review of Montaigne's views on nobility and the controversies they have produced in Montaigne criticism, see James J. Supple, *Arms versus Letters: The Military and Literary Ideals in the 'Essais' of Montaigne* (Oxford: Oxford University Press, 1984).

16. On the upward mobility of the bourgeoisie and their "tacit" ennobling, see George Huppert, *Les bourgeois gentilshommes. An Essay on the Definition of Elites in Renaissance France* (Chicago: University of Chicago Press, 1977).

17. The early modern aristocracy in France has been the subject of much recent critical work. See Arlette Jouanna, *Le devoir de révolte. La noblesse française et la gestation de l'Etat moderne, 1559–1661* (Paris: Fayard, 1989), and Kristen B. Neuschel, *Word of Honor. Interpreting Noble Culture in Sixteenth-Century France* (Ithaca: Cornell University Press, 1986). For a wider perspective, see Jonathan Dewald,

*The European Nobility, 1400–1800* (Cambridge: Cambridge University Press, 1996).

18. See J. R. Hale, *War and Society in Renaissance Europe 1450–1620* (Baltimore: Johns Hopkins University Press, 1985).

19. Montaigne proclaims that he was born of a family (*race*) "famous for integrity" (II.11, *F*311, *V*427), since way back – "de longue memoire" (III.10, *F*782, *V*1021). "Integrity" in both instances is the translation of *prud'hommie*, a virtue associated with the nobility since the late Middle Ages.

20. See especially II.11 ("On Cruelty"), which condemns the extremes of violence that the wars of religion have spawned. See David Quint, *Montaigne and the Quality of Mercy: Ethical and Political Themes in the Essais* (Princeton: Princeton University Press, 1998).

21. Montaigne observed that the demands of justice are contrary to the demands of aristocratic honour: "Whence it comes about that there are two sets of laws, those of honor and those of justice, in many matters quite opposed. The former condemn as rigorously a man's enduring being given the lie as the latter condemn his avenging it" (I.23, *F*85, *V*118).

22. See François Billacois, *The Duel: Its Rise and Fall in Early Modern France*, trans. Trista Selous (New Haven: Yale University Press, 1990).

23. Based on Deuteronomy 23:19–20, 28:12, and Luke 6:35, *Date mutuum nihil inde sperantes*, "give the loan without hoping for anything from it," in the disputed Vulgate Latin translation.

24. See in particular Charles Du Moulin, *Tractatus commerciorum et usurarum* ("Treatise on Contracts and Usury"), translated in 1547 into French.

25. For a brief overview of these debates and the presence of economic terminology in French letters, see Philippe Desan, *L'imaginaire économique de la Renaissance* (Mont-de-Marsan: Editions Interuniversitaires, 1993).

26. See II.8 (*F*281, *V*388). Gascon seems to have been a "default" language for the writer: "let Gascon get there, if French cannot" (I.26, *F*127, *V*171). That being said, Montaigne's father had him tutored in Latin as a small child.

27. On French rural life, see George Huppert, *After the Black Death: A Social History of Early Modern Europe* (Bloomington: Indiana University Press, 1986), pp. 1–13, 67–79, and Hugues Neveux, Jean Jacquart, and Emmanuel Le Roy Ladurie, *Histoire de la France rurale*, vol. 2 (Paris: Seuil, 1975).

28. See Gerhart Ostreicht, *Neostoicism and the Early Modern State* (Cambridge: Cambridge University Press, 1982), Günter Abel, *Stoizismus und frühe Neuzeit* (Berlin: De Gruyter, 1978); and Gordon

Braden, *Renaissance Tragedy and the Senecan Tradition: Anger's Privilege* (New Haven: Yale University Press, 1985), pp. 63–98.

29. See Jason L. Saunders, *Justus Lipsius: The Philosophy of Renaissance Stoicism* (New York: Liberal Arts Press, 1955).

30. Similarly, in III.1 ("Of the Useful and the Honorable"): "In truth, and I am not afraid to confess it, I would easily carry, in case of need, one candle to Saint Michael and one to the dragon, according to the old woman's plan. I will follow the good side right to the fire, but not into it if I can help it. Let Montaigne [the castle] be engulfed in the public ruin, if need be; but if not, I shall be grateful to fortune if it is saved; and as much rope as my duty gives me, I use it for its preservation" (F601, V792).

# 3 Montaigne's legacy

A legacy is something that is given by an ancestor or predecessor and handed down to future generations. A philosophical legacy is normally held by philosophers to consist of a set of questions and concepts that claim attention on their own merit. The origins and tradition of the gift have no effect on its intrinsic significance and authority. Montaigne bequeaths questions about what man can know, together with concepts of selfhood and experience. Philosophers from Descartes and Pascal to Husserl and Merleau-Ponty designate themselves heirs by *freely* assessing the philosophical merit of the bequest and moving the discussion on unhampered by any obligations to the legator. Their own authority, in turn, does not depend on the origins of their philosophical questions and concepts.

Someone who thought that the authority of a legacy with its heirs is or should be conditioned by the origins of the philosophical gift, by the moral character of its donor or author, by the social tradition identifying it as a source of guidance, would be accused of committing a fallacy.[1] Yet the majority of Montaigne's contemporaries thought in something like this way. When Montaigne received the philosophical legacy of Raymond Sebond, his freedom of response was significantly conditioned by the circumstances in which he received it from his father, by the fact that court ladies were seeking guidance from the work. But, as we shall see at the end of this chapter, it was precisely the *freedom* to judge others' philosophical legacies on their own merits that became Montaigne's own legacy. To put this another way, he retrospectively changed the character of the ancient philosophical *auctoritates* (authorities), and the spirit in which they gave their thoughts to posterity. After Montaigne, they became more doubtful, more free-spirited, more open.

For the conception of philosophy and a philosophical legacy with which I began is modern. It derives from a type of history of philosophy that emerged after Montaigne's own time. Montaigne and his contemporaries understood philosophy to comprehend vast areas of human learning, and some areas of divine learning, not just particular trains of thought about subjectivity, language, and mind. Many still believed that all humanity's knowledge was originally given by God. This was just one reason why they thought differently about legacies. In the aftermath of the Reformation, they were more anxious about questions of philosophical good faith, questions of authority and authorship, than modern historians of philosophy. Families were confessionally divided; the spiritual formation of the young was at stake. The image of sovereign power increasingly comprehended philosophical mastery of natural knowledge and priestly mastery of theological knowledge. Philosophy was at one and the same time deeply controversial and highly syncretistic. Ancient philosophical and theological disputes over the nature of man and being were being refought within an intellectual environment shaped by Christianity. The alarming proliferation of sects and schools of philosophical and religious thought produced ever more militant attempts at root-and-branch reformation and harmonization.

Montaigne did not feel that the legacy of classical philosophy had been properly collected in his time. He wanted a professional scholar like Justus Lipsius to make a book offering a methodical register of the opinions of the ancients on being and morals. The register would include their controversies, their moral reputations, the development of the various sects and schools. It would recount how, during the course of their lives, philosophers actually applied their precepts on memorable occasions that might serve as examples (II.12, F436, V578B). Montaigne's desire (not met in practice) reveals that the printed book assembled with scholarly expertise represented an important new instrument of philosophical legacy-making in the sixteenth century. It could give general access to the examples or *patrons* of ancient philosophy and theology, which could then be applied in contemporary life. Montaigne makes a more haphazard collection of the wisdom of the ancients in his own book, especially in the "Apology for Raymond Sebond" (II.12, F408, V545C).

The word "legacy" still makes us think of fathers, of heirlooms, of portraits passed down within the family. Montaigne does not think of

himself as bequeathing an abstract philosophical legacy; he is authoring a philosophical book and leaving it to "friends and family." In
its first and second editions (1580, 1582) the *Essays* closely accompanied the second edition of another work translated by Montaigne but
authored – if in a different sense – by his father: Raymond Sebond's
*Natural Theology* (1569, 1581). To understand Montaigne's philosophical legacy we have to understand the intellectual significance
of this family context.

Montaigne describes his father's legacy in one of the most famous
passages in the best known of Montaigne's *Essays* (II.12, F319–21,
V338–440A).[2] The passage tells a complicated and uncertain story
about the origins, intended applications, and fortunes of Sebond's
philosophical work. Many participants or "authors" get in on the
act of handing down the book and its meanings. There is not only
the artist, or writer. There is an ancient father who may have dictated
the work to Sebond. There is the divine original cause of the book's
subject matter. There are many readers or recipients who are agents
in the handing on of the work, in the making of its significance and
authority (or lack of authority).

Sebond's work features in Montaigne's family history as a paternal bequest with benefits and duties attached. In fact, the book
points Montaigne not only to the moment of its original writing, but also to *three* subsequent or transactional contexts. It was
given to Montaigne's father as a prophylactic against atheism and
Lutheranism in the dangerous period after the European Reformation had begun. It was then given to Michel with a duty attached to
translate it, to reauthor it in French, and to protect it from calumny.
But we are also told that the same book is circulating at court. It is
often read by court ladies of Montaigne's acquaintance who oblige
him to defend it against the objections of the "new" or reformed
theologians. Montaigne describes it as *their* book. They as recipients of the work seem if anything more important than the person we would normally describe as the "author" – the original
writer.

But was the person who wrote the book the author of its
philosophy? Based on his reading of the text, Montaigne judges it
the work of a fine mind. The mind may have been that of a Spanish
professor of medicine by the name of Sebond who lived two centuries before in Toulouse. But he consults a scholar, Adrien Turnèbe,

for an authoritative opinion. Turnèbe believes the philosophy in the work to have been derived from the ancient church father, Thomas Aquinas. But from another point of view there is actually another Book behind the book, the Book of Nature, and the author of that is God the Father. From this point of view, the object represented by the *Natural Theology*, the object that ultimately caused it to be what it is, is a work – Nature – that reveals God's agency as prime mover. Of course, the extent to which God's agency *could* be inferred by anyone from Nature was deeply controversial.

I shall return to this passage at the end of the chapter. For now, the important point is the context it offers for understanding and questioning the origins and transmission of philosophical knowledge and philosophical authority in Montaigne's time. Many authors and authorities are involved, including scholarly experts in the present. Philosophical works can be issued and defended for the sake and under the aegis of particular elite recipients or patrons. But despite all this, despite its paternal origins, Montaigne creates the impression that the authority of Sebond's book remains uncertain – this, in a way, is the whole point of the "Apology."

What of the authority of Montaigne's own book? Montaigne was a minor patron who consulted scholars, who authored a philosophical book, like his father, but who declared *himself* to be the origin of the only kind of knowledge on offer in his work, his own doubtful self-knowledge. Montaigne was a new kind of patron–author; he departed from the model left by his father's generation and continued by many of his contemporaries. He was a great critic of the authoritative patrons and models of learning of his day. He sought neither to follow nor to be one in the wonted fashion – thereby, to some early critics, becoming one.

The *Essays* attempt to bring out the inner "patron" or "master form" of a private man in his retreat, without arbitrarily imposed interruptions or interference from powerful dignitaries, classical prototypes and doctrinal models, public educational institutions, moral and professional norms. This does *not* mean Montaigne isolates himself from all external relations.[3] His privacy was very busy, full of his *commerce* with friends, scholars, patrons, and books – the *Essays* testify to this throughout.[4] But it does mean that Montaigne conducts his relations from his own "seat," as a kind of informal host into whose private domain no foreign obligations, rules, or ceremonies are admitted. He does not allow his house to become part of a civilized philosophical society. An "unusual freedom" is reserved (III.3, F625, V823–4B).

When a patroness to whom he is obliged comes to visit, Montaigne does not interrupt his textual "form," his free-flowing essay, but incorporates the visit and the corresponding dedicatory letter within it (II.37, F595–7, V783–5A). Elsewhere he tells us that when he is writing, he would prefer to do without the company of "good authors" ("bons autheurs"), both in the form of classical books and of visiting nobles or scholarly friends such as lawyers and theologians who might want to correct or perfect – author – his work, thereby making it less his. But his favorite authors do inevitably insert a helping hand, just as his most valued noblewomen friends will visit and show interest in his work, and he accommodates their presence and support in his own house-style.

Plutarch, for example, is described in the same passage as inexhaustible in riches and embellishments (III.5, F666, V874–5B). He is like a magnificent benefactor who on all occasions and subjects – whether you like it or not – extends his liberality. The benefactor's gifts create a reciprocal relationship that exposes Montaigne to risk. For accepting such gifts so liberally as parts of his own work means that others who steal from Plutarch may also be stealing from him, endangering the integrity of his own form. This is so because Montaigne freely binds himself to the support and protection of Plutarch, as he does to that of other patrons. As in the case of Sebond, however, other authors are involved, other actors play a part. Plutarch's liberality is dispensed via Montaigne's acquaintance Jacques Amyot, a scholarly bishop who selected Plutarch's book and gave it to his country (in French translation). Without Amyot, it would not have been possible for Plutarch to have lifted "us" ignoramuses out of the quagmire (II.4, F262, V363–4A).

So Plutarch, a rich and powerful Greek who became a Roman citizen and an emperor's private instructor, is to Montaigne's mind a noble patron–author of philosophical works. The Greek's chief characteristic is evident in his writings, for he is "libre par tout," free everywhere (II.10, F300–01, V413A). And early readers understood Montaigne to be emulating Plutarch and other classical models, not least in his very freedom. For La Croix du Maine, Montaigne's first bibliographer, the Essays were composed "after" Plutarch. The essayist had fashioned his self-portrait on the most esteemed, the most "recommendable" classical prototype of the moment.[5] This goes against the grain of Montaigne's own comment – added in a later edition, perhaps as a response – that he had no external classical *patron* in forming himself and his writings (II.12, V546B, F409).

Certainly, Montaigne does not appear to be as grand a personage as the classical Greek essayist and biographer. But there are some respects in which his self-portrait does recall his favorite author. He studies the natural morals of the heroes and authors of the past (II.10, F302, V414–15A). He imagines himself giving rich matter to his readers (1.40, F185, V251C). He prints his charter of Roman citizenship (III.9, F765, V999–1000B). He imagines that he could have been a private instructor to a king (III.13, F825–6, V1077–8B). He does claim, most importantly, to be *almost* free everywhere. He would have been so had he been living in free times ("To the Reader", F2, V3A). But this apparent conformity with a famous classical *patron* was not premeditated. It happened by chance, after he was already formed by nature – or so Montaigne would have it (II.12, F409, V546C).

Montaigne presents himself as a nobleman who merely dabbles in philosophy and the making of books – a patronly author, not a writerly author. He is a casual collector, like his father, of the wise opinions of the ancients and the moderns on being and morals. My point is that we have to look at the norms of patron-authorship in Montaigne's culture if we want to understand exactly what lies behind this self-portrait, exactly what Montaigne intended to be distinctly *free* about his self-image. To recover these norms is to see what Montaigne shares with the European elite's understanding of the place of philosophical books and book-learning in elite individuals' and families' histories. But I have already been using "patron" in more than one sense, and this needs explanation.

### THE PATRON AS AUTHOR

A patron is a lordly protector and supporter of others, and a moral pattern deserving imitation.[6] So in sixteenth-century English "patron" could mean both a pattern or mould to copy, and a lord protector or father. The separate senses of "patron" and "pattern" emerged during the seventeenth century. In sixteenth-century French, the two concepts were closely related. Montaigne uses the word "patron" in the sense of an example or model to be followed, but he refers to the "patronage" of seigneurs such as himself (II.37, F591, V778A), and he expects that a "grand personnage" with a reputation will also be a "patron" for imitation ("It ill befits anyone to make himself known save him who has qualities to be imitated, and whose life and opinions may serve as a model ["peuvent servir de patron"]"; II.18, F503, V663A). So the greatest patrons are the likes of Alexander and Caesar. This prince, says Montaigne of the former, is the supreme "patron" of hazardous, or beautifully courageous acts (I.24, F94, V129B). Patronage of the arts was not distinct, as now, from other forms of patronage; neither was it so distinct from the authorship of art.

For a patron could be a sponsor, or privileged consumer of art, but also an *auctor* or author. Like God, he is visible and readable in his works. So a rich and powerful citizen like Cosimo de' Medici used art patronage as a way of publicly registering and memorializing exemplary moral works of which he was the prime mover. He aimed to express the Christian charitable virtue of liberality, a virtue which shaded into "magnificence" when greatness of scale and conspicuous expenditure on art were involved. The magnificent man is like an artist. He can see what is fitting and spends accordingly. What he collects and builds reflects his own prototypical virtues as mediated by the skills of his artists.[7]

Patrons could author theological and philosophical books in the same spirit. Take a pair of items on display in the Vatican library when Montaigne visited. The first is a copy of the luxurious, monumental edition of the Antwerp polyglot Bible (8 vols., 1569–72) commissioned from Christopher Plantin by Philip II, its patron–author, and printed on parchment. An inscription on the binding tells Montaigne that this copy was a gift from Philip to the present pope. The gift had been timed carefully: a crucial and delicate moment in relations between the papacy and a France torn by religious war.[8] It stood in the Vatican library like an inscribed statue indexing the Spanish king's good faith.

To accompany it on display is an equally statuesque index of the English king Henry VIII's bad faith. As originally transacted, the special presentation copy of Henry VIII's *Vindication of the Seven*

*Sacraments* of course bore the opposite intention. Montaigne carefully reads the prefatory Latin distich written out in Henry's hand. It offers the book to a previous pope (Leo X) as a witness of the king's good faith and friendship. Montaigne also carefully reads the prefaces, one to the pope, the other to the reader and describes the style as good – for scholastic Latin.[9] The copy can serve as a model of a sixteenth-century book that an international readership understands to be authored and given by a patron.

For obvious reasons the Reformation forced the printed book into prominent service as a potential index of good faith and doctrinal command – and their "bad" opposites. This was as true in the case of Pierre Eyquem as it was in that of Henry VIII. The printed book could of course circulate more easily and in greater numbers than the luxury manuscript. Compared with other kinds of art you might commission it had obvious advantages. Instead of one statue in one location with a brief inscription you could circulate a whole series of portable statues with elaborate inscriptions. So in 1521 Henry VIII conceived a brief for a book against Luther designed to give him the right doctrinal and spiritual credentials and to win him a title from the pope to match those of the French and Spanish kings.[10] The book was to function like the commemorative self-portrait given by king René of Sicily to the king of France (II.17, F496, V653–4A). The whole point for Henry is that the book shows him to be personally involved in the intellectual debate as a learned agent on the pope's side.

From the start, however, there were doubts about Henry's authorship of the work because everyone suspected he would naturally be employing the learned expertise available at his court. Rumors persisted that Erasmus was the author. Erasmus opined that the king *and* his advisers were the author. Luther wanted to attribute it to Erasmus' enemy Edward Lee, so as to dissociate the king's name from such an anti-Lutheran tract. A consensus emerged that the king had indeed used a group of ecclesiastical and lay scholars for consultations and for collection of materials. Thomas More was later described as "a sorter out and placer of the principal matters," though Henry, upon realizing what a sharp sword he had handed to his papal opponents, was to blame More for having made him write the work.[11] By that stage, what had been designed as a public index of his good faith, had become a public index of his bad faith.

Montaigne seigneurially implies that he uses the printing-press only as a convenient way of copying his work for distribution to "friends and family" ("To the Reader," *V*3a, *F*2). Distinct and personalized copies of the *Vindication* were prepared for Henry's international "friends and family" as Cardinal Wolsey began negotiations to secure the special papal title. The title of *Defensor fidei* ("Defender of the Faith") was duly conferred.[12] As exhibited in the Vatican library long after Henry's divorce and the dissolution of the English monasteries there could hardly be a more monumental index of Henry's bad faith than the *Vindication* – from the papal point of view.

The point here is not of course that Henry's work is typical of the book in Montaigne's age. It is a luxury product exchanged between magnates. But I described above how a gift of an anti-Lutheran book was offered to Montaigne's father, then by him via his son to the public; and, however much he hedges it round with warnings about vanity, Montaigne *does*, after all, print the title of Roman citizen which his reputation as the Catholic author of the *Essays* won him at Rome (III.9, *F*765, *V*999–1000B). I am suggesting that royal transactions such as the English king's and the pope's set the mould for elite understanding of what learned – theological and philosophical – books produced by and on behalf of the aristocracy were for, and that this understanding is not as different as we might expect from their understanding of what other collected or commissioned art was for.

For such books – as the *Essays* do, in their own distinctive way – show aristocratic patrons in relations with other patrons, with artists and experts, classical and biblical prototypes, a wider public audience. They index the patron's moral and intellectual agency as mediated by these subordinate artists and ancient prototypes; they reflect his reputation and his honors on given occasions. But they are risky investments and can result in a net loss of reputation. Montaigne knows that his book will be judged against a background of investments of this kind and distinguishes it accordingly for presentation to the public. The nature and fate of Henry's learned book explains Montaigne's concerns for his own. Montaigne would have his book be judged enduringly as an index of his good faith. He would not have it perceived as a work modeled on or for external patrons, for his glory or their service.

So when Montaigne says to his reader that he has had consideration neither of "your service nor of my glory," that his forces are not capable of such a "design," he is also indicating what might normally be expected of a philosophical book by a noble ex-magistrate ("To the Reader," *V*3A, *F*2). An aristocratic project of self-portraiture which employs the printing-press and which shows signs of considerable learning would normally be expected to have such a "design." Readers might suspect scholarly intermediaries or secretaries to have been involved in servicing the patron's brief, collecting and ordering his matter. For the point of publishing a book is to show the learning at the patron–author's command. An independent and authoritative take on contemporary religio-political controversies or topical learned questions is called for, though of the kind that indicates good doctrine and intellectual judgment. Copies of the book would be personally distributed with "glorious" or honorable ends in view – from confirmation of social or professional status to specific titles and privileges. Above all, the book – the expectation went – would have been carefully, that is artificially designed and prepared to serve as a public index of the patron–author's moral and intellectual agency. It would give him the right image, the right kind of "credit." Though it could, again, rebound badly upon him. It is this blueprint for the confection of a patron–author's book that determines the counter-design of Montaigne's "natural" book. The *Essays* have not been artificially prepared. Anyone can see that. They offer a true, because shifting and unstable index of their patron's moral and intellectual agency.

WHY MAKE A LEARNED BOOK?

In "On Pedantry", Montaigne says that,

[w]e know how to say, "Cicero says thus, such are the morals of Plato; these are the very words of Aristotle." But what do we say ourselves? What do we judge? What do we do? A parrot could well say as much.

This habit makes me think of that rich Roman who went to much trouble and very great expense to procure men learned ("des hommes suffisants") in every field of knowledge, whom he kept continually around him, so that when there should befall among his friends some occasion to speak of one thing or another, [they should bring needed supplies to his position] ("ils suppléassent sa place") and all be ready to furnish him, one with an argument, one with a verse of Homer, [depending on their competence] ("chacun selon son gibier"); and he thought that this knowledge was his own because it was in the heads of [men in his pay], as those do whose ability dwells in their sumptuous libraries.

I know a man who, when I ask him what he knows, asks me for a book in order to point it out to me. . .[13]

Members of the elite invest in philosophical learning, as in other external furnishings, because it indexes their social agency as *patroni*, rich lords and masters on the ancient Roman model. A rich patron can buy or borrow the commodities and services of book learning, as he can buy or borrow luxury supplies and services of all sorts. The philosophical learning so obtained is his to dispose, but only in the sense that he can call upon one of his servants for an argument, or point to a place in a book indicated by them when he needs to. That is what being a patron with a bought reputation for *lettres* is normally taken to be about. But for an acute observer, the way in which the patron disposes ("judges") the books, servants, and textual loci he has acquired will serve publicly to index his own *lack* of *suffisance* or intellectual capacities. The result is dishonor, not honor.

Montaigne suggests that from his point of view such a situation is normal, not exceptional, amongst "us," the patrons of learning. As he puts it in a related passage elsewhere, "most men are rich with [other men's abilities]" ("La plus part des hommes sont riches d'une suffisance estrangere"; III.8, F715, V936B). So even "abilities" (various forms of artistic or intellectual agency) and "opinions" (mentalities or beliefs), are treated as commodities that can be bought and borrowed, traded and exchanged, commodities that are not in any essential moral or intellectual sense "ours" as self-possessed, judgmental agents. We are just the patrons who possess, display, and exchange them for ulterior motives.

Patrons, Montaigne tells us, can even buy or borrow the reputation that comes not just with the collecting but also with, again, the *authorship* of whole books – and even boast that they have done so. He is talking about the way "we" dress ourselves in others' faculties, others' agency, while leaving our own idle. We go begging an appetizing glory by stuffing ourselves with quotations from some German humanist's preliminary epistle. There is any number of such books

on Montaigne's shelves designed to service his need for discursive
authorities. Montaigne then gives two cases where he has seen how
a book has been put together. It is crucial that he has actually witnessed the "inside story" of these books:

> I have known books to be made out of things never either studied or under-
> stood, the author entrusting to various of his learned friends the search for
> this and that material to build it, contenting himself for his part with hav-
> ing planned the project ("d'en avoir projeté le dessein") and piled up by his
> industry this stack of unfamiliar provisions; at least the ink and paper are
> his. That, in all conscience, is buying or borrowing a book, not making one.
> It [shows] men, not that you can make a book, but, what they might have
> been in doubt about, that you cannot make one.
>
> A [chief presiding judge] was boasting in my presence of having heaped up
> two hundred-odd quotations from others in [one of his written presidential
> judgments]. By proclaiming this to everybody he seemed to me to efface the
> glory that people were giving him for it.[14]

Nowadays, when patrons put their name to something, we do not
think that they "made" it – least of all if it is a book they are sponsor-
ing. The Renaissance audience for art and for books did think patrons
made art. They thought so quite habitually. So the passage reveals
an understanding that patrons could commission books, rather as
they did buildings or gardens or statues. We saw a concrete example
of this earlier: Henry VIII's *Vindication*. The nature of the author's
involvement in the making of a book is the same as that of a patron
in a building project, and he expects to get the same thing out of it –
a monument to reflect his or his superiors' glory in an enduringly
public way. The patron provides the general brief and the "industry"
necessary to bring everything together; artisans and architects
assemble the materials themselves in line with the brief. The problem for Montaigne is that the materials have not been shaped, in
any sense, by the patron's understanding. The patron simply expects
to get the honor of having sent for the literary materials from afar
and assembled them in one place for construction by his architects
and artisans. Neither of these patrons are "authors" in good faith –
something we might not have known had we not had the chance to
observe them putting a book together.

The second example shows that a *president* or noble presiding
judge expected to be accorded a glorious reputation simply on the

basis of having amassed a discursive form of what might now be called cultural capital. He did not care to hide the fact that he had done *no more* than amass. He just needed quantities of erudite authorities to back up his point and expected his power to collect them to bring him honor. Montaigne is picking up again on an expectation that conspicuous acquisition – by expenditure or borrowing – of literary capital will routinely bring social credit. The authors are not even pretending to have been personally involved as judgmental agents in making the books. They had a *dessein* or brief that needed backing with authoritative materials. They expect "honor" to accrue from their industry in collecting the materials together in books.

Modern philosophical and literary critics are intrigued by the ontology of Montaigne's claims about the presence of his being in his book. But another way of expressing the point of the consubstantiality of the *Essays* and Montaigne, is to say that he has manifestly made a book, not bought or borrowed one. He has not just ordered the materials and wafted in to see how the workmen were doing. He is present at and in its writing. We know this because we see the inside story of his book from the start (he *lets* us see it). We see everything pass through *his* understanding onto the paper. It is not just furnished from the heads of his educated servants or from the printed commodities on his shelves. He is not just amassing erudition and collecting examples under heads. So, again, when Montaigne disavows the motives of *service* and *gloire* in his preface and throughout the *Essays* he is ironically telling us that he has not been up to commissioning a book in the manner described in this passage. His work is not the product of a deliberated brief to reflect his own or some higher patron's glory. It is not backed up by powerful classical and biblical prototypes or *patrons*. He does not have the power, the means to put together such a project. He is no Caesar, no Cosimo de' Medici, and he does not emulate their kind of glory.

There is a further distinction. As he is not trying to build a big public reputation his book can reveal all his weaknesses and bad qualities as well. His central claim is not to honor and authority for his public persona and positions but to *be*, "au naturel," the moral and intellectual agent indexed so freely by everything in the book. He is his own prototype, his own *patron*; he truly is the patron-as-author, the prime mover of a work which reflects him, which *is* him, in every changing, flawed detail.

Of course, this modest claim was in itself, at the time, highly original and distinctive. Like all Renaissance claims to discursive originality, it smacked of a return to antiquity, in this case to the free and natural philosophy of the first ancient sages and their descendants. Where Montaigne's originality and distinction were so recognized, the *Essays*, a book without *patron*, paradoxically earned him a glorious reputation as a free-ranging but authoritative philosopher on the ancient model of a Seneca or a Plutarch. There is concrete evidence of this in the personally customized exhibition laid on for him at the Vatican library.[15] The leading European humanist, Justus Lipsius, early on hails Montaigne as a new prototype, a modern Thales (one of the seven ancient sages with whom the history of philosophy began).[16] Montaigne is the only *true* patron–author, an everyday, vernacular but noble philosopher like Socrates himself. The document conferring Roman citizenship acknowledged this (by describing him as the "French Socrates").[17] The son of a merchant and provincial mayor had gone far. But it is time to go back to the family origins of his philosophical work.

## A FAMILY OF PATRON–AUTHORS

Montaigne praises his patroness Diane de Foix as a member of a *race lettrée*, a noble family with a strong reputation for letters. This family of patrons are themselves authors. Diane's uncle, the bishop of Aire, Montaigne says, gives birth every day to new works that will spread the family reputation for *lettres* to many later centuries ("which will extend for many centuries the knowledge of this quality in your family").[18] Montaigne is referring here to grand works published in the 1570s by his own publisher at Bordeaux, Simon Millanges. François de Foix de Candale (Foix-Candale), the Roman Catholic bishop of Aire, was an esteemed scientist and alchemist who produced medicines in his own laboratory.[19] In 1574 he dedicated to emperor Maximilian a philologically ambitious new Latin translation of a corrected Greek text from the *Corpus Hermeticum*, in which he had enlisted the help of the scholar Joseph Scaliger. Foix-Candale claimed in his dedicatory epistle that the ancient philosopher "Hermes Trismegistus" possessed knowledge of the divine equal to that of the apostles and the evangelists.[20] In the "Apology" there is a passage mocking an ecclesiastical dignitary who pointed in

Montaigne's company to a biblical passage that he felt validated his quest for the philosopher's stone (II.12, F442, V585–6A). Another contemporary and friend of Montaigne's, Florimond de Raemond, identified the dignitary as Foix-Candale in an annotation he added to his copy of the *Essays*.[21]

In 1579, a year before the first edition of the *Essays*, Foix-Candale published with Millanges a revised French translation of the original Greek text or *exemplaire* (*Le Pimandre de Mercure Trismegiste*) and dedicated it to the very patroness associated with Montaigne's "Apology" (II.12): Marguerite de Valois, wife of Henri de Navarre.[22] The vast commentary, requested by his brother and sister Frédéric and Jacqueline de Foix, dwarfed the slender ancient text. It included an apology for a "natural theology" of a much more ambitious and sophisticated kind than that proposed by Raymond Sebond.[23] Foix-Candale claimed that all Catholic teachings were anticipated and supported in the Hermetic "scriptures," that Hermes had been privy to the secrets of God's book of nature before Jesus Christ and before Moses.

Protestants in the same intellectual "family" based in the southwest but connected with Paris were making similarly ambitious uses of philosophical reasoning and ancient texts in theological contexts.[24] Philippe du Plessis de Mornay (Duplessis-Mornay) was a friend of Montaigne's and visited Foix-Candale's laboratory as a principal adviser in the train of Navarre himself.[25] In 1581, the same year as the second edition of Montaigne's translation of Sebond's work, the internationally famous publisher Plantin issued a work of Duplessis-Mornay's dedicated to Marguerite's husband, Navarre.[26] The work aimed to do exactly what Montaigne said Sebond had aimed to do: "by human and natural reasons to prove against the atheists all the articles of the Christian religion" (II.12, F320, V440A).[27] Like Foix-Candale's, it drew on ancient philosophers, including Hermes, to lay down rational foundations for its particular confessional stance. In his preface, Duplessis-Mornay answered two kinds of objector to his use of philosophical reason to combat opponents of the Protestant Christian faith. The first deny that you can use reason at all against those who do not accept your premises; the second accept that reason *could* be used to a limited degree to support and declare faith, but argue that it would be inappropriate.[28]

Montaigne inverts – in order to rebuff – the kind of apology made by a theological rationalist like Duplessis-Mornay. He also replies, on Sebond's behalf, to objectors of two types: those who say that Christian belief cannot be supported by natural reason; those who say that Sebond's use of natural reason in support of Christian belief is far too weak. He devotes the majority of his "Apology" to answering those – including Duplessis-Mornay – who would encourage the ladies at Navarre's court to go much further than Sebond in using natural reason and Greek philosophy either to prove or to disprove articles of the Christian faith (II.12, F327–8, V448–9A–C). Montaigne also takes up the legacy of the ancient sages but in so doing he changes its nature. He divides all ancient philosophy into three sects who differ over the outcome of the common quest for certain knowledge: dogmatists (they find it and establish their certainties as sciences), dogmatic sceptics (they affirm we can know nothing), pyrrhonists (they say they are still in search of the truth). But he goes on to reunite them as one extended family of doubtful reasoners, free exercisers of the mind who never intended to claim unquestionable authority (II.12, F370–83, V502–16). Even Aristotle's dogmatic style is described as pyrrhonism in an affirmative form (II.12, F376, V507A).

Montaigne is answering not only reformed authors amongst his acquaintance, like Duplessis-Mornay, but all authors who use natural reason and ancient texts in the refoundation of Christian dogma. More particularly, I am arguing that he is answering a noble Catholic philosopher who is still more closely a part of his own "family" than Duplessis-Mornay. Montaigne and Foix-Candale were neighbors. Both retired to take up private philosophical studies. They shared a whole set of social and intellectual relations with modern aristocratic and ancient philosophical "patrons," as well as with scholarly experts and publishers. Foix-Candale may to us sound like a more bizarre philosophical figure than Montaigne. In fact, his range of interests, his desire to produce a syncretistic philosophy for all of creation, to return to the pure sources of man's God-given knowledge, was much more at home in the prevailing philosophical atmosphere. He is an excellent example of the sort of contemporary patron–author against whom the author of the *Essays* – a "new figure, an unpremeditated and accidental philosopher" – should be set (II.12, V546C, F409).

Pierre de Brach, another of Montaigne's friends, aligned Foix-Candale and Hermes as equivalent classical and modern exemplars. Both, he says, were at one and the same time great princes, great prelates, great philosophers.[29] The *Pimandre* is a dogmatic philosophical theology stamped with the authority of the ancient prototype Hermes Trismegistus and of the imperial Catholic nobility. Montaigne answers his neighbor in a deliberately tentative style and format. He makes no obvious pretensions to philological and philosophico-theological authority. He does not remodel – and remodel himself upon – a foundational ancient *patron* like Hermes. He makes a virtue and a legacy out of *not* pretending to such grandeur, authority and learning.

The paradox, of course, is that he *does* draw on authoritative ancient models to authorize his not doing so. He also goes back to the "first philosophy" of the Greeks. He too, like Duplessis-Mornay and Foix-Candale, draws a religious conclusion from pagan philosophical texts. But the first philosophy he finds is not primeval knowledge of the causes of all things. It is a restless and endless inquiry rather like his own. So he "accidentally" rediscovers the free, never-ending inquiries of the first Greek sages, just as the late antique writer Plutarch had done. Plutarch is to Montaigne what Hermes is to Foix-Candale. Plutarch had been a philosopher and a priest, but in a different vein from the altogether mythical Hermes. One of Plutarch's theological dialogues on man's lack of communication with being is the source for the final passage in the "Apology."[30]

Montaigne's skeptical apology for his own father's "natural theology" shows the female Catholic nobility how to disarm dogmatic theological *docteurs*. Montaigne hands his patroness an intellectual weapon for the struggle against the new dogmatisms. It is the liberty and wantonness of ancient minds ("la liberté . . . et gaillardise de ces esprits anciens"), a weapon to be drawn only by the "wellborn" in extreme circumstances (II.12, F418–20, V557–9A). Montaigne is passing on the liberties of judgment and spirit of ancient Greeks from Socrates and Pyrrho down to Plutarch – but in controlled conditions.

THE MONTAIGNES' LEGACY

Like the rich Roman, Pierre Eyquem took great care to obtain the services of learned men and keep them around him. He also thought their knowledge was in some sense his. His intellectual abilities likewise dwelt in his collection of discourses and books, and in the heads of humanist visitors and the sons they educated:

My house has long been open to men of learning, and is well known to them. For my father, who ruled it for fifty years and more, inflamed with that new ardour with which King François I embraced letters and brought them into credit, sought with great diligence and expense the acquaintance of learned men, receiving them at his house like holy persons [who had been granted private inspiration by divine wisdom], collecting their sayings and discourses ("leurs sentences et leurs discours") like oracles, and with all the more [awe and devotion] as he had less [liberty] to judge them ("moins de loi d'en juger"); for he had no knowledge of letters, any more than his predecessors. Myself, I like them well enough, but I do not worship them.

Among others, Pierre Bunel, a man of great reputation for learning in his time, after staying a few days at Montaigne in the company of my father with other men of his sort, made him a [gift], on his departure, of a book entitled "Natural Theology, or Book of Creatures, by Master Raymond de Sabonde". And because the Italian and Spanish languages were familiar to my father, and this book was composed in a Spanish scrambled up with Latin endings, Bunel hoped that with a very little help he could make his profit of it, and recommended it to him as a very useful book and suited to the time in which he gave it to him; this was when the innovations of Luther were beginning to gain favor and to shake our old belief in many places.

In this he was very well advised, rightly foreseeing by rational inference that this incipient [disease] would easily degenerate into an execrable atheism. For the [mass of ordinary people], not having the faculty of judging things in themselves, let themselves be carried away by chance and by appearances, when once [you have put into their hands] the temerity to despise and [criticize] the opinions that they had held in extreme reverence, such as are those in which their salvation is concerned . . . [T]hey will soon cast easily into like uncertainty all the other parts of their belief . . . and they shake off as a tyrannical yoke all the impressions they had once received from the authority of the laws or the reverence of ancient usage. . .

Now some days before his death, by father, having by chance come across this book under a pile of other abandoned papers, commanded me to put it into French for him. . . [B]eing unable to disobey any command of the best father there ever was, I got through it as best I could; at which he was singularly pleased, and ordered it to be printed; and this was done after his death.[31]

If we combine this with other passages from 1.26 and II.12 we have a background story for the *Essays*.[32] On the model of the court of François I, a gentleman collector and patron forms a cultural legacy for his house, to be transmitted from father to son with other social privileges, possessions, and signs of status. Collecting, receiving, educating, commissioning, and giving (including to the public) are closely linked in this story. For collecting *sentences* and *discours*, receiving learned men as guests and learned books as gifts into the house, directing your son's institution using the latest pedagogical methods, organizing the translation and publication of works in your collection – all of these contribute to the attempted formation of an enduring reputation for *les lettres*.

There are hints as to how investment in collections of books, humanists and their *sentences* and *discours* spreads, and how it relates to the acquisition of social *credit* or reputation. The news of the religious passion of other European patrons like the papacy and the Medici for collecting manuscripts and humanist advisers convinced François I in the early 1520s to brief Guillaume Budé to expand the royal library at Fontainebleau.[33] This and other royal activities raised the reputation of *les lettres* throughout France, attracting investment from minor provincial patrons – those who, like Pierre Eyquem, were keen to move their families on. This is not to say that Pierre did not genuinely reverence the humanists and their discourse. Far from it. The whole point is that, lacking the *loi*, the liberty or power to judge, he "bought" wholesale the aura they set out to give to humane letters.

Pierre was looking to transfer this aura to his *maison*, by giving it a reputation with the humanists, a reputation for receiving humanists and their books. He believed that the future of his dynasty depended in important ways on its reputation for *les lettres*. He invested in it by hiring learned guests and buying their ideas to educate his son (1.26). One of these guests, on a particular occasion, offered him a timely gift-remedy in the form of a philosophical book with a pro-phylactic prescription against the disease of licentiously critical reasoning, whose first host was Luther. What appears to have mattered to Pierre about Sebond's book was that it marked a social transaction with a man of great reputation for learning. There is no hint that he personally formed any real acquaintance with the book and its contents. It seems to have been discarded under a pile of papers. When he happened across it again by chance, he used it to index an act of obedience from a son who, thanks to his investment, was capable of translating it from Latin into French. As patron, he made a new copy from a book in his collection and he ordered it to be published. It duly appeared posthumously under his name.[34] It is his public legacy, his *dying* legacy, as Michel emphasizes. With his gift-book Pierre was handing the moral and literary credit of his *maison* into the hands of his son, along with other possessions, rights, and privileges. He may also have entertained an intention – Bunel's intention, originally – to keep the recipient on the straight and narrow of the old faith by philosophical means.

It is arguable that from Michel's perspective the translated book *does* index the moral agency of a good father and head of household. Pierre is, morally, its author. It is just that Pierre's "good work" is mediated by the "borrowed" *suffisance* and judgment of his own son, and by the intention of the humanist who made the timely gift of a remedy in the first place. If Montaigne makes an implied criticism of his father, it is that borrowing someone else's intellectual intention in this way, and making a book without having "loi d'en juger," could be a risky business, especially when it came to the new culture of printed theologico-philosophical polemic. It could end up damaging your reputation or getting you embroiled in controversies.

But of course "Montaigne" does not publish the work without "loi d'en juger." The son and heir provides it. Sebond's text and its *risqué* prologue are carefully adapted in translation, and there is a lengthy apology to accompany it in the *Essays*.[35] It is important to understand, however, that Michel uses his own intellectual judgment and resources not so much to defend or betray the letter of Sebond's text as to realize the spirit of the original gift-remedy in his own terms and in his own moment. Bunel's intention – an intention co-opted by his father – had been to provide a textual prophylactic against the spread of licentiously critical reasoning. Sebond was an author held by Montaigne's betters and patrons to be of assistance in preserving true Catholic piety, even though the Roman Church was highly suspicious of Sebond's intentions as expressed in his prologue. But it was in many ways a "weak" book designed for readers with relatively little formal learning, readers such as Pierre Eyquem and the ladies at court (II.12, *F*320, *V*440A).[36] It looked flimsy and inadequate when put up alongside other works being produced by court theologians and philosophers like Duplessis-Mornay and Foix-Candale. It needed protection and support from its patron (Pierre), were it to serve the purpose intended by Pierre's learned guest, and vicariously by Pierre himself. In his father's name, Michel brings in some heavy-duty argumentative resources from Sextus Empiricus to provide this protection and meet this purpose. The new wrapping changes the nature of the gift – it now undermines rather than rebuilds the foundations of man's rational knowledge – but it serves the same purpose.

This is not, though, just a virtuoso display of philosophical judgment and learning on Montaigne's part. At stake here is the transmission of a carefully circumscribed natural liberty (*loi*) to judge freely of philosophical opinions, social customs, and works of art. On the one hand, the *Essays* do abrogate to themselves a well-born man's natural liberty to speak and judge more or less as he would, public reverence permitting. In so doing, they add to the Montaignes' legacy by "chiming" accidentally and fortuitously with the legacy of ancient philosophy – now received as an endless and doubtful inquiry. Montaigne takes this *loi*, this liberty knowing that some readers – not only official censors – might grant and some deny it him. Guez de Balzac, for example, wrote that Montaigne should have given himself less *liberté* when traveling as a stranger in Latin country (i.e., in judging classical Latin authors), that he should not have acted as a magistrate in a country in which he had no citizenship ("droit de bourgeoisie"). Etienne Pasquier is more indulgent; he allows Montaigne his "liberté particulière," his natural immunity from restraint.[37]

On the other hand, we have also heard how the theological scholar and humanist Luther gave ordinary people (*le vulgaire*) the boldness freely to criticize doctrines – such as those on their salvation – which they used to hold in awe. This legacy threatens to produce a diseased society full of people who would take nothing on authority, who, like kings, would only receive things to which they had assented by their own decree. Though he does not say it explicitly here, Montaigne knows that his great friend La Boétie's discourse in honor of liberty and against tyrants had *unwittingly* done something similar. It had handed arms against the "tyrannical" Catholic king to the public for Huguenot justifications of rebellion (1.28, *F*135, *V*183–4A; *F*144, *V*194A). So Montaigne had to be very careful about how and to whom and for what applications he bequeathed the well-born man's natural liberty to criticize, to judge. Otherwise, he might become the Luther of the secular philosophy of man (exactly what he *did* become, in many people's eyes).

So *docteurs* from the Lutheran and Calvinist reformers to the Catholic Hermeticists (like Foix-Candale) were bandying about the *loi* fundamentally both to critique and to re-rationalize the old religion. Montaigne's "Apology for Raymond Sebond" shows the patroness how to take that licentiously abrogated right from the hands of the *docteurs* using a still more extreme form of liberty taken from Greek sources. In so doing, the essay, and the *Essays* as a whole, aim to preserve, under particular conditions, the at once natural and ancient image of a free-ranging, lay critical discourse, a discourse different in kind from the esoteric theosophies and hermeneutics founded on ancient models by Duplessis-Mornay and Foix-Candale. The *Essays* were to have preserved it in polished form in that very discourse on liberty, inspired by a *sentence* in Plutarch and written by La Boétie, which was to have appeared in the middle of book I.

There is no paradox here if one accepts a philosopher's will and testament, the way he grants a legacy to beneficiaries with restrictive clauses, as part of the legacy itself. The *Essays* are the product of a careful balancing act. They would transmit, to a selective audience of the "well-born," a carefully circumscribed *liberté* to judge independently and freely of opinions, customs, and works of art. It is circumscribed in that it is proscribed from application to the bringing down of the established religious doctrines and political authorities of a fragile society. So when, for example, Montaigne abrogates to himself the liberty to criticize the harsh sentences handed out by magistrates and princes to witches, he immediately seeks to proscribe practical *applications* of that liberty against public reason or established custom (III.11, F790, V1033B). The conditional nature of this transmitted liberty is most apparent in the *absence*, in the event, of the intended publication of La Boétie's work from book I, a work that in the circumstances Montaigne judged too delicate to release again into the diseased public air. At the same time, however, Montaigne refuses to be publicly marked as a partisan supporter of the status quo. Where appropriate, indeed, he puts down markers of his defiance, such as his refusal to concede to the magistrate at Rome a right to censor his opinion that a heretic was one of the best poets of the century (III.10, F775, V1013B).

In the process of apologizing for the gift-remedy that Pierre would offer in French to the world (Sebond's book), Michel takes the liberty of criticizing – gently and implicitly – his own father. He shows how important it is for a patron not to welcome philosophical gifts and prescriptions with *undue* reverence (as his father had done). He turns his "apology" for Sebond into an extended display of the skeptical spirit in which all learned gifts and authoritative opinions are *personally* digested and self-applied by one noble collector of discourse who is studying his own natural *moeurs*. He continues to think and speak freely on all other topics – within certain limits – in order to reveal himself more fully. In offering us a register of this process as continued over half an adult lifetime he claims to be giving us the extraordinary fruits of a unique ethical experiment, one more potentially valuable than the alchemical and medical trials conducted by other noblemen. For many other patron–authors in Montaigne's social class were experimenting, were making collections from books, books from collections. But they were invariably doing so with third-hand, extraneous purposes and ready-made patterns in mind. And their practical curiosity was at work in areas of knowledge like natural philosophy, divinity and law, not the most fundamental knowledge of all, self-knowledge. That is what would make Montaigne's legacy so distinct. That is what made him the patron saint of the well-born person's liberty of speech and thought.

NOTES

1. See Steve Fuller, *The Struggle for the Soul of Science: Kuhn vs. Popper* (Cambridge: Icon Books, 2003), pp. 182–8.
2. Most of the passage is quoted in the final section of this chapter, below.
3. For Montaigne's *"patron"* or pattern within see III.2, F613, V807B. For "maistresse forme" see 1.50, F219, V302c; III.2, F615, V811b; M. A. Screech, *Montaigne and Melancholy: The Wisdom of the "Essays"* (London: Duckworth, 1983), p. 102.
4. For an essential corrective to the romantic modern view of a Montaigne isolated from all outer relations in his ivory tower see George Hoffmann, *Montaigne's Career* (Oxford: Oxford University Press, 1998).

5. Olivier Millet, *La Première réception des Essais de Montaigne (1580–1640)* (Paris: Honoré Champion, 1995), p. 53.

6. In this chapter I use *patron* in italics to denote an exemplar and "patron" for a person (who may also be a model).

7. Dale Kent, *Cosimo de' Medici and the Florentine Renaissance: The Patron's Oeuvre* (New Haven and London: Yale University Press, 2000), pp. 5, 214, 219–21; Aristotle, *Nicomachean Ethics*, 1122a.

8. Montaigne, *Journal de voyage*, ed. François Rigolot (Paris: Press Universitaires de France, 1992), p. 112 (*F950*); Franca Caldari Bevilacqua, "Montaigne alla Biblioteca Vaticana," in E. Balmas, ed., *Montaigne e L'Italia: Atti del Congresso Internazionale di studi di Milano-Lecco, 26–30 ottobre 1988*, Gruppo di studio sul cinquecento francese (Geneva: Slatkine, 1991), pp. 363–90 (374).

9. *Journal de voyage*, p. 112 (*F950*).

10. See in general Nello Vian, "La Presentazione e gli esemplari Vaticani della 'Assertio septem sacramentorum' di Enrico VIII," in *Collectanea Vaticana in Honorem Anselmi M. Card. Albareda a Bibliotheca Apostolica edita*, Studi e Testi 220 (Vatican City: Biblioteca Apostolica Vaticana, 1962), pp. 355–75.

11. Vian, "La Presentazione," pp. 360–62.

12. Vian, "La Presentazione," pp. 362–7, 369, 371.

13. I.25, *F100–01*, *V137A–C*.

14. III.12, *F808–9*, *V1055–6B–C*.

15. The manuscripts of Seneca and Plutarch shown to Montaigne were not part of the standard exhibition shown to visitors.

16. Millet, *La Première réception*, p. 51.

17. Giuseppe Marcenaro and Piero Boragina, *Viaggio in Italia: Un corteo magico dal Cinquecento al Novecento* (Electa: Milan, 2001), p. 116, citing Rome, Biblioteca Apostolica Vaticana, MS. 9693 (I have not seen this document myself).

18. I.26, *F110*, *V149–50A*.

19. *Dictionnaire de biographie française*, ed. J. Balteau et al. (Paris: Letouzey et Ané, 1933–). Foix-Candale is sometimes referred to as François Foix de Candale or just François de Foix.

20. *Mercurii Trismegisti Pimandras utraque lingua restitutus, D. Francisci Flussatis Candallæ industria. Ad Maximilianum Caesarem eius nominis quartum* (Bordeaux: S. Millanges, 1574). Foix-Candale believed Hermes Trismegistus to be the ancient Egyptian author of philosophico-religious treatises in Greek known collectively as the *Hermetica*. He believed him to date from the period of the first pharaoh, before the time of the Old Testament Abraham.

21. The passage talks about textual interpreters authoring *erreurs* or heresies, about the pseudo-authorities or Sybils in whose words interpreters find whatever prognostication they like. Montaigne may be alluding directly to Foix-Candale's work on the *Hermetica*. For Raemond's identification see Alan Boase, "Montaigne annoté par Florimond de Raemond," *Revue du Seizième Siècle*, 15 (1928), pp. 237–78 (271–2).

22. For the "Apology" and Marguerite de Valois see II.12, F418–20, V557–9A; Elaine Limbrick, "Métamorphose d'un philosophe en théologien", in Claude Blum, ed., *Montaigne, "Apologie de Raymond Sebond": De la "Theologia" à la "Théologie"* (Paris: Honoré Champion, 1990), pp. 229–46 (236–8); François Rigolot, "D'une *Théologie* 'pour les dames' à une *Apologie* 'per le donne'" in Blum, ed., *Montaigne*, pp. 261–90 (264–7).

23. *Le Pimandre de Mercure Trismegiste de la Philosophie Chrestienne, Cognoissance du verbe divin, & de l'excellence des oeuvres de Dieu, traduit de l'exemplaire Grec, avec collation de tres-amples commentaires, par Francois Monsieur de Foix, de la famille de Candalle, Captal de Buchs, & c. Evesque d'Ayre, & c. Tres-haute, tres-illustre, & tres-puissante Princesse, Marguerite de France, Roine de Navarre, fille & soeur des Rois tres-Chrestiens* (Bordeaux: S. Millanges, 1579).

24. See the excellent article by Jeanne Harrie, "Duplessis-Mornay, Foix-Candale and the Hermetic Religion of the World," *Renaissance Quarterly*, 31 (1978), pp. 499–514.

25. Harrie, "Duplessis-Mornay," pp. 502n.15. For Montaigne's contact with Duplessis-Mornay see the index to Donald Frame, *Montaigne: A Biography* (London: Hamish Hamilton, 1965).

26. Philippe du Plessis de Mornay, *De la Verité de la Religion Chrestienne contre les Athées, Epicuriens, Payens, Juifs, Mahumedistes, et autres Infideles* (Antwerp: C. Plantin, 1581).

27. Duplessis-Mornay uses different strategies depending on the position of his opponent. Against atheists and Epicureans he uses natural reasoning, and against "false Naturalists" he uses natural reasoning and Greek philosophy together.

28. I have used the edition published by Claude Micard at Paris in 1585, as the first edition is defective.

29. Pierre de Brach wrote a sonnet for the preliminary matter of *Le Pimandre*.

30. After the long hidden quotation from Plutarch, Montaigne goes on: "To this most religious conclusion of a pagan I want to add etc. . . . ." (II.12, F455–7, V601–03A).

31. II.12, *F*319–20, *V*438–9A. In the phrase "moins de loi d'en juger" I have translated *loi* as "liberty" in the older English sense of a specific privilege or right to do something, a specific immunity from restraint. In old French, *liberté* has a similar connotation.

32. For a related reading of this passage see Michel Simonin, "La Préhistoire de l'Apologie de Raymond Sebond," in Blum, ed., *Montaigne 'Apologie de Raymond Sebond'*, pp. 85–116 (94–100). Simonin argues convincingly that Montaigne's background story is likely to be confected in many respects.

33. Arlette Jouanna, *La France du XVIe siècle 1483–1598* (Paris: Presses Universitaires de France, 1997), p. 254.

34. *La Theologie Naturelle de Raymond Sebon* (Paris: Michel Sonnius, Guillaume Chaudière, and Gilles Courbin, 1569). Pierre's name appeared at the head of his son's dedication.

35. See the introduction to Montaigne, *An Apology for Raymond Sebond*, trans. and ed. M. A. Screech (London: Penguin, 1987), and the essays collected in Blum, ed., *Montaigne, 'Apologie de Raymond Sebond'* (especially Hendrick and Simonin). Although it is still not clear which Latin text Montaigne used, it is increasingly accepted that his translation – especially of Sebond's prologue – was heavily adaptive.

36. Limbrick, "Métamorphose," pp. 234–8; Rigolot, "D'une Théologie 'pour les dames' à une Apologie 'per le donne'," pp. 261–90.

37. Alan Boase, *The Fortunes of Montaigne: A History of the Essays in France, 1580–1669* (London: Methuen, 1935), p. 297; Millet, *La Première réception*, p. 144.

# 4 Montaigne and antiquity: fancies and grotesques

[I]f . . . he had adopted a plan such as mine, of putting his ideas (*fantasies*) in writing, we should see many rare things which would bring us very close to the glory of antiquity.

(1.28, F135, V184)

Montaigne's appreciation of La Boétie uses terminology that one has come to consider the highest accolade for the Renaissance writer: the contemporary author is seen as comparable with classical antiquity, its true heir, imitator, and emulator. It is a remark that Montaigne endorses at the close of his essay, declaring that La Boétie's "mind was molded in the pattern of other ages than this" (*F*144, *V*194). There appears to be no finer compliment. Yet by an irony that is rarely far from Montaigne's work, the essayist's veneration of his friend is couched in terms that are the opposite of his evaluation of himself and his own enterprise: where La Boétie is outstanding "in the matter of natural gifts" (*F*135, *V*184), Montaigne's "ability does not go far enough for [him] to dare to undertake a rich, polished picture, formed according to art" (*F*135, *V*183). The difference is intensified precisely because one writer is alive and the other dead; La Boétie has become absorbed into that classical pantheon that reverses the movement from past to present that is an assumption of the Renaissance intellectual heritage. As one reads on, it becomes apparent that La Boétie's surviving writings, of which Montaigne is the literary executor, are only a pale shadow compared to what might have been had he lived. The full paradox of the situation now becomes apparent, inasmuch as La Boétie can be the unified writer, a model rivaling past ages, because death has robbed him of the necessity of facing the difficulties of dealing in the present with the heritage of

antiquity – difficulties of difference and assimilation that are written
into the issue of mimesis. Perhaps only in death and through the lens
of friendship can the status of the classicizing writer become fully
conferred.

This small vignette of the relationship between two writers is
indicative of a crucial strand in Montaigne's thinking about classical
antiquity. Among all his essays, the titles of most of which begin with
the word "on," none directly deals with this topic. Its absence is not
fortuitous, for Montaigne's thought is imbued with classical antiquity, which is present in a variety of forms throughout his *Essays*
as well as his *Travel Journal*: thus antiquity is not of antiquarian
interest for him. It is not received as a set of abstract propositions
or an inert corpus of knowledge, but as a body of writing within a
body of writing, woven piecemeal into the texture and text of the
*Essays* as part of the act of composition; so that each essay will be
in an important sense a fresh start, a new way of approaching antiquity. Montaigne's description of La Boétie, that we quoted earlier,
highlights a central feature in this process: the *Essays* have an intimate connection with *fantasie(s)*, a word that (as here) frequently
means "thought(s)" or "idea(s)," but is etymologically linked with
the faculty of *fantasie* or imagination, and through that with fancy,
dream, illusion, or – by association, as we shall see – the grotesque.[1]
The present chapter will attempt to trace the emergence and operation of this cluster of ideas in three principal areas of Montaigne's
work that deal with classical antiquity: the use of quotation; classical philosophy; and the question of models of behavior. "These
are my fancies, by which I try to give knowledge not of things, but
of myself," Montaigne emphasizes in "Of Books," adding, "As my
fancies present themselves, I pile them up" (II.10, F296–7, V407,
409): with the *Essays*, antiquity enters a medium in which writing
(*écriture*) and the essay form are the primary focus, not incidental
features.

## BOOKS: "POETRY HAS FINGERS"

Antiquity as a textual presence is most immediately seen in the quotations from and allusions to classical works that densely pack each
page of the *Essays*.[2] Montaigne's evolving tastes in this regard have
been the subject of various studies,[3] and it is worth dwelling for a

moment on the nature of his preferences. Alongside his liking for Plutarch and Seneca[4] stands Montaigne's passion for Latin poetry, particularly Horace, Lucretius, Ovid, and Virgil in his early writing career (during the 1570s and up to the first edition of the *Essays* in 1580). During the 1580s this interest in Latin poetry broadens, with the addition of Catullus, Juvenal, Lucan, Martial, Persius, Propertius, and Terence to the corpus of works he draws on. Between 1588 and his death in 1592, he makes few new references to poetry or indeed to Plutarch but shows a marked liking for historians (notably Diodorus Siculus, Herodotus, Livy, and Tacitus) and for philosophy, as represented by Aristotle's *Nicomachean Ethics*, Cicero, and Diogenes Laertius. These broad characteristics do not however do justice to the range, depth, and innovation of Montaigne's readings of the classics. The *Essays* reflect mobile tastes rather than fixed preferences and the extensive quotations that saturate Montaigne's work are far from ornamental: they deepen the resonance of his views, add extra dimensions of significance or critical distance, comment, query, or ironize. Moreover, in the original editions of the *Essays* the Latin quotations are the only segments of text that interrupt the continuous stretches of print comprising each chapter.[5] Far from merging with the surrounding French, the quotations would have stood out from it even more than they do now, and thus acted as moments of pause or points of reference.

Some instances, increasing in range from micro-contextual to macro-contextual, will help illustrate these characteristics. The opening of essay 1.28, "Of Friendship," compares Montaigne's work to that of a painter who fills the frame around his picture with "grotesques," paintings of creatures half-human, half-animal that were a feature of Renaissance art and architecture. Montaigne then elaborates the comparison – the *Essays* likewise are just "grotesques and monstrous bodies" (*F*135, *V*183) – and, seemingly to accentuate the comparison, quotes a line from the beginning of Horace's *Art of Poetry*: *Desinit in piscem mulier formosa superne* ("a lovely woman tapers off into a fish," *F*135, *V*183). The quotation tallies beautifully with Montaigne's point; and thus the classical authority appears to support the modern writer's stance. In its original context, however – and ideally each Latin quotation cited by Montaigne should be compared with its original context – Horace is also discussing a painting, but making the opposite point: the work of art should *not* be the kind of heterogeneous production that reminds one of a fish's tail stuck on to a beautiful woman's body. What Montaigne is thus implicitly emphasizing is the difference between classical esthetics symbolized by Horace and the type of writing that will be associated with the essay form. Unlike classical writers and indeed unlike the writer that La Boétie would eventually have become, Montaigne characterizes his own work as the product of disjointedness and heterogeneity, a home for fancy and the grotesque.[6]

Essay 1.8, "Of Idleness," is a compact example of the interaction of text and co-text over the course of a single short essay. It might even be considered as reinforcing, at a significantly early stage, the point about non-systematic, disorderly, incongruous writing in essay 1.28 and the valorization, alongside grotesques, of the imagination. Essay 1.8 brings these elements together. It begins with an extended double comparison. The first deals with fallow land that needs careful weeding and sowing so as to be made serviceable. The second is drawn from Renaissance medicine: the shapeless pieces of flesh (spontaneous abortions or still-births) produced by women likewise indicate the need for proper seed. The point of the comparisons is then clarified: the mind too, if not bridled and controlled, will cast itself in disorderly fashion into the "vague field of imagination" (F21, V32). The disorderly aspect with which the imagination is connected is soon after emphasized by a Latin quotation from Horace: *velut aegri somnia, vanae / Finguntur species* ("like a sick man's dreams / They form vain visions," F21, V32). The original context is once again Horace's *Art of Poetry* and once again it is a passage where Horace is criticizing an excessive propensity for variety in art (the poet's art and the painter's art). Such excessive variety produces incoherence, a sick man's dreams, idle fancies. While Horace's point underscores Montaigne's at this stage, the essayist will go further than his classical counterpart in the second half of this short essay, which in effect takes up the initial image of the fallow field. Taking retirement from his post in the *Parlement* of Bordeaux, the essayist had sought to give his mind the leisure to get to know itself and settle into itself. But the result has been the opposite: his mind has behaved like a runaway horse, begetting fantastical delusions and monsters, which the essayist has decided to write down. The economy of Montaigne's technique is apparent here, as the closing lines of the essay echo the imagery of childbirth, delusion, and idleness that had been evoked in the first part of the essay. Their implications are telling: there is no introspection without leisure, but leisure breeds wild, skittish thoughts, the vain idlings that Horace had condemned. Writing for Montaigne involves risk – delusions, dreams, fancies, ridiculousness, and incongruity pushed to the point of apparent incoherence. Montaigne's project is once again the opposite of classical esthetics, and the interaction between his thought and quotations from four Latin poets (in addition to Horace, there are Virgil, Martial, and Lucan) enables him to delineate his position, one that is fully consonant with the opening of essay 1.28 and with his pronouncements elsewhere.[7]

The examples studied so far have attempted to show how Montaigne enters deeply into dialogue with the classical authors he quotes, defining in the process his own characteristics and initiative. One final example in this section reveals Montaigne using quotations as a structural principle on a larger scale than in 1.8. Essay III.5, "On Some Verses of Virgil," makes use of three extensive quotations from Latin poetry, placed approximately at the beginning, middle, and end of this lengthy essay whose innocuous title conceals the fact that it deals largely with attitudes towards sexual behavior and gender. In each case, the quotations serve as a focus for Montaigne's reflections, summarizing what he has been saying or anticipating a point that follows. In effect, the whole essay could be seen as a lengthy gloss on the quotations, so inverting the assumed order of priority of text and quotation and demonstrating at the same time how Montaigne can approach a difficult, even taboo topic allusively and indirectly.

Montaigne, indeed, states that love is depicted more vividly in poetry than in real life and then proceeds to substantiate his claim by quoting nine lines from book 8 of Virgil's *Aeneid* dealing with the union of Vulcan and Venus, the man and wife deities of fire and love respectively. The second quotation is intended directly to echo the first: "what Virgil says of Venus and Vulcan, Lucretius had said more appropriately of a stolen enjoyment between her and Mars" (*F*664, *V*872). This too is a story of love, but of adulterous, not married, love, and these lines from Lucretius' *De rerum natura* (*On the Nature of Things*), though in themselves remarkable, give rise to a no less remarkable critical appreciation of this and the previous passage from Montaigne himself:

When I ruminate that *rejicit* (flings), *pascit* (devours), *inhians* (wide-mouthed), *molli* (soft), *fovet* (fondles), *medullas* (marrow), *labefacta* (trembling), *pendet* (suspended), *percurrit* (runs through), and that noble *circumfusa* (blended), mother of the pretty *infusus* (out-poured), I despise those petty conceits and verbal tricks that have sprung up since. These good people needed no sharp and subtle play on words; their language is all full and copious with a natural and constant vigor. They are all epigram, not only the tail but the head, stomach, and feet . . . When I see these brave forms of expression, so alive, so profound, I do not say "This is well said," I say "This is well thought." It is the sprightliness of the imagination that elevates and swells the words. (F664–5, V872–3).

The poetry of Lucretius and Virgil is personified in anthropomorphic terms: it has not a tail only, but a head, a stomach, and feet. Montaigne says a little later that the Latin poets' words are not wind, but flesh and bone. It is a striking confirmation of Montaigne's earlier comment, drawn from Juvenal, that poetry has fingers (F645, V849) – that it is invested with a power of touch, of feeling, and of excitement that allows the words to mean more than they say. Montaigne deftly suggests that the imaginings of poetry may have an intensely physical tangibility and effect on the reader or listener. Around and between these quotations, he weaves considerations on no less physical, intimate features of human activity – love, marriage, sex, adultery, pleasure, the erotics and reticences of language. By the time he reaches his final major Latin quotation – from Catullus, LXV, an extract itself about eroticism and reticence – he has moved on to the sexual oppression of women and the problem of gender difference. He persuades us that poetic fancies are not a sick man's delirium, but ways of representing what is most intimate and least expressible in human society and thought. Only in poetic imaginings, and in Montaigne's own quirky imaginings, can such inexpressibles be given the voice for which they yearn. "On Some Verses of Virgil" is a pre-eminent example of how a potentially remote corpus of writing inherited from antiquity can be perceived as a living body instinct with the power to convey and even shape the most private thoughts and feelings of the reader. Poetry has fingers, and it is in Montaigne's essay that these fingers reach out to touch.

### PHILOSOPHY: INTERROGATIVE IMAGINATION

Montaigne's relationship with classical philosophy – our second area of investigation – is unusually complex. In the first edition of the *Essays* in 1580, he criticizes both Plato and Aristotle in the essay "Of the Education of Children" (1.26) in the following terms: "But as for gnawing my nails over the study of Plato or Aristotle, or stubbornly pursuing some part of knowledge, I have never done it" (F106–07 modified, V146). The key to his hostility is given in the phrase "stubbornly pursuing some part of knowledge": the two Greek philosophers symbolize at this early stage the bookish, stultifying learning that for Montaigne is the opposite of authentic intellectual inquiry. After 1588, however, Montaigne will alter his attitude at least towards Plato, who is now removed from the above quotation and becomes the object of Montaigne's attention, largely because of the figure of Socrates (to whom we shall come in due course). The central section of "Of Physiognomy" borrows from Plato's *Apology for Socrates*, while "Of Coaches" will make use of the *Symposium; Laws, Republic, Timaeus, Gorgias, Phaedo* as well as the Dialogues all likewise contribute something to the *Essays* after 1588. By contrast, the essayist's attitude to Aristotle remains more ambiguous. He is the object of severe criticism: the Stagirite is the "monarch of modern learning" (F107, V146) and "the god of scholastic knowledge" (F403, V539). These two quotations, particularly the second, reveal the reasons for Montaigne's dislike: the doctrinal status of Aristotle in late medieval Scholasticism had led to intellectual rigidity, and Montaigne directs especially withering criticism at the *Organon*, the collection of Aristotle's logical works that was a source (frequently parodied) of Scholastic jargon.[8] Nonetheless, Montaigne's express statements about Aristotle should not be taken entirely at face value. Recent research has shown that he was fully conversant with Aristotelian ethics, rhetoric, and dialectic and that these form the conceptual framework for his reflections in a variety of spheres.[9] Montaigne seeks all the same a philosophical outlook that is more consonant with the tentative, exploratory, non-systematic nature of his own enterprise. He finds it in Pyrrhonian skepticism.[10]

Pyrrho of Elis (ca. 365–ca. 270 BCE), the "founder" of Pyrrhonism, left no writings of his own. Montaigne became acquainted with his philosophy from two sources: the biography of Pyrrho to be found in Diogenes Laertius' *Lives of the Philosophers*, a Latin translation of which had appeared in the fifteenth century; and Sextus Empiricus' *Outlines of Pyrrhonism* (sometimes also known by the older title *Pyrrhonian Hypotyposes*), a Latin translation and edition of which was published by the French humanist Henri Estienne in 1562. In the "Apology for Raymond Sebond" – the twelfth essay in the second book and the longest in his whole work – Montaigne gives an account – rather a piecemeal one, admittedly – of the chief tenets of Pyrrhonism such as are central to his own concerns. In essence, Pyrrhonism is based on the attainment of *ataraxia* (*ataraxie* in French, "imperturbability" in English) through the suspension of judgment (*epochē*, "surceance et suspension de jugement" for Montaigne, F374, V505), as a reaction to what Pyrrhonists see as the indeterminacy of the truth about sense perception and their consequent advocacy of the need to follow appearances (*phainomena*) without worrying about their truth value. In essay II.12 itself, Pyrrhonism is used as a tool to dismantle the claims of human reason to be a source of epistemological certainty. The claims and counter-claims of a large range of classical philosophies that Montaigne surveys in the course of his argument – from the Pre-Socratics to Stoicism and Epicureanism – only help demonstrate for him the vanity of human intellectual aspirations, all asserting a privileged relationship with the truth, whereas they are in fact for Montaigne so contradictory as to be readily falsifiable and bear witness less to knowledge than to ignorance.

What is less often noticed in this radical relativism is the extent to which Montaigne's Pyrrhonism is linked to the idea of imaginings and so ties in with the uses of fantasy that are apparent elsewhere in his work. In the "Apology," Montaigne states: "I say the same thing about philosophy; it has so many faces and so much variety, and has said so much, that all our dreams or reveries ("songes et resveries") are found in it. Human fancy ("phantasie") cannot conceive anything good or evil that is not in it" (II.12, F408, V546). This ironically derogatory remark is aimed at the contradictions and excesses of classical thought that Montaigne reviews in the course of his essay. Against the fixed intellectual positions that these systems of thought represented, Montaigne proposes a philosophy that renounces dogmatism and in so doing can itself appear as fantastical. Thus in discussing the Pyrrhonists' "sacramental word" *epechō* ("I refrain," *F*374, *V*505), Montaigne typifies their outlook in this way: "whoever will imagine (*imaginera*) a perpetual confession of ignorance, a judgment without leaning or inclination, on any occasion whatever, he has a conception of Pyrrhonism. I express this point of view (*fantasie*) as well as I can, because many find it difficult to conceive" (*F*374, *V*505). He later adds: "The Pyrrhonians, when they say that the sovereign good is Ataraxy, which is the immobility of the judgment, do not mean to say it in an affirmative way; but the same impulse of their soul that makes them avoid precipices and take cover in the cool of the evening, itself offers them this fancy (*fantasie*) and makes them refuse any other" (*F*435–6, *V*578). The paradox in Montaigne's descriptions of this variety of classical skepticism is that the Pyrrhonians themselves opposed the human fantasy of possessing the truth: "the fantastic, imaginary, false privileges that man has arrogated to himself, of regimenting, arranging, and fixing truth, he [= Pyrrho] honestly renounced and gave up" (*F*374, *V*505). The "fantasy" of Pyrrhonism is thus pressed into service to combat the human fantasy of fixing and holding the truth.[11] Less a ready-made theory than a methodological approach that fits in well with the exploratory nature of the essay form itself, skepticism in Montaigne's hands is not a means for casting indiscriminate doubt upon everything – and hence a form of easy cynicism – but a method of inquiry, a way of judging and weighing dogmatic assertions of many kinds. As he says at the opening of essay II.3, "If to philosophize is to doubt, as they say, then to play the fool and follow my fancies ("niaiser et fantastiquer"), as I do, is all the more to doubt. For it is for learners to inquire and dispute, and for the master to decide" (*F*251, *V*350). Truth itself is not thereby discarded as an outmoded intellectual category – Montaigne specifically says the opposite[12] – but rather suspended in favor of the examination of the premises under which inquiry after the truth is conducted or represented in human thought. Pyrrhonism is hence best seen not so much as the result of a putative skeptical crisis, supposedly situated in the mid-1570s,[13] as the outcome of Montaigne's trying out of various solutions to the issues that preoccupied him (epistemology and ontology are among the most obvious) until he discovered a classical philosophy consistent with his own investigative enterprise. It is this harnessing of philosophical approach and literary form that gives the methodology of the *Essays* in this domain its particular acuity and strength.

Although the "Apology" provides the best-known instance of Pyrrhonism, it is but one example of a generalized phenomenon. In keeping with Sextus Empiricus' statement that skeptical "medicine" can be administered in stronger or weaker doses according to need,[14] Montaigne varies the quantity as the case requires. The procedure is heuristic rather than uniformly systematic; sometimes it will be a word, expression, or allusion that inaugurates the skeptical method or perspective, while at other times the skeptical treatment is more extensive.[15] "Of Cripples" falls into the latter category.[16] It shares with the "Apology" a distrust of human reason and its propensity for idle speculation about causes rather than establishing and examining facts:

I was just now musing, as I often do, on how free and vague an instrument human reason is. I see ordinarily that men, when facts are put before them, are more ready to amuse themselves by inquiring into their reasons than by inquiring into their truth. They leave aside the cases and amuse themselves treating the causes ... They pass over the facts, but they assiduously examine their consequences. They ordinarily begin thus: "How does this happen?" What they should say is: "But does it happen?" Our reason is capable of filling out a hundred other worlds and finding their principles and contexture. It needs neither matter nor basis; let it run on; it builds as well on emptiness as on fullness, and with inanity as with matter. (III.11, F785, V1026–7)

A case in point is the essayist's initial reference to the reform of the calendar put into effect by pope Gregory XIII in October 1582; fears about the upheavals it would bring in its wake proved groundless.

Yet Montaigne is aware that not all such instances are easy to deal with, seeing that: "Truth and falsehood are alike in face, similar in bearing, taste, and movement; we look upon them with the same eye" (F785, V1027). And nowhere do difficulties arise more pressingly than in legal cases where witnesses are adduced to testify to the truth of allegations, a feature especially common, Montaigne adds, "in things of which it is hard to persuade others" (F785, V1027). This last remark leads on to the question of witch trials, which flourished in the latter part of the sixteenth century:[17] "The witches of my neighborhood are in mortal danger every time some new author comes along and attests to the reality of their visions (*songes*)" (F788, V1031). This quotation displays one of Montaigne's targets in this essay: the credence given to what are essentially illusions (*songes*). Accusations of witchcraft based on opinion, rumor, or hearsay glorified with the status of legal evidence seem to Montaigne dubious; they would, he says, require divine guidance to adjudicate which are true and which false – but it precisely such divine guidance that is, with some exceptions, lacking. Witnesses in this matter are not themselves necessarily credible:

How much more natural and likely it seems to me that two men are lying than that one man should pass with the winds in twelve hours from the east to the west! How much more natural that our understanding should be carried away from its base by the volatility of our untracked mind than that one of us, in flesh and bone, should be wafted up a chimney on a broomstick by a strange spirit! (F789, V1032)[18]

In the meantime, Montaigne advocates prudence – in this instance, the benefit of the doubt: "I follow St. Augustine's opinion, that it is better to lean toward doubt than toward assurance in things difficult to prove and dangerous to believe" (F789–90, V1032), while emphasizing on various occasions in the course of the essay the degree of certainty that is needed before human life can justifiably be taken.[19]

The questioning that Montaigne directs at such cases is backed up by recourse to Pyrrhonian terminology as such: his profession of ignorance and refusal to speak of things "didactically and dogmatically" ("par precepte et resolution"; F788, V1030) are clear instances of such terminology. Similarly when he proceeds to scrutinize the very vocabulary by which we formulate propositions:

I like these words, which soften and moderate the rashness of our propositions: "perhaps," "to some extent," "some," "they say," "I think," and the like. And if I had to train children, I would have filled their mouths so much with this way of answering, inquiring, not decisive – "What does that mean? I do not understand it. That might be. Is it true?" (F788, V1030)

The description "this way of answering, inquiring, not decisive" ("enquesteuse, non resolutive") points to the Pyrrhonian origin of these terms[20] as ways of introducing doubt into assertion and highlighting the provisional, non-absolute quality of all statements. We recall that Montaigne had introduced his own querying of any inquiry into causes with an interrogative form: "They ordinarily begin thus: 'How does this happen?' What they should say is: 'But does it happen?'" (F785, V1026–27), and in the "Apology," he deems such interrogative forms particularly appropriate to Pyrrhonism.[21]

It is not the only occurrence of a Pyrrhonian outlook here. It recurs specifically in the discussion that gives the essay its title, namely the reputed prowess of the lame in love-making. Montaigne offers several explanations for this phenomenon (remarking also, in passing, that the same tale is told of women weavers) before standing back to evaluate these stories:

> Do not these examples confirm what I was saying at the beginning: that our reasons often anticipate the fact, and extend their jurisdiction so infinitely that they exercise their judgment even in inanity and non-being? Not only is our invention flexible in forging reasons for all sorts of dreams [songes], but our imagination [imagination] is equally prone to receive impressions from the very unreliable appearances given by falsehood. (F791, V1034)

As with witchcraft, the example of the lame proves another instance of the mind's preference for speculation over fact; thus the closing reflections are consistent with the argument that Montaigne advances throughout. The suspension of judgment that he advocates in this matter is coupled, here as previously, with an investigation into the mind's capacity for forming opinions; and foremost in consideration is the imagination. We recall that the imagination and imaginings characterize Pyrrhonism in the "Apology," the skeptical outlook being itself both a fancy and an attack on the vain fancies of human reason. The same principle is adopted here: we can forge reasons, Montaigne says, for all sorts of dreams (the same word that had been applied to witches' delusions in an earlier passage).

The final page of "Of Cripples" will deal with a further set of fancies, this time relating to Carneades (ca. 213–129 BCE), the founder of the New Academy and a skeptic of such radical disposition that he rejected all notion of seeking the truth through the exercise of judgment. Montaigne comments: "This very vigorous idea (fantasie) of Carneades sprang up in antiquity, in my opinion, from the impudence of those who profess to know and from their immoderate arrogance" (F792, V1035). A little later, he explains further: "The pride of those who attributed to the human mind a capacity for all things produced in others, through spite and emulation, the opinion that it is capable of nothing. These men maintain the same extreme in ignorance that the others maintain in knowledge" (F792, V1035). Carneades' philosophical position comes about as an extreme reaction to dogmatic claims on behalf of the human mind (often associated in skeptical thought with Stoicism). On one side stand "impudence," "immoderate arrogance," "pride," "knowledge;" on the other side, "fancy," "spite and emulation," "opinion," "ignorance." A similar characterization occurs in essay II.12 when Montaigne describes those ancient philosophical schools that claimed to possess the truth; those that abandoned any such hope; and those that suspended judgment about the truth.[22] The last-named position is that of the Pyrrhonists. So too in this context: the philosophical extremes that Montaigne describes are equally fantasies, born out of opposition to each other, and so constitute a dialectical construct rather than an objective position. Between these two poles, Montaigne the Pyrrhonist patiently proposes suspension of judgment as a means of resisting rash opinion and delusion (though the essayist also willingly admits his own fallibility in this regard),[23] as he equally patiently investigates the misrepresentations that the mind builds up in defiance of a clear-sighted view of the evidence.

CONDUCT: SHAPING FEATURES

The relationship of Montaigne to antiquity that this chapter has sketched out up to this point has emphasized the inventiveness of the essayist in shaping inherited forms in ways that mark the singularity of his project – his difference from antiquity as much as his indebtedness to it. The final part of this chapter will turn to an area in which the influence of classical antiquity has a peculiarly determining role: the question of models of conduct. While the *Essays* may seem to modern readers of eminently bookish conception and execution, the essayist himself consistently underscores their non-bookish or indeed anti-bookish qualities, drawing the reader's attention to the importance of action and living, and the consequent need to understand human behavior and motivation. It is the model of conduct that acts as a link between the existential and the writerly. In one sense, this area develops a Montaignean version of Plutarch's

*Parallel Lives*, for which the essayist had a predilection,[24] since the discovery of the self that the *Essays* describe and explore has its counterpart in the discovery of other selves whose potential as guides for conduct or emulation can be investigated.

The essay "Of the Most Outstanding Men" (II.36) affords an insight into Montaigne's tastes at an early stage of development. It considers three such examples of excellence: Homer, Alexander the Great, and Epaminondas, a juxtaposition of a writer (and a poet at that), a conqueror, and a soldier–statesman that is itself instructive. The three men are considered separately, in sequence, yet also compared with each other, and with other examples of pre-eminence: so Alexander is also compared with Julius Caesar, Epaminondas with Scipio Aemilianus. The two military leaders are prized for their moral qualities (while conversely Homer is valued for his military advice!), but special consideration is reserved for Epaminondas, as an admired blend of soldier, statesman, and Pythagorean philosopher. In this essay, Montaigne displays in microcosm his preferred approach to the question of figures of influence: he is attracted to those who display a spectrum of talents, particularly those who combine the active life and life of the writer (Julius Caesar and, in a minor key, Xenophon, fall into this category).[25] As with the essayist himself, aspects of their characters are refracted prismatically throughout the *Essays* and the picture of them that emerges is many-layered and multi-faceted. Cato the Younger – the object of a lengthy life by Plutarch – is a special favorite with Montaigne in the early days. Essay 1.37 is entirely devoted to him, and celebrates him as "truly a model chosen by nature to show how far human virtue and constancy could go" (F171, V231). And it is notable that in the process of extolling Cato, Montaigne here also extols the poetry that commemorates him, quoting from Martial, Manilius, Lucan, Horace, and Virgil in his praise. Once again, excellence and writing about excellence go hand-in-hand. Elsewhere, the essayist comments positively on Cato's courage and also on his attitude to his chosen manner of death, suicide.[26] Yet when he later considers Cato's virtue in "Of Physiognomy," he finds it so far above the attainment of ordinary mortals as to be inimitable.[27] By contrast, in his dealings with skepticism, Montaigne purposely stresses that Pyrrho is a flesh-and-blood man, not just the embodiment of a philosophy.[28] Géralde Nakam not unreasonably claims that Pyrrho is a major model of

imitation in the *Essays* of 1580, whereas in and after 1588 this role
has been taken by Socrates.[29] There is, however, an overlap rather
than a clean break, and it can be argued that Socrates epitomizes
the diverse strands that, throughout the *Essays*, constitute the figure of conduct as such. He has, for instance, interestingly enough,
intrinsic connections with Pyrrhonism, inasmuch as a philosophical
tradition, referred to by Montaigne in the "Apology," made him (and
indeed Plato) representatives of the skeptical outlook.[30] Like Pyrrho
(again), he is the champion of ignorance, as a counterbalance to the
philosophical "wisdom" that claims more than it can prove; like the
Cato the Younger, he is the embodiment of virtue (II.11, *F*308, *V*423);
in essay III.8 (*F*705–6, *V*925), he is the representative of that art of
vigorous debate that Montaigne clearly sees as a prime feature of
his own work. He equally turns attention away from the mere accumulation of knowledge to its practical application in the business
of living, at the same time that he examines the premises of such
knowledge, revealing it to be often no more than opinion or fancy.
Above all, he embodies the search for self-knowledge that is of central concern to the author of the *Essays*; in "Of Experience" (III.13,
*F*823, *V*1075), Socrates will indeed be directly connected with the
imperative to know oneself. He is, in short, "the master of masters"
(III.13, *F*824, *V*1076).

"Of Physiognomy," essay III.12, gives pride of place to Socrates. He
is viewed from the very outset as the ideal product of Nature understood as a guiding principle that can be known through *expérience*
(experience, but also *essai*, testing-out) of one's own nature; and he
is by the same token the opposite of the artifice and artificiality
that Montaigne thinks of as characteristic of his own age. Socrates
is now preferred even to Cato, as behaving "in the ordinary way
of human life" (*F*793, *V*1038); he becomes by so doing one of the
"interpreters of the simplicity of nature" (*F*805, *V*1052). In a move
common elsewhere in Montaigne's assessment of models of behavior, this simplicity finds expression in literary form – in this case
a passage from Socrates' address to his trial judges, quoted from
Plato's *Apology for Socrates*, which is deemed "the pure and primary impression and ignorance of Nature" (*F*807, *V*1054–5). And
Montaigne concludes: "Truly it is much easier to talk like Aristotle
and live like Caesar than it is to talk and live like Socrates. There lies
the extreme degree of perfection and difficulty; art cannot reach it"

(*F808, V1055*). Simplicity, ordinariness, living according to Nature supplant the alternative biographies, the other parallel lives, that Montaigne has investigated up to this point.

There is, nonetheless, a flaw in this perfection. It arises from a characteristic for which Socrates was renowned in classical antiquity: his physical ugliness. It might be said that Socrates is a natural fantastic, a kind of living grotesque, a flesh-and-blood example of what Montaigne describes his own *Essays* as being.[31] From that standpoint, Socrates might in other circumstances be an appropriate emblem for the work in which he appears. Yet in the present context, where Montaigne is dealing approvingly with the alignment of mental and physical beauty, such grotesqueness presents a difficulty, and the essayist attempts to tackle it:

About Socrates, who was a perfect model in all great qualities, it vexes me that he hit on a body and face so ugly as they say he had, and so incongruous with the beauty of his soul . . . There is nothing more likely than the conformity and relation of the body to the spirit. (*F809, V1057*)

Montaigne's discussion of this problem only serves to embroil the dilemma it poses.[32] He quotes anecdotes from two classical sources, Cicero's *Tusculan Disputations*, IV.37 and *Of Fate*, V, in both of which Socrates admits that his physical ugliness betrays an ugliness of soul, but claims that he has corrected it (depending on the anecdote) either by training and discipline or by reason. Socrates, the perfect product of Nature and the antithesis of artifice, needs to supplement his own nature by recourse to art – the practice of a discipline that will tame the deficiencies of his personality. Montaigne is visibly embarrassed by this situation and asserts that Socrates is merely being ironical, it being impossible for someone of such excellence to be self-made. Yet the crux remains, and it is compounded by the fact that the same phenomenon – a beautiful soul in an ugly body – affected La Boétie (albeit to a lesser extent, Montaigne maintains, by way of palliating the problem): thus even the revered friend, the classicizing writer who rivals antiquity, with whom we began this study, also proves in the end to be a sort of grotesque, and no less so than the work that commemorates him or the Socratic model of behavior that it proposes to its reader for emulation. Montaigne himself then marks his difference from Socrates – "I have not, like Socrates, corrected my natural disposition by force of reason, and have not troubled my inclination at all by art" (III.12, F811, V1059) – leaving the reader to ponder in turn on the anomaly of a parallel life that is suddenly not quite so parallel.

Models and their implementation, differences of personality and individuality, questions of transmission and reception: these issues derive ultimately from the overarching problem of mimesis, the question of how to write in the wake of classical antiquity that was a necessity and an anxiety in Renaissance literary activity.[33] In this tension between assimilation and difference, Montaigne traces a purposely wayward path and adopts a hybrid form, insisting that his work is unworthy of its classical antecedents and underscoring by contrast its experimental nature with its combination of an esthetics of *non finito* and an ontology of incompleteness. In short, through an emphasis on the fantastical and the grotesque, Montaigne creates the seemingly unlikely conditions for the emergence of the *essay*, redefining as he does so classical antiquity as both a rich legacy and a problematic inheritance.

NOTES

1.  See Olivier Guerrier, *Quand "les poètes feignent": "Fantasie" et fiction dans les "Essais" de Montaigne* (Paris: Champion, 2003); John O'Brien, "Reasoning with the Senses: The Humanist Imagination," in Philippe Desan and Ullrich Langer, eds., *Reason, Reasoning, and Literature in the Renaissance, South Central Review*, Special issue, 10/2 (1993), pp. 3–19.

2.  See Terence Cave, "Problems of Reading in the *Essais*," in *Michel de Montaigne, "Modern Critical Views*," ed. Harold Bloom (New York: Chelsea House, 1987), pp. 79–116; Floyd Gray, *Montaigne bilingue: Le latin des "Essais"* (Paris: Champion, 1991); Mary McKinley, *Words in a Corner. Studies in Montaigne's Latin Quotations* (Lexington, KY: French Forum, 1981) and *Les terrains vagues des "Essais"* (Paris: Champion, 1995); Michael Metschies, *La citation et l'art de citer dans les "Essais" de Montaigne*, trans. Jules Brody (Paris: Champion, 1997).

3.  For an overview, see now Mary McKinley, "Auteurs latins," and John O'Brien, "Auteurs grecs," in *Dictionnaire de Montaigne*, ed. Philippe Desan (Paris: Champion, 2004).

4. See 1.26: "I have not had regular dealings with any solid book, except Plutarch and Seneca, from whom I draw like the Danaïds, incessantly filling up and pouring out" (F107, V146); Plutarch is "so perfect and excellent a judge of human actions" (11.2, F250, V346), a sentiment echoed in essay 11.31, where Plutarch is deemed "admirable throughout, but especially where he judges human actions" (F539, V714). On this topic, Robert Aulotte, *Amyot et Plutarque* (Geneva: Droz, 1965) and *Plutarque en France au XVIe siècle* (Paris: Klincksieck, 1971).

5. The artificial division of each chapter of the *Essays* into paragraphs is a later editorial invention.

6. On the grotesque in Renaissance art and literature, see Michel Jeanneret, *Perpetuum mobile: Métamorphoses des corps et des oeuvres de Vinci à Montaigne* (Paris: Macula, n.d.), esp. pp. 123–60.

7. Cf. essays 11.18, F504, V665: "In order to train my fancy even to dream with some order and purpose . . . there is nothing like embodying and registering all the little thoughts that come to it. I listen to my reveries because I have to record them," and 111.9, F734, V962: ". . . in these ramblings of mine."

8. Cf. 1.26, F119, V161: "It is *Baroco* and *Baralipton* that make their disciples dirt-caked and smoky."

9. Cf. Ullrich Langer, *Vertu du discours, discours de la vertu: Littérature et philosophie morale au XVIe siècle en France* (Geneva: Droz, 1999); Ian Maclean, *Montaigne philosophe* (Paris: Presses Universitaires de France, 1996); John O'Brien, "Reasoning with the Senses," and "The Eye Perplexed: Aristotle and Montaigne on Seeing and Choosing," *Journal of Medieval and Renaissance Studies*, 22/2 (1992), pp. 291–305; Edilia Traverso, *Montaigne e Aristotele* (Florence: Le Monnier, 1974).

10. On Montaigne's Pyrrhonism, see Frédéric Brahami, *Le scepticisme de Montaigne* (Paris: Presses Universitaires de France, 1997) and *Le travail du scepticisme (Montaigne, Bayle, Hume)* (Paris: Presses Universitaires de France, 2001); Terence Cave, *Pré-histoires: Textes troublés au seuil de la modernité* (Geneva: Droz, 1999); Marie-Luce Demonet, *A plaisir: Sémiotique et scepticisme dans les "Essais"* (Caen: Paradigme, 2003); Emmanuel Naya, *Le phénomène pyrrhonien* (thesis, University of Grenoble, 2000).

11. Cf. 11.12, F374, V505: the Pyrrhonians "use their reason to inquire and debate, but not to conclude and choose."

12. Cf. "Of Prayers," 1.56, F229, V317: "I put forward formless and unresolved notions (*fantasies*), as do those who publish doubtful questions to debate in the schools, not to establish the truth but to seek it," and later in the same essay, F234, V323: "I set forth notions (*fantasies*) that

are human and my own, simply as human notions (*fantasies*) considered
in themselves, not as determined and decreed by heavenly ordinance and
permitting neither doubt nor dispute; matter of opinion, not matter of
faith."

13. Pierre Villey, *Les sources et l'évolution des "Essais"de Montaigne*, 2nd
    edn. (Paris: Hachette, 1933), vol. 2, p. 146ff., contested by (e.g.) André
    Tournon, *Essais de Montaigne, Livre III* (Paris: Atlande, 2003), p. 48.

14. Sextus Empiricus, *Outlines of Pyrrhonism*, III.280–81; and for an appli-
    cation, see John O'Brien, "Si avons nous une tres-douce medecine
    que la philosophie," in Marie-Luce Demonet and Alain Legros, eds.,
    *L'écriture du scepticisme chez Montaigne* (Geneva: Droz, 2004),
    pp. 13–24.

15. Cf. for punctual uses of words or expressions, John O'Brien, "Aristotle's
    Prudence, and Pyrrho's" (on essay II.15) in Ullrich Langer, ed., *Au-delà
    de la* Poétique: *Aristote et la littérature de la Renaissance/Beyond the
    Poetics: Aristotle and Early Modern Literature* (Geneva: Droz, 2002),
    pp. 35–45, and Kirsti Sellevold, "*Phonai skeptikai* et expressions modal-
    isantes. Ressemblances et différences," in Marie-Luce Demonet and
    Alain Legros, eds., *L'écriture du scepticisme chez Montaigne* (Geneva:
    Droz, 2004), pp. 25–37.

16. Cf. André Tournon, "L'argumentation pyrrhonienne: Structures d'essai
    dans le chapitre 'Des boyteux'," in Françoise Charpentier and Simone
    Perrier, eds., *Montaigne: Les derniers essais, Cahiers Textuels*, 2 (1986),
    pp. 73–85.

17. Cf. Robin Briggs, *Witches and Neighbours: The Social and Cultural
    Context of European Witchcraft* (London: Fontana, 1996), and Stuart
    Clark, *Thinking with Demons: The Idea of Witchcraft in Early Modern
    Europe* (Oxford: Oxford University Press, 1997).

18. Note that these two sentences in the original French are questions, not
    exclamations.

19. "To kill men, we should have sharp and luminous evidence" (F789,
    V1031); "After all, it is putting a very high price on one's conjectures to
    have a man roasted alive because of them" (F790, V1032).

20. Cf. Sextus Empiricus, *Outlines of Pyrrhonism*, 1.187–204, and Mon-
    taigne, II.12, F373–4, V505.

21. II.12, F393, V527: "This idea is more firmly grasped in the form of an
    interrogation: 'What do I know?' – the words I bear as a motto, inscribed
    over a pair of scales."

22. II.12, F371–2, V502: "Whoever seeks anything comes to this point: he
    says either that he has found it, or that it cannot be found, or that he is
    still in quest of it. All philosophy is divided into these three types. Its
    purpose is to seek out truth, knowledge, and certainty. The Peripatetics,

Epicureans, Stoics, and others thought that they had found it . . . Clitomachus, Carneades, and the Academics despaired of their quest, and judged that truth could not be conceived by our powers . . . Pyrrho and other Skeptics or Epechists . . . say they are still in search of the truth. These men judge that those who think they have found it are infinitely mistaken; and that there is also an overbold vanity in that second class that assures us that human powers are not capable of attaining it . . . So the profession of the Pyrrhonians is to waver, to doubt, and inquire, to be sure of nothing, to answer for nothing."

23. III.11, F786, V1028 (tendency to exaggeration and hyperbole), F791, V1034 (his gullibility in respect of the proverb about the lame).

24. Cf. II.10: "those who write biographies . . . are most suited to me. That is why in every way Plutarch is my man" (F303, V416); and 1.26, F115, V156: "What profit will he not gain in this field by reading the *Lives* of our Plutarch?"

25. Some instances: Caesar: II.10, F303, V416 (praise of Caesar as author), II.18, F503, V663 (military and literary activity), II.34, F556–63, V736–43 (whole essay devoted to Caesar's methods of war); Xenophon: 1.6, F18, V29 (writing, military leadership, philosophy), II.18, F503, V663 (military and literary activity).

26. 1.44, F198–9, V271–2 (courage), II.11, F308–9, V425 and especially II.28, F532, V703–4 (suicide).

27. III.12, F793, V1037–8.

28. II.12, F374, V505: "He did not want to make himself a stump or a stone; he wanted to make himself a living, thinking, reasoning man, enjoying all natural pleasures and comforts, employing and using all his bodily and spiritual faculties in regular and upright fashion."

29. Géralde Nakam, "Figures et espace du rêve," in *Montaigne: la manière et la matière* (Paris: Klincksieck, 1992), p. 123.

30. II.12, F377, V509: "Moreover, some have considered Plato a dogmatist, others a doubter; others, in certain things the one, in certain things the other. The leader of his dialogues, Socrates, is always asking questions and stirring up discussion, never concluding, never satisfying; and says he has no other knowledge than that of opposing." On this tradition, see Paul Woodruff, "The Sceptical Side of Plato's Method," *Revue internationale de philosophie*, 156–7 (1986), pp. 22–37, and Julia Annas, "Plato the Sceptic," in James C. Klagge and Nicholas D. Smith, eds., *Methods of Interpreting Plato and his Dialogues*, Oxford Studies in Ancient Philosophy supplementary volume (Oxford: Oxford University Press, 1992), pp. 43–72.

31. Cf. III.12, F793, V1037: "Under so mean a form we should never have picked out the nobility and splendor of his admirable ideas."

32. See the discussion in Timothy Hampton, *Writing from History: The Rhetoric of Exemplarity in Renaissance Literature* (Ithaca: Cornell University Press, 1990), pp. 181–8.

33. See the fine study by Thomas Greene, *The Light in Troy: Imitation and Discovery in Renaissance Poetry* (New Haven: Yale University Press, 1982).

# 5 The *Essays* and the New World

Montaigne' *Essays* are perhaps the first and greatest reflections on the impact of the discovery and colonization of the New World upon Europe and early modern consciousness. Oceanic travel and the effects of the Columbian discoveries mark the work indelibly. A seasoned reader may often wonder if the author's project of self-portraiture, in which he wishes that "I want to be seen here in my simple, natural, ordinary fashion, without straining or artifice" ("To the Reader," *F2*, *V3*), could not be done without the newly found alterity or the discoveries brought from the New World. Montaigne does not expound on the marvel and wonder of new lands. Rather, he offers the first anthropological speculation on what the New World might be. He furnishes both imaginative and reasoned studies of the natural and human conditions of a world whose geographical limits were close to being determined and concluded. Montaigne makes clear the importance of the historical moment when God's creation finds itself called in question: when, all of a sudden, in the gaps and crevasses of biblical and classical texts, a general incapacity to explain the very being of the New World casts authority in the shadows of doubt.

The publication of the *Essays* comes on the heels of revisions that had been brought to Ptolemaic geography. The Alexandrian geographer's *Cosmographia* had recently been abandoned in favor of new and different ways of projecting and describing the world. New atlases, principally the creations of Abraham Ortelius and Gerard Mercator, offered copperplate engraving of the eastern and western hemispheres; with the new views came a heightened consciousness of history reaching beyond the beginning of man.[1] Humanistic cartography that had been taught in European universities was quickly

revised in the hands of cartographers and engineers executing draw-
ings and nautical charts calling in question hypothetical or allegorical representations of the globe. Present in the minds of many French
citizens were narratives, first, of Verrazano's and Cartier's discoveries
of the eastern seaboard of the North American coastline and Cana-
dian lands extending from the shores of the St. Lawrence River and,
second, of the failed colonial expeditions – one by Nicolas Durand
de Villegagnon at the mouth of Rio de Janeiro, the other by René de
Laudonnière on the eastern coast of Florida – that in fact anticipated
some of the local and national conflicts in the wars of religion begun
in 1562.

Copious evidence affirms how people concurred that the New
World was simply "there," that it existed in its own right, but also
that by and large it had little effect on the dilemmas of a nation at war
with itself and its European neighbors.[2] Contrary to a majority who
either gave little thought to the New World – who preferred to fit it
into allegorical schemes that would promote the Christian ideology
of redemption, or serve arguments in favor of colonial programs[3] –
Montaigne treats the discoveries as an object of both history and
fantasy. In his view they need to be appreciated first for what they
were before they were discovered, and how the adamic state they
occupy in the imagination can be called in question.[4] And second, in
the passage of almost a century between the first voyage of Columbus
and subsequent conquest up to the initial publication of the *Essays*,
Montaigne wonders what they have become.

The *Essays* remain a keystone in the literature of discovery. They
grant to the space and peoples of the New World a relation mirroring
that which the essayist holds with himself, one that welcomes the
presence of the unknown, something of the order of what students
of the psyche call "la relation d'inconnu," a relation that is vital for
the perpetuation of life itself.[5] Without empathy for things unknown
or for potential beings and places that remain over and beyond the
horizon of a person's own experience, sentience tends to wither. Life
becomes deadened if a relation with the unknown is forgotten. Montaigne brings this relation into geography when the unknown, seen
on maps in the name of *terrae incognitae*, has begun to disappear.
The essayist is required to look inward in search of spaces and places
that might bear mental promise similar to the unknown in physical
space. The voyage of self-discovery and self-portraiture in the *Essays*

has as a foil those of recent travelers. As he notes about voyage and writing in "Of Vanity," "the soul is continually exercised in observing new and unknown things" (III.9, F744, V973).

In his enduring study of the evolution of the *Essays* Pierre Villey noted that the project of self-portraiture develops slowly, *chemin faisant*, as the writer moves from the role of a commentator and a translator into that of a writer.[6] He begins, as attest the style and aspect of the shorter essays, by annotation and summary reflection. Autobiographical incursions become more frequent before the essayist succumbs to a crisis of faith, made clear by the presence of a demonstrative "anti-essay," the monstrous "Apology for Raymond Sebond," set at the core of the second volume, prior to his access in the later essays to mature and extensively self-invested reflections on life, travel, and experience. At crucial junctures the essayist, wondering about the nature of the world, co-ordinates his reflections on the unknown with visual points of vanishing. He plots into the text areas that visibly indicate where, like the converging lines in a painting based on Renaissance perspective, physical and spiritual worlds touch one another. The text of the *Essays*, as Montaigne avows at the beginning of his chapter on friendship (I.28), adopts these visual strategies of composition.

It is hardly by chance that the New World figures in proximity with these areas. As a result the geography of the *Essays* becomes part of the essayist's speculation on the nature of the world into which he, like every human subject, has shared the fate of having been born. Yet it would be a mistake to think that Montaigne entertains thoughts on the New World for the purpose of self-aggrandizement, narcissism, or solipsistic pleasure. Rather, its spaces also figure in a politics, neither utopian or dystopian, that displace adamic myths about oceanic discoveries and that admonish Iberian plunder and colonization. The politics of Montaigne's assessment of the state of "Antarctic France" and the Americas inform not only the project of self-portraiture but also the nascent anthropology of the *Essays* as a whole.

Politics, art, and self-study are related to the new lands. The New World serves as plot-point in a field of tension that extends between the eastern and western hemispheres. The reader discovers a strongly motivated spatial plan in which the printed matter figures in an arcane rapport with ciphers and layers or strata of writing. A textual geography can be discerned through the presence of two vanishing points marked by the New World. The one, "Of Cannibals" (1.31), is situated near the midpoint of the first volume. Set in close proximity to "Of Friendship" (1.28), an essay that might conceivably be construed to figure as the left panel of a triptych in which "Of Moderation" (1.30) figures at the center, "Cannibals" would be a dexter panel. The thirty-first essay is close to the place where all the lines of force of the first volume tend to be directed.

Likewise, "Of Coaches" (III.6), published eight years later, figures on the other side of the volume, in the virtually "new" world of the third volume that is written by a wizened and "older" author with respect to the first, and also at a point to the left of the center. Referring to his "Cannibals" in the text of "Coaches" Montaigne invites a comparative reading that arches over and back from one world of the *Essays* to another. Arranged in an emblematic configuration with "On Some Verses of Virgil" (III.5), a rhapsodic and probing chapter on love and Eros, "Of Coaches" heralds an enigmatic title that bears on the minuscule chapter that follows, "Of the Disadvantage of Greatness" (III.7), in which the site that kings occupy – at the allegorical center of their kingdom – is ostensibly the vanishing point of the third volume: it is found between two equal units of six chapters each, and as a set it is shown to be as precarious and unsettling as a coach, a boat, a litter, a battlewagon, or any of the modes of transport taken up in the immediately preceding essay. Both of these chapters treat of the New World, and each offers a distinctly different picture of the author's relation with what he has learned about it. Both invite comparative readings, and both are of similar textual and figural tenor.

TEXT AND BODY OF "CANNIBALS"

"Of Cannibals" belongs to textual composition in which the reader is invited to see the author espousing alterity through his display of empathy. In his reflections on the New World Montaigne writes in a manner that welcomes the arrival of the "other," of the native inhabitants of the Americas, in a context where they would otherwise be estranged. By contrast, "Of Coaches" is an elaborate allegorical machinery, building on the foundation of "Cannibals," that offers counsel about national and foreign policy through what seems to be a series of off-handed observations about the virtues and vices of carriages and other horse-drawn vehicles. In the earlier essay, when he fancies how he might discern truth from falsehood in the accounts of anthropophagy in the New World, Montaigne admits a need to consult topographers to correct the inexact observations of cosmographers who have distorted views about the shape and form of information ranging from description of flora and fauna to cultural phenomena. A retrospective reading shows that these observers might indeed be Amerindians, quite possibly Tupinambas of Brazil, who can look at their environs without turning what they see into abstractions. In the later essay Montaigne envisions the end of the world in an apocalypse through allusion to the Indians of Peru and of Mexico.

The complexity of Montaigne's rapport with the Columbian discoveries can be discerned through these two chapters and the positions they assume in the greater whole of the *Essays*. Each seems to refract each other's lines of reasoning through different modes of textual play. The appeal to topography in the former is countered in the latter by an apocalyptic vision of the end of the world. A caustic critique of European expansion and of barbaric atrocities committed in the Americas in the latter has subtle counterparts in the former. Neither essay, however is exactly a mirror-image of the other. The chapter in the first volume takes up alterity and ends with a critique of French political economy while that in the third is a devastating account of the destruction and imminent end of the world.

"Cannibals" begins by referring to Pyrrhus who, during his Italian campaign, noted that the Roman legions standing before his eyes were hardly as barbarous in their aspect as he had been told. He saw a well-disposed army that immediately disclaimed any connection a person would be tempted to make between a foreign or *strange* nation – the Greek etymon of *barbare* equating "strange" with people who stutter and babble in the eyes and ears of the observers – and an uncivil one. The impression leads Montaigne to reflect on his acquaintance of a rustic character who had lived for "ten or twelve years in that other world which has been discovered in our century, in the place where Villegaignon landed, and which he called Antarctic France" (1.31, F150, V203).

He momentarily forgets the man when thoughts about the classical accounts of the origins of the new lands come forward. Were they, as Plato contended, originally an island? Or a continent? Did they belong to an archipelago, as current *isolarii* (atlases of islands) would have us believe? Did the movements of the earth's surface, what we now know in geology as tectonics, yield a "firm and continent land" with the East Indies on one side and the lands under the two poles on the other? Answers are sought in his impressions of the changes wrought in the Dordogne River that had (because Montaigne lived before dams have since domesticated the rivers of France) shifted lands and sands so much and in such different directions that "the face of the world would be turned topsy-turvy" (1.31, *F*151, V204). Or were they, according to Aristotle, an island that the Carthaginians discovered and to which people emigrated so readily that citizens feared the nation would find its population crippled and decimated?

That neither of the authors can furnish the history of the discoveries leads Montaigne back to the "simple and crude" qualities of the man he knew, the man who possessed traits crucial to a veracious account of the shifting and conflicting accounts from the new world. Then, suddenly, he asserts,

We ought to have topographers who would give us an exact account of the places where they have been. But because they have over us the advantage of having seen Palestine, they want to enjoy the privilege of telling us news about all the rest of the world. I would like everyone to write what he knows, and as much as he knows, not only in this, but in all other subjects; for a man may have some special knowledge and experience of the nature of a river or a fountain, who in other matters knows only what everybody knows. (1.31, *F*152, V205)

He who knows or experiences "the nature of a river" would be Montaigne himself. It is the essayist who tries to derive greater truths from whatever shards of information he obtains from accounts of the new lands. All of a sudden the chapter begins to float as if it were an island in a greater sea of writing. Its own position becomes unmoored and unknown to itself, prey to the uncertain knowledge of its author and his failing memory. Yet it is also a "continent," a firm and molar mass when it immediately returns to its beginning, when a somewhat overwrought (but now, in the eyes of humanists, highly celebrated) maxim is cited to bring the essay back to its point of departure. As important as the equation linking impressions of barbarity with unfamiliarity may be, the figure of the topographer melds with that of an ethnographer or observer of local practice:

> Now, to return to my subject, I think there is nothing barbarous and savage in that nation, from what I have been told, except that each man calls barbarism whatever is not his own practice; for indeed it seems we have no other test of truth and reason than the example and pattern of the opinions and customs of the country we live in. (1.31, F152, V205)

The test or sighting point (*mire*) of truth belongs to the topographer's lexicon while it also indicates the axis that the essay might be for those, like the author, who wish to estrange familiar ways of doing things. Montaigne virtually becomes cannibal. There follows the conceit that praises nature in the New World for a naked beauty – that includes the nudity of its inhabitants – that surpasses the overly refined and overly vested, stifling and smothering quality of western inventions. Discoverers have found places and beings that neither Lycurgus nor Plato could have imagined in their descriptions of the golden age. They could not have fathomed "such a pure and simple" way of living of the kind that the sixteenth-century travelers discover in their own experience.

What would be a premonition in the sentences that follow, addressed to Plato, about noble savages living in Arcadia becomes a threshold for an extensive description and a topographic account crafted from images and texts of André Thevet, Jean de Léry, and other chroniclers of Antarctic France. Montaigne describes the long house and the hammock, two attributes of the Tupi and other South American tribes; their *caouin*, or malted drink and their dietary regimes; their religious assemblies, communions, and divinations; their wars with nations "beyond their mountains, further inland, to which they go quite naked" (1.31, F155, V208); their butchery and cooking of prisoners whose bodily parts they roast and eat in common and send to their absent friends, not for nourishment, but "to represent an extreme vengeance." Montaigne is led to reflect on western barbarity of dismembering, eating, and giving bodily parts of living beings to dogs and pigs, common practice (infers the text) during the wars of religion, practices that surpass by far the habit of roasting and savoring carefully cooked flesh.[7]

The description inspires a vision of a homeostatic world in which a need is never felt to engage "the conquest of new lands" as do

westerners. "So we may well call these people barbarians, in respect
to rules of reason, but not in respect to ourselves, who surpass them
in every kind of barbarity" (1.31, F156, V210). The cannibals' art of
warfare, he continues, is based on principles of honor, valor, courage,
and fair play. Like the heroic images of natives at war in the woodcuts
of Thevet's *Les Singularités de la France antarctique* (1557) and his
*Cosmographie universelle* (1575), combat and treatment of prisoners
are taken to be the equal of Greek and Roman models. Those who
await their demise warn their captors that they will be eating the
skin and muscle of their own ancestors, an invention "that certainly
does not smack of barbarity" (1.31, F158, V212). Time and again the
essay returns to the substantive in order to show that barbarity is
often in the eyes of those who name it as such. It is not, he implies,
a commanding trait of the peoples of the Caribbean whence the cannibal is derived. By the end of the chapter the concept has been seen
and studied from all possible angles.


### POLITICS AND FRIENDSHIP

The descriptions of Tupi culture and language give way to an autobiographical anecdote that caps the essay. It inaugurates an entire
literature and politics that eighteenth-century *philosophes* – Montesquieu, Voltaire, Diderot – will exploit to foment change in the
*Ancien régime*.[8] In the texture of the essay the anecdote is a dialogue of two parts. The first, recounted in the third person, tells of
three Amerindians, brought to Rouen in 1562, during the kingship of
the adolescent Charles IX (1560–74). They were visited by the king
himself, who showed them "our ways, our splendour, the aspect of
a fine city" (1.31, F159, V213)[9]. One person in the entourage asked
questions of them that prompted three responses. Without yet admitting that he had been there, Montaigne notes that unfortunately only
two of the answers remain in his memory.

They mentioned three things, of which I have forgotten the third, and I am
very sorry for it; but I still remember two of them. They said that in the first
place they thought it very strange that so many grown men, bearded, strong,
and armed, who were around the king (it is likely that they were talking
about the Swiss of his guard) should submit to obey a child, and that one of
them was not chosen to command instead. (1.31, F159, V213)

The natives remark that the Swiss guards, mercenaries hired to protect the king, were taller than he. Thus, if the topographer's perspective is held in view, the foreigners would naturally be better
leaders because of their capacity to see the world around and below
them.[10] Their secondary sexual traits unsettle inherited hierarchies.
*Barbe*, the beard they "wear," makes the Europeans more *barbarous*
than Amerindians. The three prisoners in Rouen are implied to have
less bodily hair than their European counterparts and thus closer
in aspect to the pubescent Charles. Their naiveté causes them to
resemble Montaigne's friend at the outset of the essay, "simple and
crude" in vision, who is of a manner "proper to bear true witness" to
things. The anecdote brings confusion to a received order of values.
It bears revolutionary potential in the way it reformulates Etienne de
La Boétie's political manifesto, the *Discours de la servitude volontaire*, that Montaigne had invoked a few pages earlier at the beginning
of "Of Friendship."

The second remark in the first part of the conclusion suggests that
the same cannibals are familiar with scientific reasoning by the way
that they take rational account of their observations. The complement is based on the term *moitié*, or "half," that the natives use to
name one another in an egalitarian fashion. The point almost jumps
out of the parenthesis that contains it: "(they have a way in their
language of speaking of men as halves of one another)" (1.31, F159,
V214). These human "halves" in their own lands are "have-nots" in
the western world, a world riddled with social and economic inequal-
ities. Montaigne's biting irony rings in the echoes of signifiers that
redound and change valence in the course of the account: "They
had noticed that there were among us men full and gorged with all
sorts of good things, and that their other halves were beggars at their
doors, emaciated with hunger and poverty, and they thought it
strange that these needy halves could endure such an injustice, and
did not take the others by the throat, or set fire to their houses" (1.31,
F159, V214). The men who are stuffed ("gorgez") with commodities
ought to be strangled ("à la gorge") for having imposed intolerable
injustice in the social compact. The Amerindians are shown living
outside of a hierarchy. *Moitiés* that they are, they never stray far
from their bonds of *amitié*. If friendship, as Montaigne indicated
in the adjacent essay (1.28) of that title, engages commerce where
no gain or exchange can alter the equality of the relation,[11] it is

implied that befriending is tantamount to halving or splitting the self
for the betterment of others. In *moitiés* are found, visibly and con-
cretely, the presence of what defines them, the essence of *amitié*. The
perfect relation about which Montaigne organizes the first volume of
essays around and about a vanishing point has as its immediate ana-
logue, on the other side of its line of divide, the Amerindian half, the
friend and other whose words are volatile enough to foment sedition
in the Old World.[12]

The second panel of the conclusion begins with an intervention in
the first person. Montaigne relates how he spoke at length with one
of the two Indians. "I had a very long talk with one of them ("à l'un
d'eux")" (1.31, *F*159, *V*214). The expression carries the homonym of
the author speaking to "one two," a ciphered formula that unites and
splits the self who speaks to the other. Once again – and here is placed
the third point that Montaigne had forgotten or shunted aside –
courage and valor are shown when the leader, he tells the essayist,
can march first into war and be followed, in a "piece of ground"
(III.31, *F*159, *V*214) that with his arms he indicates to include four
or five thousand men. In time of peace the same pleasure is afforded
when his subjects clear a path for him through the rows of their
forests.

The famous last words, the parting shot of the essay, "All this is
not too bad – but what's the use? They don't wear breeches" (1.31,
*F*159, *V*214) affirm that the captain was not that wrong because he
and his compatriots are nude. Many readers point to the irony that
the native emperor cannot wear "new clothes" or be seduced by his
subjects' sycophantic admiration. The essayist is also thinking topographically and naively, along the lines of the natives, for the reason
that Europeans walking along the same paths would find their ample
clothes torn by twigs and branches, whereas the Indians ambulate
effortlessly and in stealth. The nude Indian who passes along the
hedgerows of his forests marks a strong contrast to the king and his
retinue who make costly and ultimately senseless royal entries into
the cities they visit.

The political parables at the end of "Cannibals" become a telling
reflection on ethnocentrism and its inverse. In its form the essay
does not promote relativism or sanctify the idea of the noble savage. It is a critique of foreign and domestic political economies from
which an ethnographic consciousness emerges. The latter is resonant

when the essay is situated in the greater "marquetry" of the *Essays*, a term Montaigne uses to describe his complex network of reflection as they can be seen and read together.[13] "Cannibals" bleeds into the following chapter, "We Should Meddle Soberly with Judging Divine Ordinances" (1.32), that begins by taking up the relation with the unknown that the essayist had inaugurated through his identification with the Tupi natives in Rouen. Barbarity, sensed to be a defensive reaction to the fear of alterity, was shown not to be so barbarous amongst the most cruel of all human creatures. Now the same fear of the unknown is seen in religious practices that confer aura and authority upon alterity. The beginning of the chapter is conceived as an emblem. Its first words are a subscription or legend bearing implicit commentary on the "inscription" or visible body of the essay below.

The flow of "Of Cannibals" into the essay that follows leads the reader to see how its representations of the New World are related to "Of Moderation," a chapter on the extremes of human comportment – torture and excess – that ends with an anecdote taken from Lopez de Gómara's chronicle of the conquests of Hernando Cortez. Montaigne notes that as "in these new lands discovered in our time, still pure and virgin compared with ours" (1.30, F149, V201), the bloodthirsty practice of human sacrifice is rampant. The idols of the New World are starved for blood. Offerings include bodies half-roasted and immolated in order to have their hearts and entrails torn away, or even women skinned alive.

One group of Aztecs sacrifices fifty men to welcome the arrival of Cortez. To cap the account (and the chapter) Montaigne adds a last item, also from Gómara, that he turns into a riddle. The nations that Cortez had defeated dispatched, in search of friendship, several messengers: "Some of these people, having been beaten by him, sent to acknowledge him and seek his friendship" (1.30, F149, V201). The envoys offered to the Spaniard "three sorts of presents, in this manner: 'Lord, here are five slaves; if you are a cruel god that feeds on flesh and blood, eat them, and we'll bring you more. If you are a good-natured god, here are incense and plumes. If you are a man, take these birds and fruits" (1.30, F149, V201).

Which does he choose? Montaigne removes Gómara's conclusion that glorifies Cortez's barbarity by praising his decision to have the envoys mutilated. Cortez's soldiers amputated their hands and feet before sending them back to their leader.[14] Montaigne lops away the end of the Spanish historian's account. The event becomes a gruesome variant on the judgment of Paris. Read topographically, the final words tell Cortez – and the reader, also addressed in the second person – to take the birds and fruits *que voicy*, that "you see here."[15] The offerings would indeed be the printed words of the essay that follows, itself resembling birds and fruits in the form of a plea for moderation and acceptance of the inhabitants of the New World. The exotic flora and fauna of Mexico would be assimilated into the generous vision of "Cannibals." Furthermore, the Mexican envoys came from a space in Mexico approximating that of the literal context of the *Essays*, where the foundations of friendship have been pondered in "Of Friendship," the neighboring chapter that more and more is seen as a complement to the cannibals. Immoderation of sacrifice and unusual cruelty in the New World are exceeded by Spanish brutality. Friendship, the unique relation that Montaigne shares with Etienne de La Boétie, is transformed into empathy through harsh criticism of Iberian colonial policy.

"Cannibals" is nestled in a textual architecture of memorial design. In the first edition Montaigne reserved the space of chapter twenty-nine for twenty-nine sonnets of the signature of his dead friend. After 1592 the sonnets are removed, but his preface to them (addressed to Diane de Grammont) remains, affirming the congruence of the number of the poems and that of the chapter. A tombal area, a crypt, is hollowed out to receive the memory of the defunct *ami*. They take the shape of an ornamental surround in the form of grotesques, that are "fantastic paintings whose only charm lies in their in variety and strangeness" (1.28, *F*135, *V*183). Very close to this vanishing area decorated with the charmingly *strange* figures is the friend from the Old World on the one side; on the other are found the cannibals of the New.

### "OF COACHES": A RIDDLE AND AN EMBLEM

A similarly arcane disposition of essays is found along the edges of "Coaches," the chapter adjacent to "Of the Disadvantage of Greatness" (III.7), a study of thrones situated at the center of the third volume, and placed below "On some Verses of Virgil" (III.5), a rhapsodic reflection on love and melancholy. The sixth chapter "sits" at a juncture of world, old and new, embroiled in a vision of global degeneration and imminent apocalypse. Montaigne's arcane construction seems to hinge on two riddles placed below the title, that in themselves seem unfit for any extended speculation. Causality, an issue taken up elsewhere in the *Essays*, is occasion for thoughts about rhetoric and truth: "It is very easy to demonstrate that great authors, when they write about causes, adduce not only those they think are true, but also those they do not believe in, provided they have some originality and beauty. They speak truly and usefully enough if they speak ingeniously" (III.6, *F*685, *V*898–9). When an ingenious or handsomely crafted cause is attributed to an ineffable or even derisory effect the proof becomes no less worthy than a true one.

But here the *cause* is embroiled in the effect. The *coche*, a word bearing aural and visual resemblance to "cause," is defined by the nature of its tenor (the horse or animal that pulls, conveys, or conduces it) and its own effect as vehicle (the coach itself). In the wit of the essay the end or *cause* of the chapter is the cause of the effect, the essay on coaches. The relation of the title to the *incipit* determines how the essay can be read, especially in a commanding riddle that follows, in which Montaigne asks his reader whence originates the custom of blessing people who sneeze. The question elicits an ostensibly flippant response:

Do you ask whence comes this custom of blessing those who sneeze? We produce three sorts of wind. That which issues from below is too foul; that which issues from the mouth carries some reproach of gluttony; the third is sneezing. And because it comes from the head and is blameless, we give this civil reception. Do not laugh at this piece of subtlety; it is, they say, from Aristotle. (III.6, *F*685, *V*899)

In the guarded diction people who sneeze (*estrenuent*) are precisely those people who traffic in *estres nus*, nude beings or slaves brought from overseas by virtue of wind, the force propelling the vessels carrying the human commodities and a common figure of the economy of the world. Sneezing (*estrenuement*) is blessed because it comes from higher regions of the mind. In the context of his virulent attack on Spain's inhuman treatment of Amerindians in the rest of the essay the words infer that sneezing is a portmanteau word for slaving. Trade in *estres nus* (nude beings) is implicitly blessed among higher authorities. In this instance they are both Aristotle, who is mentioned, and pope Alexander VI, a figure having an allusive presence in the essay. Aristotle's arguments for slavery (on the grounds that natives were mechanical and not rational beings) had been a lynchpin in Juan Gomez de Sepúlveda's arguments in the debates held with Bartholemé de Las Casas in Valladolid (in 1552) over the proper actions to be taken and solutions with respect to the "native American question." Pope Alexander had long before underwritten the Spanish conquests of the West Indies.[16]

All of a sudden the "ambitious subtlety" of Montaigne's title becomes clear. "Des coches" is a homonym of the imperative order "to shoot" (or "to sneeze," as might a harquebus aimed at a victim or a long bow that will release (*descocher*) an arrow whose nock snugly holds the bowstring pulled taut by the strong arms of an archer. The essay makes this clear in an excursus on how Hungarians loaded their *coches* with harquebuses, a *rondellier* and a musketeer: like tanks in modern combat, they broke up and fired on the ranks of Turkish foot soldiers. They "undid" (*descochaient*) their squadrons by smashing into their lines of troops. A war-coach gives way to the golden coach of Roman times, a sign of munificence, that leads the essayist to criticize nations that consume themselves in useless display and who pillage the New World in their thirst for gold. The critique of Spanish policies in the New World has the counterpart of a hypothetical national program for improved defense and infrastructure – "in ports, harbours, fortifications, and walls, on sumptuous buildings, churches, hospitals, colleges, and the improvement of streets and roads" (III.6, *F*688, *V*902) – that will be contrary to deficit spending of the kind witnessed in Spain.

In order to engineer an allegory of the world and time that combines the sign of the wheel with the open mouth, along with the typographic letter (in the instance of "Coaches," the majuscule Roman "O"), Montaigne appeals to the likeness of the capital letter (heralding the sign of gold, of *or*) to the shape of the Roman coliseum, round on the extrados, of an elliptical intrados, where excesses of every kind were given to the populace. Inside is found a site where flora and fauna were "vomited" from its cavernous spaces and where its arena, filled with water to simulate a sea, "marine monsters" where drawn, like coaches, to represent naval battles. These scenes, made vivid in the text through quotation of Calpurnius, are set adjacent to the

Spanish pillages described from the point of view of the Amerindian victims. On the one side of the essay stand Rome and its excess, and on the other Spain and its conquests. At the fulcrum figures a remark on which both worlds are in the balance. Montaigne imagines how the natives saw

the unexpected arrival of bearded men, different in language, religion, shape and countenance, from a part of the world so remote, where they had never imagined there was any sort of human habitation, mounted on great unknown monsters, opposed to men who had never seen not only a horse, but any sort of animal trained to carry and endure a man or any other burden; men equipped with a hard and shining skin and a sharp glittering weapon, against men who, for the miracle of a mirror or a knife, would exchange a great treasure in gold and in pearls, and who had neither the knowledge nor the material by which, even in full leisure, they could pierce our steel; add to this the lightning and thunder of our cannon and harquebuses – capable of disturbing Caesar himself, if he had been surprised by them with as little experience and in his time – against people who were naked (except in some regions where the invention of some cotton fabric had reached them), without other arms at the most than bows, stones, sticks and wooden bucklers; people taken by surprise, under color of friendship and good faith, by curiosity to see strange and unknown things; eliminate this disparity, I say, and you take from the conquerors the whole basis of so many victories. (III.6, F694, V910)

A free indirect discourse allows Montaigne and the reader to experience, as might the native, the arrival of the unknown, metallic humans astride equine monsters. The descriptions of pillage and murder were cause enough for censors to expurgate these passages from most Spanish editions of the *Essays* for the greater portion of the twentieth century.[17]

The black legend stands in contrast to the architectural description of the magnificent road that local populations built from Quito to Cuzco without machinery other than their arms and legs. The setting of a great highway that is not destined for coaches is ironic in view of the final image of the essay, the death of Attaualpa at the hands of Pizarro and his phalanx of conquistadors. When Montaigne returns to the topic of coaches by "falling back" to them he again, as he had with the scene of the Americans' first encounter with the European soldiers, mimes a moment of death not only of the king of Peru but also, in the context of apocalypse, of everything that the New World had been:

Let's fall back to our coaches. Instead of these or any other forms of transport, they had themselves carried by men, and on their shoulders. The last king of Peru, the day he was taken, was thus carried on shafts of gold, in the midst of his army. As many of these carriers as they killed to make him fall – for they wanted to take him alive – so many others vied to take the place of the dead ones, so that they never could bring him down, however great a slaughter they made of these people, until a horseman seized him around the body and pulled him to the ground. (III.6, F698–9, V915)

Myriad images, of coaches and of Attaualpa, in circulation at the time of the writing of the essay, are woven into this passage.[18] The text has a strange aura in its reflection of gold (*or*) in words that would slake the Spaniards' desire to topple the monarch from his litter. Pizarro, the human beast who wrestles him to the ground, is cast as an animal who figures in a strange and disquieting flicker of words in a montage that reproduces a double movement, forward and backward, of men collapsing and being replaced by others.

In cartographic images the New and Old worlds had been imagined in a balance of eastern and western hemispheres. At the end of this essay they fall to a point of annihilation. Montaigne writes in accord with the topic of the world in degeneration, in a vision of apocalypse, that he now extends to the New World.

Our world has just discovered another . . . no less great, full, and well-limbed than itself, yet so new and so infantile that it is still being taught its A B C; not fifty years ago it knew neither letters, weights and measures, nor clothes, nor wheat, nor vines. It was still quite naked at the breast, and lived only on what its nourishing mother provided. If we are right to infer the end of our world . . . this other world will only be coming into light when ours is leaving it. The universe will fall into paralysis; one member will be crippled, the other in full vigour. I am much afraid that we shall have greatly hastened the decline and ruin of this new world by our contagion . . . (III.6, F693, V908–9)

Space, indeed the guarantee of possibility and hence of the presence of God, is seen shrinking and declining. In a premonition of ecological disaster owing to human causes, the death of one hemisphere will anticipate that of the other before the universe shrivels away. Where other writers, such as Lancelot du Voisin, had reserved a "third world," the idea of a southern continent in the Pacific, as sign of a divine presence and cause for colonization by the reformed Church, at the middle (in its vision of apocalypse) and the conclusion of the chapter (the fall of the Attaualpa from his litter) Montaigne anticipates the end of all expansion and, more drastically, an erasure of space.[19]

In these pages collapse, decadence, and exhaustion are key. They sum up the effect of the most important chapter of all of the *Essays*, the "Apology for Raymond Sebond" (II.12), in which Montaigne uses the new discoveries to impugn the power of cosmography and theological reason that had constructed the ladder of being and put the human species on one of its upper rungs. Especially remarkable, in both the abyssal episode of "Of Coaches" and the premonitions of the "Apology" is the sense that the space of the world is finite and seems to shrink under the pressure humans exert upon it. In the "Apology," in a celebrated reflection spurred by the new discoveries and their impact on the received opinions of cosmographers, "an infinite extent of terra firma, not an island or one particular country, but a portion nearly equal in size to the one we know" (II.12, *F*430, *V*572) reveals not infinite plenitude, but compression, for geographers have seen and concluded from now on that "now all is discovered and all is seen" (II.12, *F*430, *V*572). The thought prompts him soon to add that "we have no communication with being" (II.12, *F*455, *V*601) because human nature is unconnected, rootless, and in limbo between birth and death. In the midst of infinite differences and singularities that the New World has shown to exist the human creature can assure itself an illusion of its being – its ontology – only through what it can fathom – through epistemology – what it might know. In the context of the Iberian conquests of the New World the end of "Coaches" makes clear the devastating observation that mobilizes so much of the "Apology."

### PAINTING IN THE NUDE

In the vision of the New World in its infancy Montaigne writes of it being "completely naked at the breast" or in the lap of a nourishing mother who does not go by the name of Nature. The cannibals who had been praised for an unassuming nudity bear upon the subject and the object of the writing of the *Essays* in general. Throughout the three volumes nudity is treated diversely, and always in the context of the esthetics and the politics of the author's self-discovery. Time and again Montaigne wonders what indeed clothing really is. Is it decorative or protective? Is it functional, ornamental, or even the pliable architecture of social relations? Is the subject in a truer state of being when it is disrobed? Or is skin a bodily cloth that natives wear as Frenchmen their breeches and bonnets? In "Of the Custom of Wearing Clothes" Montaigne wonders, in the midst of the winter season, "whether the fashion of going stark naked in these lately discovered nations is forced on them by the warm temperature of the air, as we say of Indians and the Mores, or whether it is the original way of mankind" (1.36, F166, V228).

The deliberation on the variety of customs leads the essayist to reflect on the biological fact that humans are the sole being to enter into the world in a defective and indigent state. They would die without "external aid" ("sans secours estrangier"). Amerindians can live in the nude because their skin is conditioned to protect them from inclement weather and the toil of the seasons. They are so hardened that he can discern a greater distance between himself and his garb and that of the peasants of his country than what distinguishes the latter from a man "dressed only in his skin" (1.36, F167, V226). At stake in the denomination of customary dress are an esthetics, an anthropology, and a politics, like those of the greater essays, but with the difference that nudity is drawn into the very project of the speculation: the essay itself dresses and undresses its topic in the movement of the reflection that shifts as much as the king of Mexico who has the habit of changing his clothes four times a day. Clothing, the wondrous effect of mendacity and dissimulation, two vital traits that need to be espoused in the project of self-portraiture, owe their force in part to the newly found nudity of the peoples of the New World.

In "Of Giving the Lie," the essay in which the idea of the self-portrait in writing is witnessed in its birth, clothing and sumptuary effects become the pertinent attribute of the pictures of "our friends and ancestors" with the "form of their clothes and armor" (II.18, F503, V664) that he observes inhering in their writing, seals, books of hours, and armaments. He adds that in the New Indies, a place utterly destroyed by conquest, priests offered to their gods blood drawn from the tongues and ears of the population to expiate the sin of prevarication. He avows parenthetically that the names and customs of these nations have been extinguished: unsaid is the point that their nudity was no doubt what betrayed any expression of mendacity. Montaigne's own envelope, his cortex, indeed his printed writing, yield effects that cannot be revised for reason of the implied nudity of the figure he projects of himself in the movement of his self-portrait. He becomes consubstantial with the inhabitants of the New World through the very nature of the project of the *Essays* in their continuous nascence.

That is why it is salutary to recall that in the first words Montaigne addresses to the reader the self-portrait stands at the crux of a design that seems perpetually inchoate. "I want to be seen in my simple, natural ordinary fashion, without straining or artifice: for it is myself that I portray" ("To the Reader," *F2*, *V3*). Anticipating the impossibility of disavowal, in the spirit of affected modesty he adds that his faults will be read in their living state, along with his natural form, to the degree that is allowed by public respect. Prior to stating that "I am myself the matter of my book" (*F2*, *V3*) he speculates on the relation with the New World and its peoples that permits the self-portrait to be drawn in the first place: "Had I been placed among these nations which are said to live still in the sweet freedom of nature's first laws, I assure you that I should very gladly have portrayed myself here entire and wholly naked" (*F2*, *V3*).

Writing is equivalent to a process of painting of the kind practiced by the Caduveo Indians and other tribes.[20] He would have written his text in the ink and dye of Brazilwood in order that his entire body be at once clothed and disrobed when tattooed with the whorls and volutes of lines in the shape of both figures and letters. In this ironic remark the essayist avows that he would have become an Indian had he been an Indian. The temptation to have painted himself "naked" does not mean that he has removed clothing to show that the self-portrait depicts a nude body; implied is that painting of the body resembles that of the self in ink on the skin of the page. Without the New World or without the presence of the Indian the project would not have been so radical. The *Essays* owe much of their power to the New World that, over and again, they inspire us to discover and discern. In the absence of New Worlds in our time the *Essays* are today our most precious sign both of what they had been and of the many new adventures and unknown relations they continue to bring forward. The first and last places where we encounter the New Worlds are in the writing of the *Essays*.

NOTES

1. Walter Goffart remarks that editions of Ptolemy in the early and middle years of the sixteenth century, in which "old" and "new" maps were juxtaposed to show that the atlas itself was a historical document, gave way to collections that claimed themselves of greater exactitude: in *Historical Atlases: The First Three Hundred Years* (Chicago: University of Chicago Press, 2003), p. 16.

2. Claude Lévi-Strauss follows the words of Lucien Febvre, who saw among Europeans expression of a "mediocre astonishment" following the news of the voyages of Columbus, Cabral, and Magellan, in: "En relisant Montaigne," *Histoire de lynx* (Paris: Plon, 1992), pp. 277–8.

3. Guillaume Postel, *Les Merveilles du monde, et principallement des admirables choses des Indes et du Nouveau Monde* (Paris, 1553). Monique Pelletier discusses this work in *Cartographie de la France et du monde de la Renaissance au siècle des lumières* (Paris: Bibliothèque Nationale de France, 2001), pp. 13–15.

4. The heritage of the reception of the New World is taken up at length in Giuliano Gliozzi, *Adamo e il nuovo mondo. La nascità dell'antropologia come ideologia coloniale: dalle genealogie bibliche alle teorie razziali (1500–1700)* (Florence: La Nuova Italia, 1977).

5. Guy Rosolato, *La relation d'inconnu* (Paris: Gallimard, 1978), but also the same author's *Eléments de l'interprétation* (Paris: Gallimard, 1986), pp. 166–86.

6. Pierre Villey, *Les Sources et l'évolution des "Essais" de Montaigne*, 2 vols. (Paris: Hachette re-edition, 1933).

7. Among other representations, the latter are amply and graphically illustrated in Richard Verstegen, *Theatre des cruautez des Hereticques de nostre temps* (Anvers: Adrien Hubert, 1588), a compilation of grisly images that circulated widely in Europe and England after its initial publication. The religious issues at work in the essay – its apparent inversion of Catholic mass – are taken up in George Hoffmann, "Anatomy of the Mass: Montaigne's 'Cannibals,'" *Publications of the Modern Language Association of America*, 117/2 (March 2002), pp. 207–21.

8. Albert Thibaudet calls it "a program of an entire literature that will flourish in the eighteenth century," in *Montaigne*, ed. Floyd Gray (Paris: Gallimard, 1963), p. 388.

9. The third term of the enumeration does not fit with "fashion" and "pomp." It may refer to a city-view, a topographical perspective on

a European metropolis as they had been known in Georg Braun and Hogenburg's *Civitates orbis terrarum* (1517) or in Sebastian Münster's *Cosmographia universalis*, an illustrated work that circulated widely. Montaigne had a French translation (1565) of Münster in his library.

10. In "Of Coaches," the companion-essay to "Cannibals," Montaigne launches a critique of deficit spending where monies go outside of French borders. In the context of Montaigne's pervasive criticism of national economic and military policies that send monies outside of the state and that employ foreigners to defend national land, the guards are a sign of spendthrift ways. In "Of Physiognomy" (III.12), he shows little appreciation for mercenaries who bring strife and dissent to the nation. "Our armies are no longer bound and held together except by foreign cement; of Frenchmen one can no longer form a steadfast and disciplined army corps. How shameful! There is only so much discipline as borrowed soldiers show us; as for ourselves, we follow our own lead and not our leader's, every man his own way. The leader has more trouble within than without" (III.12, F796, V1042).

11. Montaigne's friendship, notes Ullrich Langer, "consistently must refuse subordination to an end other than itself," in *Perfect Friendship: Studies in Literature and Moral Philosophy from Boccaccio to Corneille* (Geneva: Droz, 1994), p. 169.

12. The point is developed further in my "Friendship in a Local Vein: Montaigne's Servitude to La Boétie," *South Atlantic Quarterly*, 97/1 (1998), pp. 65–90.

13. In "Of Vanity" he refers to his essays as "an ill-fitted patchwork" (III.9, F736, V964) to which are attached, here and there "some extra ornaments" (III.9, F736, V964), in other words, a figure, an emblem, or a cipher in the texture of the printed writing. Such would be the numerical design of the chapters around and about "Cannibals."

14. Lopez de Gómara, *Cortez: The Life of the Conqueror*, trans. Lesley Byrd Simpson (Berkeley: University of California Press, 1964), chs. 47–8, pp. 105–7.

15. Montaigne alters the original, putting "fruits" in the place of Gómara's "bread and cherries" ("pan y cerezas"), no doubt because bread was not a comestible known to the Aztecs, a point made clear in "Cannibals" where he notes that the natives eat a white matter, resembling preserved coriander, in place of bread. In his "De la immoderación de Hernán Cortés a 'De la moderation' de Michel de Montaigne," Juan Durán Luzio remarks this change and others, and observes that the ending of "Of Moderation" prepares the way for a political reading of the following essay, "Of Cannibals," a first chapter intended for a polemic around the

conquest of the New World (*Montaigne Studies*, 6/1–2 (1994), pp. 167 and 172).

16. See Olive Dickason, *The Myth of the Savage and the Beginnings of French Colonialism in the Americas* (Edmonton: University of Alberta Press, 1997).

17. Juan Durán Luzio, "Montaigne ante la censura hispanica," *Montaigne Studies*, 7/1–2 (1995), pp. 203–12 (esp. 208–9).

18. See Théodore de Bry, *America pars sexta* (Frankfurt, 1592), copies of which are appended to Gérard Defaux's, "A propos 'Des Coches' de Montaigne (III, 6): De l'écriture de l'histoire à la représentation du moi," *Montaigne Studies*, 6/1–2 (1994), pp. 135–61 (160–61). In his reflection on vehicles Montaigne appeals indirectly to a common iconography of time, seated on a coach in guise of Saturn devouring his children: see my *Graphic Unconscious in Early Modern French Writing* (Cambridge: Cambridge University Press, 1992), ch. 8.

19. See Lancelot du Voisin, sieur de la Popelinière, *Les Trois Mondes* (1582), ed. Anne-Marie Beaulieu (Geneva: Droz, 1997).

20. Claude Lévi-Strauss, "Une société indigène et son style," in *Tristes Tropiques* (Paris: Plon, 1955), pp. 205–27.

# 6   Justice and the law: on the reverse side of the *Essays*

At the beginning of the chapter "Of Experience" (III.13), the last of the *Essays*, Montaigne completes his critique of kinds of knowledge with an indictment against jurisprudence, the science of deceptive comparisons between "cases" which cannot be reduced to legal rules, and against, more generally, the defects of the legal order – "There is nothing so grossly and widely and ordinarily faulty as the laws" (III.13, *F*821, *V*1072) – with their consequences, "condamnations plus crimineuses que le crime" (condemnations more criminal than the crime) (*F*820, *V*1070–71).[1] These attacks are obviously inspired by his own very strong requirement for justice: in other words, by his desire to see the virtue of justice being put into practice. This virtue should inspire legislators and judges, and determine social relations; the philosopher observes with bitterness that such is not the case: "we call 'justice' the hodgepodge of the first laws that fall into our hands, and their application and practice, often very inept and very iniquitous" (II.37, *F*580, *V*766); and if he remarks immediately that "those who ridicule it and accuse it do not thereby intend to malign that noble virtue, but only to condemn the abuse and profanation of that sacred title" (*ibid.*, *F* 580–81, *V* 766), his critique of judicial institutions is all the more severe. Montaigne accuses these institutions of discrediting by a kind of sacrilege the ethical and political principle whose pre-eminence they are intended to ensure. It was long thought that Montaigne's systematic rejection of everything deriving from the law arose from some sort of personal repugnance, and perhaps also from incompetence. One of his biographers, Roger Trinquet, even questioned his study of law.[2] Wrongly so, since that would have assumed, without any kind of proof, after his brief work at the *Cour des Aides* of Périgueux (1556–7), that he submitted his opinions for thirteen years, as counselor at the *Chambre des Enquêtes* of the *Parlement* of Bordeaux (1557–70),[3] without any knowledge about the texts on which his verdicts were based. The refutation of this traditional falsehood was recently corroborated by an examination of the archives of the *Parlement*: Katherine Almquist has discovered fifty decrees, during a period of less than four years (from June 1563 to August 1567), that Montaigne signed as *rapporteur* charged specifically with the examination of the file (10 autograph signatures, 40 dictated to a court secretary), and 337 decrees in whose margins his participation in the debates and the judgment was noted.[4] These documents attest to Montaigne's intense involvement. In the commemorative inscription announcing his retirement, to be sure, Montaigne declared himself to be "worn out" (*pertaesus*). We should examine which elements in his initial exposure to and practice of the law provoked this discomfort, especially since these elements became, retrospectively, philosophical problems.

### THE PROBLEMS OF THE LAW: HUMANISM AND JURIDICAL TRADITION

These problems are quite evident. Law in the Renaissance is an area of controversy more so than an area of investigation. Medieval glosses are contested by humanist jurists not only in their exegetical details but in their very proliferation, which was thought to be (for example by Cujas in the exordium to his *Paratitla*) parasitical in relation to the *Corpus juris civilis*. In the practice of the tribunals, however, the medieval glosses remain authoritative, and the new interpretations are suspect, especially since their authors (Alciati in particular), by their own antidogmatic logic, recognize that their interpretations are just as conjectural as those that they refute. The original text alone remains beyond all question. But towards the middle of the sixteenth century even the original text is the object of criticism: even the *Pandectes*, an assemblage of extracts of the *Prudentes* of the early empire that the jurist Tribonian selected by order of the emperor Justinian, come to be accused of incoherence, and according to the most aggressive polemicists (François Hotman, in his *Antitribonien* of 1567), their faults reveal a plan to modify the original equity that presumably inspired the most ancient jurists. Official doctrine is thus undermined at its base, as much by methodical criticism as by a nostalgia for mythic origins. However, the humanists, in their efforts to restitute the *responsa*[5] of the *Prudentes,* could not recover them in full, since they had been cut up and mutilated, so the humanists say, from the late empire on. Nor could they translate into practice their historical and philological research, as a counterweight to the *consilia*[6] that the medieval doctors had artificially grafted on the *Corpus* in order to respond to the needs of a society entirely different from ancient Rome. Hence legal knowledge in the sixteenth century presents itself in the form of a set of prescriptions whose foundations are acknowledged to be uncertain and partly factitious, and whose articulations are obscure or full of gaps. Moreover, in distinction to theology, legal knowledge cannot claim for itself a sacred authority.

What is more, the law's articulation and modes of expression demonstrate these diverse traits: some commentaries are discontinuous (the glosses) and superposed in strata in the margins of legal compilations, while others are co-ordinated in synthetic treatises, but constantly and profusely refer to concurrent texts, glosses, and treatises. These forms of presentation show up the number and the variety of exegeses, and the precariousness of incidental notes which are always subject to statements vested with a superior authority. At the same time the compilations and treatises assign to these dispersed or co-ordinated notes a role in elucidating the law, giving them a formal status in spite of their disparate nature and even their confessions of uncertainty. Montaigne uses them as an argument in his reflection on knowledge, at the beginning of the chapter "Of Experience." According to him, in order to "adapt" the laws "by some roundabout, forced, and biased interpretation" (III.13, F819, V1070) to concrete cases that are infinite in their variety, where "resemblance does not make things so much alike as difference makes them unlike" (*ibid.,* F815, V1065), jurists and judges multiply distinctions and unusual likenesses, dispersing meaning with "subtleties." They "make the world fructify and teem with uncertainty and quarrels. . . . We were perplexed over Ulpian, [let us be once more] perplexed over Bartolus and Baldus" (who claimed to shed light on Ulpian's *responsa*) (*ibid.,* F816–17, V1066–7). However, he also recognizes in these superimposed glosses – agents of interference that render their object unintelligible (*ibid.,* F818, V1068) – the movement of critical investigation, a movement which continually overtakes acquired knowledge. This movement is typical of the "hunt for knowledge" (*F817, V1068*) as he conceives it ("Agitation and the chase are properly our quarry," III.8, *F708, V928*). After characterizing as sterile books in which "we only provide glosses for each other," he observes that the *Essays* are also articulated through internal commentaries, reflecting on their own statements: "How often and perhaps how stupidly have I extended my book to make it speak of itself!" (III.13, *F818, V1069*). In this way juridical knowledge becomes the model for the aporias of knowledge and for its harmfulness as "natural infirmity of [the] mind" (*ibid., F817, V1068*), but it also becomes the model for knowledge's resources and for the intellectual processes of the person who denounces its faults. Elsewhere the "verdicts" which proceed from these processes are cited as examples of assertions without responses but at the same time as examples of "the discussion and stirring up of the diverse and contrary reasonings which the matter of the law allows" (II.12, *F378, V510*), which in turn reveals the secret Pyrrhonism of the holders of doctrinaire knowledge. Hence one finds in the law the principal problems of Montaigne's theory of knowledge, in the disconcerting forms that he was able to give them.

### LAWS AND CUSTOMS: THE CIVIC FOUNDATIONS OF THE LAW FOR MONTAIGNE

But it is not only a question of a theory of knowledge, for underneath the disparateness of jurisprudence we find outlined the question of the foundations of the social and political order, and of its legitimacy. Two models of law were operative in the deliberations of the *Parlement* of Bordeaux. On the one hand, there was "written law," conceived as emanating from sovereign authority and imposing its supremacy. The compilation of royal ordinances concretized this law, and the "laws" of the Roman *Corpus*, functioning in southern France as a supplemental system and as a model of "reason," rested on the same principle. On the other hand there was "custom," emanating from the collective entities in which it was in use. Legitimized by an anonymous tradition, without a legislator or a system of authoritative prescription, custom expressed itself in the form of statements: in our region, the dividing up and transmission of goods, the differing status of persons, loans, guarantees etc. are regulated in this or that manner. That's the way it is. In principle the two kinds of legal models did not conflict with each other: royal laws were "received" in the provinces, local customs were "authorized" by the king and sometimes "reformed" by him after consultation with the provincial assemblies. But the political writers of the sixteenth century, in particular Jean Bodin,[7] clearly distinguished between the two sorts of legitimacy that proceeded from them: one was inscribed silently in the "common consent" of the social body and in its practices, while the other took form and efficacy from the sovereign injunctions of the prince who reigned over the social body, and from the agents of his power. This distinction reduces itself to the opposition between autonomy and heteronomy, between civic discipline and subjection. Montaigne was sensitized to this sort of problem by the *Discours de la servitude volontaire* by his friend La Boétie, and he did not fail to question its institutional foundations. In the seventeenth century the Bordeaux lawyer Etienne Cleirac copied and annotated a *Coustumier de Guyenne*, a compilation of regional customs, which he claimed to have "obtained from the study of Sir Michel de Montaigne, author of the *Essays*"[8]; this text is not identical to the "reformed" custom of 1520 (which was the only legally valid one), nor is it identical to the older version written in the fourteenth century. The very fact that Montaigne owned and studied this document reveals his attentiveness to past and present vestiges of his fellow citizens' autonomy. But above all the political concepts expressed in the *Essays* are witness to this interest.

Simple indications of these concepts are obvious, such as Montaigne's approval of the efforts by a "Gascon nobleman" to resist Charlemagne's imposition of "Latin and imperial laws" (1.23, F85, V117), or the defense of a customary disposition (F84, V116). What counts more is the fact that Montaigne requires of laws the immemorial permanence that legitimizes customs: "no laws are held in their true honor except those to which God has given some ancient duration, so that no one knows their origin or that they were ever different" (1.43, F198, V270 – everyone knows, on the other hand, the "origin" of royal laws, and the date on which they are promulgated by edict). Even more significant is his concept of the role of the magistrate who represents their authority: he exercises a regulative function on the "affairs of the city . . . lend[ing] a shoulder to make them easy and light" (III.10, F783, V1024), and even remaining inactive (*ibid.*, F782, V1021) if everyone conforms spontaneously to collective discipline, as is the case with "a state that is in a healthy condition" (1.23, F89, V122). In the case of disorder, his action, as energetic as it may be, is directed merely to re-establishing the "useful mutual confidence" (1.24, F 96, V131) which is intended to maintain harmony among citizens. The sovereign proclamations that Bodin expects from a representative of power are thus not his affair; Montaigne suspects them of hiding personal ambitions (III.10, F 782, V1023). This explains the professed conservatism in the final pages of the chapter "Of Custom, and Not Easily Changing an Accepted ["received"] Law" (1.23). It applies to "received" laws, that is ratified by the practice and assent of the civic body, following the model of custom, whatever their origin. If these "laws" are fundamentally contingent, judging by their diversity (manifested by his intentionally disorganized recording of exotic customs that invade the chapter after 1580, F80–83, V109–14), they share the characteristic of presupposing the autonomy of the group that observes them, and of distinguishing this group, to the very extent that they may appear aberrant to others. It is for this reason that the Indians refuse monotheism even though they "like" the reasoning that proposes it; for paganism, an error to which they remain faithful, "having followed it so advantageously for so long" (III.6, F695, V911), is a trait of both their cultural identity and their freedom. Thus it is perfectly logical to declare simultaneously that the rules which are observed spontaneously or agreed to ("received") are deprived of rational justifications, and that they must be maintained without modification, except when the exigencies of the moment make them disastrous for the city in which they are observed. One more step in the first direction, and Montaigne states that "laws remain in credit not because they are just, but because they are laws. That is the mystic foundation of their authority; they have no other" (III.13, F821, V1072). He comments bitterly in the Bordeaux copy of the *Essays*, referring to "laws" promulgated officially: "And that is a good thing for them. They are often made by fools, more often by people who, in their hatred for equality, are wanting in equity; but always by men, vain and irresolute authors" (*ibid.*, F821, V1072; see also II.12, F436, V579 – the last remark is responding to the then current idea that the legislating prince is the spokesman for divine justice). A further step in the other direction, and we have his repeated declarations of loyalty in the form of his refusal of "innovation" (1.23, F86–8, V119–21; 1.28, F144, V194) and of unshakable loyalty to "the cause of the laws and the defense of the old-time order" (III.1, F602, V793; see also III.9, F760, V994). These two series of statements simply develop the two sides of the same idea of citizenship.

These are dispersed elements of a political and legal thought whose coherence can only be perceived in the *Essays* as a pattern of threads, through an overview of several chapters – in particular 1.23, 24, 31, II.12 (F436–40, V578–83); III.1, 6, 10, 13. Montaigne refrained from proposing a synthesis undoubtedly because of his suspicion of all doctrinal exposition, even his own, but also because he found reasons to hesitate in the historical circumstances. At the end of the sixteenth century, the customary model retained only the vestiges of its former political meaning: the "reform" of customs which was being completed after having been accelerated since the time of François I marked the preponderance of royal will. It was said repeatedly in the *Parlements* that from now on no local custom could constitute an obstacle to the application of ordinances, so much so that the idea formulated by Guy Coquille, that "the people of each province has the right to establish the laws that govern them," became obsolete. What is more, the desire for regional independence was being exploited in various places and moments by the seditious elements among the Protestants or the Catholic *Ligue*, threatening to cause the dismemberment of the kingdom, "its dissipation and disintegration, the worst of our fears" (III.9, F734, V962). Under these conditions a theory of collective autonomy risked being abused and falsified, as had been the case with the demand for freedom inscribed in the first pages of La Boétie's *Discours de la servitude volontaire*. Montaigne thus did not formulate his political thought as a system, but as a *problem* at the foundation of law and civic discipline, just as La Boétie had postulated the premise of liberty only by examining the mechanisms of alienation.

### JUDICIAL PRACTICE AND THE REAL

The aforementioned problems had no direct influence on judicial practice, although this practice posed other questions of no less

significance in the form of discrepancies between legal procedure
and reality. The most obvious discrepancy concerned truthfulness
of statements. During a period in which investigatory methods were
rudimentary, the main part of a case consisted of testimony gathered during preliminary investigation. Once testimony was declared
admissible (sometimes at the end of long debates over "reproaches" –
reasons for impugnment – alleged by the parties), its coherence
caused the "confidence" (*foi*) of the tribunals, as long as other depo-
sitions had not contradicted it. The judge could thus dispense with
examining the risks of false testimony. In cases of disagreement,
though, he had to choose between the contradictory statements, a
task that the numerous treatises *De testibus* (*On Testimony*)[9] find
difficult, despite the strategies that they propose (examining the attitude of the witnesses, cross-checking, requiring more detailed statements . . . ). The most expeditious way was to weigh the testimony
according to the status of the witnesses in the social hierarchy, and
to accept the testimony of those whose weight was greater. This
procedure hardly conformed to the requirements of any real search
for the truth. A reform that was enacted during Montaigne's years
as magistrate would certainly have drawn his attention to the problem. In 1566, article 54 of the ordinance of Moulins requires the
establishment of a notarized contract for any transaction involving a
value of more than a hundred *livres*, and prohibits recourse to proof
by witnesses in cases where the transaction is contested. The first
commentator, Jean Boiceau de la Borderie,[10] explains the reasoning
behind the law, which becomes the criterion for its application: witnesses are too often corrupted and make false testimony. This reason ends up casting suspicion on statements made under oath, in
spite of the trust that was accorded them previously. In his preface
Boiceau quotes the arguments of those opposed to the ordinance: "by
prohibiting proof by testimony this law has, so it seems, prohibited
men from trusting each other, as if there were no longer any good
faith (*fides*) among them." The problems raised go beyond the strict
domain of the law. Montaigne seems to echo them in relation to
his own book: he claims its sincerity, as the only guarantee of the
work, but knows that nothing can guarantee his sincerity, since a liar
could say the same thing. He observes this in the chapter "Of Giving
the Lie" (II.18), immediately following "Of Presumption" where he
evaluated his own capacity to think and say the truth about himself.
Having answered a possible charge of self-display, he suddenly poses

a more incisive question: "But *whom shall we believe when he talks about himself*, in so corrupt an age . . .?" (ii.18, *F*505, *V*666, my italics). The context does not offer an answer; however the entire project of the *Essays*, as it is defined in the prologue to the reader, is thus being questioned, and the question extends beyond the *Essays*, to any search for truth in another person's word. On the basis of what criteria can one decide that an assertion is truthful? In the framework of epistemology the problem poses itself in terms of verification, and Pyrrho's doubting attitude, which Montaigne adopts (ii.12, *F*371–5, *V*502–5, *F*422, *V*562, *F*454–5, *V*600–01), is well known. Concerning human relations, the problem poses itself in terms of truthfulness and confidence, and Montaigne's response is first of all personal: at times it takes the form of a nostalgia for absolute faith in the other (i.28, *F*140, *V*189–90, speaking of La Boétie: "I should certainly have trusted myself to him more readily than to myself"), at times the form of a requirement for "perfect and entire communication" (ii.8, *F*287, *V*396) between persons close to each other. At the intersection between the two domains the philosophical dialogue takes place, in the broadest sense of the term: any exchange of statements that is held to be correct by the person who utters them. Truthful statements are possible, but without any other guarantee than the mutual and reflexive control that is practiced in the "conversation" that Montaigne wishes for (iii.8) and that he proposes discreetly, at a distance, for his reader (iii.9, *F*749–50, *V*980–81). In this way he sketches the image of a *precarious truth*, in direct relation to the crisis of the "proof by witnesses" which the ordinance of Moulins had officially uncovered.

The issue of the judge's word gave rise to the same troubling observations. In principle, far from being exposed to suspicion, it formulated official truth, since it benefited, as soon as it was pronounced, from the "authority of the adjudicated thing." But his word ceased to benefit from this authority when the case was under appeal, as was the case with most of the affairs examined in the *Chambre des Enquêtes*. The counselors in this chamber needed simultaneously to consider the decision of an inferior tribunal as revocable – because of error – and their own decision as an irrevocable formulation of the truth: all of which could appear troubling. In addition, the process by which sentences were arrived at contained constraints that were difficult to reconcile with a naive concern for the truth. The magistrates were held to make pronouncements *secundum allegata et probata*, "in accordance with the texts cited and the proved facts," leaving out any information that had not left traces in the procedure. A judge who, through personal information, knows the accused to be guilty is obliged to release him if the official charges are not sufficient to convict him (the jurists evoke less willingly the opposite example, of the judge required by the case of the prosecution to condemn an accused person whom he knows to be innocent). In sovereign courts the rule was a bit less constraining, since one could bypass the *allegata* of the law through recourse to "equity," but the regulations ("style") prescribed its use only in very rare circumstances. So this reduced prerogative increased the responsibility of the magistrate without truly giving him greater power. The *Chambre des Enquêtes* was all the more evidently limited to the texts and facts of the case since the persons subject to judgment did not appear before the court: trials were judged "by writing," and the counselors had at their disposal only elements that had been in the record before, or rather the report that one of them gave, the "reporter" (*relator*) who was helped in this by two colleagues who verified the conformity of his statements with the elements of the case. There was obviously, then, a permanent risk of discrepancy between what really had happened and the documents that presented the facts. The reporter was in a position to notice other types of discrepancies. After having exposed the cause by arguing *pro et contra*, and having given his opinion, he participated in the debate and in the vote, then composed the *dictum* that resulted. This could easily not be in agreement with his own opinion; however, he signed it along with the president as guarantor of the majority's decision. Then the *dictum* was transmitted to the *Grand'Chambre*, where it was "pronounced" by the presiding magistrate, which made of it an *arrêt*, a judgment, and thus executable. But during this last stage the decision could still be modified. The counselor experienced, in other words, a triple alienation of his own voice: he needed to found it on the data of the case which he had evaluated without being able to control their exhaustiveness nor even their exactitude; he risked being deprived of his words by the majority of the *Chambre* whose decision he had to sign; and the resulting judgment could depend on a superior instance. When in 1571 Montaigne described his judicial activities as a *servitude* (*servitium*) from which he had just freed himself, he probably was thinking of this type of subjection which diminished his official role as magistrate entrusted with rendering justice, more so than the work which he needed to undertake in accomplishing his tasks.

A final constraint leaves profound traces in the *Essays*: the obligation to judge. The magistrate cannot simply reserve his opinion, since he would be guilty of a "denial of justice." If he hesitates, and if he cannot find more competent colleagues to help him, he must have the temerity to settle the question and to take responsibility for his decision. Montaigne refuses to endorse this duty. In order to demonstrate its worst effects, he ventures beyond his competence as counselor of the *Chambre des Enquêtes*, which only dealt with civil law cases. He declares à propos of the Martin Guerre case, a criminal trial for usurpation of identity, judged in Toulouse, in which the arguments and evidence presented by the accusation and the defense balanced each other out, "Let us accept some form of sentence which says 'The court understands nothing of the matter'" (III.11, F788, V1030) – which would have prevented a death sentence from having been pronounced without decisive proof.[11] He also argues in the chapter "Of Cripples," that those accused of witchcraft should benefit from the doubt inherent in this type of affair, "since we see neither causes nor their means" (III.11, F788, V1031). If people are burned at the stake, it is because the judges cannot or do not want to recognize that they "understand nothing about" the wonders that rumor attributes to Satan and his hell hounds. He condemns from a similar perspective the application of judicial torture to a presumed criminal: "Are you not unjust when, *in order not to kill him without cause*, you do worse to him than kill him? As proof that this is so, see how many times he would rather die without *reason* than go through this *investigation* that is more painful than the execution" (II.5, F266, V369, my italics). The scrupulous judge has a confession wrung out by torture, believing that he can dissipate his doubts. Those are the perverse effects of the obligation to arrive at a verdict. And Montaigne generalizes: "Many abuses are engendered in the world, or, to put it more boldly, all the abuses in the world are engendered, by our being taught to be afraid of professing our ignorance, and our being bound to accept everything that we cannot refute" (III.11, F 788, V1030). The formula is undoubtedly inherited from Pyrrho or Carneades, through Sextus Empiricus or Cicero, but its vehemence, accentuated on the Bordeaux copy of the *Essays*,[12] probably derives from his own reflection on the injustices, cruelties, and murders committed in the name of the law, by its "abuses" that are perfectly within its regulations, in sixteenth-century France.[13]

One can see, given this background, what counselor Montaigne's resignation must have signified, or at least the meaning that he gave it, during the years that he composed the *Essays*. It remains for us to understand how his book integrates and inflects the experience of his judicial activities.

## LEGAL "JUDGMENTS," INVESTIGATIONS, AND THE *ESSAYS*

At a moment of transition in the "Apology for Raymond Sebond," between the praise of Pyrrhonism and the examination of the "asinine stupidities of human [sagacity]," Montaigne steps aside from the philosophical forum in order to return to the courtroom floor: "Let us take an example from *ourselves*. Judicial sentences form the ultimate point of dogmatic and decisive speaking" (II.12, F377, V509–10, my italics). In fact *we*, the magistrates of sovereign courts, make dogmatic pronouncements by professional obligation, content to have our virtuosity admired when we adduce our reasons, and once the judgment is pronounced, any objection is prohibited. The most imperious of masters could not dream of a safer situation, except perhaps at the Holy See. But Montaigne the counselor at the *Chambre des Enquêtes* resigned his position, and here he is among the ranks of thinkers without constraints, deprived at the same time of authority and of its blinkers: "We *who deprive our judgment of the right to make [decrees]* look mildly on opinions different from ours; and if we do not lend them our judgment, we easily lend them our ears" (III.8, F 704, V923). That changes all, to the point that one can ask if his Pyrrhonism is not the reflective and elaborated expression of his refusal of the dogmatic way of speaking that was required in the tribunals and determined the lives of the persons brought before justice. That way of speaking combines two kinds of tyranny, "both in words and in acts" (III.8, F711, V931), that the philosopher cannot accept, after having experienced their misdeeds while he occupied his position at court. His renunciation of the "right to pass judgments" has the effect in any event of radically transforming the ways of thinking that he was able to borrow from his practice of law.

Thus Montaigne's investigations into humanist knowledge are modeled on the structures of commentary transmitted by the glosses, but also assign functions to these structures that change their nature. Whereas the goal of ancient and modern jurists was to determine the exact meaning and the application of the statements that they annotated, Montaigne's refusal to pronounce judgments allows him to inspect without any limitations the possible meanings of the maxims and the anecdotes on which he grafts his "fantasies," and to exploit their diversity in order to free himself from them and to extend his meditations. He uses the tendency of multiple glosses to undermine evident truths to his advantage, against the intellectual and moral routines from which we must free ourselves so as to "[refer] things to truth and reason" (1.23, F85, V117). Better yet, this regenerative power which he attributes now to the commentary, to restart the "hunt for knowledge" on a "road in another direction" (III.13, F817, V1068), has repercussions on the commentary produced: "[its] theme turns in upon itself" (III.13, F818, V1069). The statements inscribed in this reflective framework allow, sooner or later, for remarks that tend to open them to questioning, even if they are ratified or deepened (as is demonstrated by the additions to the first versions of the Essays, which in fact are traces of multiple re-examinations). The dynamics of the reflexive essay thus stand up to the apparently definitive fixity of the maxims that punctuate and occasionally are produced by the essay, situating them at a critical distance and thus enabling investigations, "boundless and without form" (III.13, F818, V1068), of their meaning and their reasons.

The same thing can be said about the traces left on Montaigne's book by the concepts and the procedures issuing from judicial practice. Although he himself does not claim knowledge and authority, Montaigne sometimes seems to grant his assertions the status of testimony. This is what his vocabulary of proof seems to indicate: the words tesmoing(s) (witness(es)), tesmoignage(s) (testimony), and the verb tesmoigner (to witness, to give testimony), in all its forms compose the largest part, that is, 210 occurrences in all, far more than the 58 occurrences of the verb "to prove," and the 7 occurrences of the word "demonstration." Only the verb "to show" (montrer) and its

noun *montre* have comparable frequencies (142 and 45), but for half
of their uses they denote simply "exhibiting" and sometimes simply
"appearance" (9 of the noun's occurrences). So witnessing produces
proof, not in order to attest globally to the truthfulness of the book
(we have shown above the difficulties of such a proof), but in order to
confirm points of detail. Montaigne seems to respond to the expectations of a reader in search of veridical elements, but he does not
agree to restrict his field of investigation to that which he can guarantee, as a witness needs to do. In the epilogue to his chapter "On the
Power of the Imagination," he declares: "In the examples that I bring
in here of what I have heard, done, or said, I have forbidden myself
to dare to alter even the slightest and most inconsequential circumstances. My conscience does not falsify one iota; *my knowledge, I
don't know*" (1.21, F76, V106, my italics). The final words authorize
him to take account not only of his direct experience, as one expects
of a witness,[14] who has "heard, done or said" something, but also
of examples drawn from books whose exactness he cannot control.
That does not really matter: "for I refer the stories that I borrow to
the conscience of those from whom I take them [. . .] Whether they
have happened or no . . . they exemplify, at all events, some human
potentiality, and thus their telling imparts useful information to me"
(1.21, F75, V105). He thus allows himself recourse to "fabulous testimonies" (they "serve like true ones," *ibid.*), and occasionally he
modifies his borrowings. False witness? Not at all: he does not claim
to establish facts, but only to examine what is possible, to "talk
about what can happen" (1.21, F75, V106), when he finds matter for
reflection.

Montaigne accords himself the same freedom when analyzing the
data. As the "reporter" of a case he would have analyzed them in
distinct "articles," giving each of them an evaluatory mark (one of
the official notes *parum, bene, optime* [*probat*] – [proves] scarcely,
well, best), and would only have kept those whose value as proof
he acknowledged, in order to derive from them the substance of an
argument. As a philosopher, he likes to "put . . . in writing," when
they appear, the "chimeras and fantastic monsters" of his mind, "in
order to contemplate their ineptitude and strangeness at [his] pleasure . . . hoping in time to make [his] mind ashamed of [them]" (1.8,
F21, V33; see also III.9, F761–2, V994–6). He adopts the same attitude
with respect to the "fantasies" which he borrows from the ancients,

or from his contemporaries. Selection and elimination are replaced by critical reflection which takes into account all that has been registered, without being compelled to ratify everything, extending its activity potentially indefinitely. There remains, however, one criterion inherited from the *Chambre des Enquêtes* which Montaigne applies to his philosophical investigations: the *relevance* of statements, guarantee of their "order" as it is defined in respect to "conversation" by the example of children's disputes: "their turbulence and impatience never sidetrack them from their theme" (III.8, F 706, V925). In juridical deliberations this criterion is the only one which is truly controlled by the "reporter" of a case. Perhaps he does not possess the means of evaluating the certainty of allegations and the truthfulness of testimony, but he is always in a position to judge if they are relevant to a cause. It is the same in the case of dialogue, where the essential point is to exchange arguments which are always relevant to the subject, and to avoid veering off the subject except in order to "see about the way to treat it" (III.8, F706, V926), that is, in order to exert critical control over the procedures of the discussion and thus to better assure their relevance. This control is necessary; even if the inquiry into a subject does not come to a finding, "we are not excusable if we conduct it badly and irrelevantly" (III.8, F708, V928). This suggests the sort of concern with intellectual rigor required of a magistrate who is attentive to the validity of procedures and inferences in spite of his possible doubts about the information which is at his disposal and about the chances of arriving at a truthful conclusion.

As to the last phase of the process at the *Chambre des Enquêtes*, there is no approximate equivalent in the philosopher's way of proceeding. Not only will Montaigne not pronounce a verdict, but the deliberation itself does not result in a *dictum* anticipating a judgment. So we are left in suspense, in expectation of an intervention by some superior agent (but who, in the *Essays*, would be seated in the *Grand'Chambre*? – the only conceivable Judge [that is, God himself] rarely discloses his decisions). The problem is more complicated, for Montaigne does not compromise in his project to see himself and others clearly, and he does not hesitate to express firm opinions, sometimes vehemently. But he avoids giving these opinions the form of verdicts, in two ways. On the one hand he denies them all authority: "I talk about everything by way of conversation, and about nothing by way of advice" (III.11, *F* 790, *V*1033; the sentence is inscribed after 1588 on the Bordeaux copy at the end of an irrefutable argument against preliminary investigation during witchcraft trials). On the other, the reflexive perspective of the *Essays* lets the reader glimpse, beyond each firm assertion, the contingent attitude of the subject who asserts: "For in what I say I guarantee no certainty except that it is what I had at the time in mind, a tumultuous and vacillating mind" (*ibid.*; see also II.10, *F*296–7, *V*407). Under these conditions, the validity of statements depends on the assent of the reader, who is no less contingent, and the *Essays* solicit this assent to the very degree that it is imposed by no privileged power or knowledge. Thus the model of the tribunal seems inappropriate to the type of control and evaluation at work in the intimacy of the self. Montaigne does write "judgment holds in me a magisterial seat" (III.13, *F*823, *V*1074), but holds his verdicts in suspense: "It lets my feelings go their way, both hatred and friendship, even the friendship I bear myself, without being changed and corrupted by them. [. . .] [I]t plays its game apart" (*ibid.*). The main point is to keep oneself at a distance from the roles assumed (see III.10, *F*773–4, *V*1011–12) and from the thoughts registered, by a doubling which the unfolding of the self-reflective book makes visible, and which could be corroborated by the virtual reader associated with the examination. Instead of an instance of deciding and of sanctioning, we have a dialogic meditation that includes the hope of a convergence of points of view.

## THE CONCERN FOR JUSTICE AND MONTAIGNE'S AUTONOMY

The *Essays* do, however, have to do with "[internal jurisdiction]" (III.8, *F*710, *V*930), with its laws and its verdicts (III.2, *F*613, *V*807), and Montaigne takes the measure of its requirements: those deriving from a permanent desire for justice, which is inscribed in his ethics as much as in his civic concepts and involvement. This concern is irreducible to judicial obligations: "The sentence I pass upon myself is sharper and stiffer than that of the judges, who only consider me with respect to common obligation; the grip of my conscience is tighter and more severe" (III.9, *F*738, *V*967). In fact the point is to stake out a space of freedom in which the *virtue* of justice can be practiced, the mere obeying of laws being its worthless *Ersatz*.

The principle is simple: if one defines legal obligations by the prohibitions that correspond to them, it is clear that they trace limits not to be transgressed, limits which are placed under the surveillance of a judge and the police. But within these limits the individual can do as he or she pleases. Thus the individual can prescribe his or her own rules, affirming his or her sovereignty as private legislator. This is the way Montaigne proceeds: he limits his projects or his claims by extending them only within the boundaries constituted by external constraints: "I have my own laws and court to judge me, and I address myself to them more than anywhere else. To be sure, I restrain my actions according to others, but I extend them only according to myself" (III.2, F613, V807). In other words, it is the other (the representative of the state, the judge, the notary) who lets me know that I *do not have the right* to do this or that, but among the things I have the right to do, I am the one who decides what is, in my opinion, *just or unjust.*

The reader might find paradoxical this way of freeing oneself from the injunctions of justice by imposing on oneself even stricter personal laws. It is anticipated, however, in the *De officiis* (III.15), where Cicero approves of the buyer who pays a sum for a property that is superior to the arranged price, since he judges it to be worth more. Montaigne connects here with the spirit if not the letter of Roman law. His behavior derives in effect from a recognized legal principle, the *bona fides* invoked in judgments on equity (*ibid.*, III.17), not in order to extend the domain of the licit beyond what is stipulated by the law in a strict sense, but rather in order to prevent the law from being misused through juridical subtleties. It is well known that crafty quibblers can take advantage of the way the law is set out, for example by using the pretext of a procedural error in order to have a contract they signed annulled. In these cases equity does not surpass the law, but restores it by an additional measure of rectitude. The person who refuses to exploit to his advantage all of the resources offered by the law makes a personal practice of this type of equity. He or she decides in complete autonomy to distinguish the licit and the illicit, within the space of what is authorized by the law of the city (for Montaigne, a heteronomy). Thus the requirement of justice can be thought about and practiced independently of codes and tribunals. Montaigne expresses this in an approximate way in the very pages where he refuses personal involvements that would entail constraints: "Yes, even in undertakings in which I am alone concerned and wholly free, if I say what I plan to do, it seems to me that I prescribe it for myself, and that to give knowledge of it to another is to impose it upon myself. It seems to me that I promise it when I mention it. Thus I seldom air my plans" (III.9, *F*738, *V*967). To translate: in the intimacy of one's self, any declaration establishes a duty towards oneself, prescribed (*préordonné*) through a spontaneous initiative. One more step, and the model perfects itself in himself, through an exact coincidence between the declaration and the individual decree as it is promulgated and registered. The subject lays down his own law for himself and observes it, delineating freely his private jurisdiction, in the margins of the common rules which he respects in any event. This can work silently within a conscience, but can also be written, over many years, and can form an ethical identity acknowledged and transformed into a personal code, in the form of a book. Montaigne discovers that he has accomplished precisely this, fifteen years or so after having set out to "put in writing" his *Essays*, when he re-examines them: "I feel this unexpected profit from the publication of my behavior, that to some extent it serves me as a rule. Sometimes there comes to me a feeling that I should not betray the story of my life. This public declaration obliges me to keep on my path, and not to give the lie to the picture of my qualities" (III.9, *F*749, *V*980). At the conclusion of his disagreements with the judicial institutions and the legality whose guardians they are supposed to be, he recognizes in his work as a philosopher a sort of law appropriate to this double requirement of justice and of autonomy, a requirement undoubtedly all the stronger for having been frustrated during his activities as magistrate.

### DOCUMENTS

*Coustumes generalles de la Ville de Bordeaux.* Jean Guyart, 1532. Bibliothèque Municipale de Bordeaux, Br.8046 Rés. Coffre.
*Coustumier de Guyenne nommé Roolle de la Ville de Bourdeaux, contenant partie des privileges, franchises, lois, moeurs et formes de vivre des anciens Bordelais; sur lequel la coustume reformée en l'an 1520 a été extraite. Tiré de l'Estude de Messire Michel de Montaigne, autheur des essais, avec quelques notes pour l'intelligence et l'explication tant du langage que de l'histoire, adjoustées par Monsieur Estienne Cleirac,*

*advocat au Parlement* (copied by L. Gautier–Lagardère and verified by H. Barckhausen on the basis of the [now lost] original, 502 pp.). Bibliothèque de Droit de l'Université de Bordeaux, MS. 5

La Roche Flavin (Bernard de), *Treze livres des Parlemens de France.* Bordeaux: Millanges, 1617

*Stilus Curiae Parlamenti [. . .] a G. de Broglio* (Guillaume De Breuil) – *Stilus Camerae Inquestarum*, MS. Bibliothèque Municipale de Bordeaux, MS. 362. See Guilhiermoz, *Enquêtes et procès.*

A numbered list of the *dicta* of the *Chambre des Enquêtes* in which Montaigne participated, for the period of 1563–7, has been established by Katherine Almquist (in *Bulletin de la Société des Amis de Montaigne*, (January 1998), pp. 34–8, following her reproduction and commentary of four autograph *dicta*, pp. 13–33). This completes the sketchy list by Bonnefon, published under the misleading title "Arrêts de Montaigne et La Boétie," in the *Archives Historiques du Département de la Gironde*, 28 (1893), pp. 121–47.

NOTES

1. The text quoted has been modified to conform to the Bordeaux Copy of the *Essays* (Paris: Langelier, 1588, containing Montaigne's handwritten additions and corrections), in particular in respect to its partitioning, falsified since 1595 (see the prologue to the edition of the Imprimerie Nationale, Paris, 1998, in which the original text division has been restored).

2. *La jeunesse de Montaigne: Ses origines familiales, son enfance et ses études* (Paris: Nizet, 1972), ch. 15, pp. 513–20, and 17, p. 599, where Montaigne is supposed to have only "skimmed the generalities of the law."

3. Some brief explanations of French judicial terms are in order (others will be explained below):

The *Cour des Aides* treated matters concerning royal taxation; the Périgueux court was disbanded soon after Montaigne's nomination, so it is not certain that he participated in its work. Created in 1462, the *Parlement* of Bordeaux was the supreme court of appeals for the Guyenne region. It consisted principally of the *Grand'Chambre* to which was adjoined the *Chambre des Enquêtes*, in which Montaigne sat. This chamber deliberated on civil legal matters, on written trials ("procès par écrit"), inquiries already brought to a conclusion by commissioners charged by the *Grand'Chambre* with conducting preliminary investigation of complex cases, or inquiries conducted by inferior tribunals whose judgments could be appealed. The counselors of the *Enquêtes* deliberated on each of the files and concluded with a *jugé* (finding); their conclusions were transmitted to the *Grand'Chambre* which pronounced the definitive *arrest.*

4.  "Quatre arrêts du Parlement de Bordeaux, autographes inédits de Montaigne," *Bulletin de la Société des Amis de Montaigne*, (January 1998), pp. 13–38. The title of the article refers to the signed decrees reproduced and studied by Almquist; in an appendix she lists 387 decrees that carry the signature or the name of Montaigne (pp. 34–8). The list of names inscribed by the clerk is different for each decree: only counselors who had effectively examined and deliberated on a cause are mentioned. Causes, which were presented almost always on appeal, were seldom simple.

5.  Originally, *responsa* were simply the opinions given by legal experts (the *Prudentes*) to the praetor, the Roman magistrate who decreed the laws (*leges*). Collected, chosen, and classified by the jurists of the empire upon the orders of Justinian, these *responsa* had taken on the force of laws, by reason of the imperial authority that conferred to the assembled texts the status of *corpus juris civilis*, the "body" of civil law.

6.  Treatises concerning "questions" posed in relation to specific "cases." They based themselves on Justinian's *Corpus*, but adapted it to medieval institutions by approximations and sometimes by distortions.

7.  *Six livres de la République* (Paris, 1576), I.10, p. 162: "Custom acquires its power gradually, over years, by common consent of all, or of the greatest number. But the law emerges in one instant, and derives its force from the person who has the power to command everyone. Custom flows softly and without coercion. Laws are ordered and published by force, and very often against the will of the subjects." Bodin attributes true authority to law only. Guy Coquille orients his *Questions, réponses et méditations sur les articles des coutumes* very differently: "the people of each province has the right to establish laws that apply to themselves: these are customs and non-written law." (*Oeuvres*, Paris, ed. A. de Cay, 1646, p. 1).

8.  A copy of this document can be found in the Law Library of the University of Bordeaux (MS. 5). The text contains annotations anterior to the notes by Cleirac, as well as a reclassification of the articles; these features of the text cannot be attributed with certainty to Montaigne. See on this point A. Tournon, *Montaigne: La glose et l'essai* (Paris: Champion, 2002), pp. 196–8, or the appendix of Tournon, "Le magistrat, le pouvoir et la loi," in *Les écrivains et la politique dans le Sud-Ouest de la France autour des années 1580* (Bordeaux: Presses Universitaires, 1982), pp. 67–86.

9.  They are assembled in the *Tractatus de testibus probandis aut reprobandis variorum authorum [. . .] per Johannem Baptistam Ziletum, Venetiis, apud Jacobum Simbenum, MDLXVIII*. The information used here is repeated from treatise to treatise; it is exposed with admirable clarity in the treatise by Nelli in San Geminiano, *Tractatus de testibus et*

*eorum reprobatione* (pp. 117–67 of the collection). The work of Andrea Frisch will shed new light on this question.

10. His *Traité de la preuve par témoins*, published in Latin in Poitiers in 1582, was translated in 1599, then re-edited with important commentary by Danty in 1697.

11. Only this refusal to judge could prevent it. For if the court had released the accused, Arnaud du Tilh, by benefit of doubt, it would have been obliged to incriminate the accuser, Pierre Guerre, with false accusation, and condemn him to the punishment which he had demanded for his adversary.

12. The amplification "or . . . all the abuses . . ." is a hand-written addition, as well as the explanation "and *our being bound* to accept" which indicates an obligation and could refer to the "style" of the tribunals, which is the explicit subject of a contiguous addition. One should also note that it is only in the Bordeaux copy that the condemnation of torture, mentioned above, takes on its full force. In the versions of 1580 and 1582, the chapter "Of Conscience" (II.5) tended to justify its use, precisely because of the "effort" of conscience: "the innocent man's conscience seems to fortify him against his torture to tell the truth" writes Montaigne, adding on the subject of torture: "torture is a means full of uncertainty and danger. But at all events, it is the least ineffective way that human weakness has been able to invent"; in 1588, a change in the punctuation rectifies the intention: "the innocent man's conscience seems to fortify him against his torture. To tell the truth, torture is a means full of uncertainty and danger. [. . .] But at all events, it is the least ineffective way" (II.5, F266, V369). On the Bordeaux copy, the excuse of the lesser evil and of "human weakness" is put into doubt by a "they say" before being refuted in the final addition, "Very inhumanly, however, and very uselessly, in my opinion" (*ibid.*).

13. This protest was not without echo in legal circles. Bernard de La Roche Flavin, in his *Treize livres des Parlements de France* (Bordeaux: Millanges, 1617), transcribes Montaigne's statements literally in his chapter "D'aucunes punitions ou condamnations trop sévères, rigoureuses, voire cruelles" (XIII, lxxiii, §§ 9, 10, 12–14, 28–30).

14. The treatises compiled by Ziletus are all in agreement on this point: what exceeds perception is not the object of witness testimony. It is up to the judge to account for what the witness perceived through his senses. Thus Nelli a S. Geminiano, *Tractatus de testibus. . .*, § 130: *Testis debet reddere rationem sui dicti per eum sensum per quem percipit id de quo testificatur* ("the witness must render account for his statements by the sense through which he perceived that about which he testified"), and § 135: *Si testis testificatur super his quae non*

*percipiuntur sensu corporis: sed oculo mentis seu rationis: non valet ejus dictum* ("if the witness testifies about something that was not perceived by corporeal senses but with the eye of the mind or of reason, then his statements are not valid"). Thus, according to Baldus (*Tractatus circa materiam testium*, III.35), hearsay testimony is acceptable in the form of "I *heard* it being said that . . ." (the auditory perception of a rumor is attested, not, of course, its veracity, which a judge must evaluate); in the form of "One says that . . ." the testimony would not be acceptable.

# 7   Montaigne and the notion of prudence

A translation of the Greek *phronēsis* (Aristotle, *Nicomachean Ethics* [henceforth *NE*], VI) and of the Latin *prudentia*, prudence "is the choice between good and evil" (II.12, *F*369, *V*499 = *Ad Herennium*, III.3 and Cicero, *De Inventione*, II.160): it is the discernment of what is good for us, or as the *OED* defines it, the "ability to discern the most suitable, politic, or profitable course of action, especially as regards conduct," i.e., "practical wisdom, discretion." The "prudent" leader, like a good helmsman, knows how to steer the ship of the state amidst all the reefs and guide it to a safe port (towards its supreme good). This *savoir-faire* or skillfulness comes from one's *memoria*, the knowledge acquired through experience; from one's *intelligentia*, an understanding of the present situation or *casus*; and from one's *providentia*, one's capacities of anticipation – *providentia* being seen by the Romans as the very etymology of *prudentia*. In the sixteenth century, prudence is *the* concept used to think about action and especially political action. It is omnipresent in the *Essays*. Montaigne begins them emblematically with a discussion of military prudence, and the title of I.1 announces a reflection on the ways and "means" of arriving at a given "end." He describes himself as a man of action, for he seeks "remedies" for ailments of the soul (III.4, *F*632, *V*832) as well as procedures to follow for arriving at his desired ends ("It is bad procedure to oppose this passion," III.4, *F*630, *V*830; "we should proceed in the opposite way from the reed," III.10, *F*779, *V*1018).

The majority of modern commentators are unaware of the concept of prudence but have reflected on Montaigne's attitude regarding human actions. Their results are divided along two main axes. The first emphasizes, and rightly so, Montaigne's conservatism: for him, to act is ultimately not to act. The second, less frequent axis argues that his book aims to transform its readers: "an ethical reform of [Montaigne's] class is at the heart of the political project of the *Essais*."[1] I will be following Quint's particularly powerful reading. After having pointed out its limitations, I will show that Montaigne portrays himself (1) as a nobleman, (2) as a *prudens*, and (3) as an "artist."

Those who support the argument regarding Montaigne's conservatism draw a conclusion whose limpidity is nearly tautological. If action concerns a matter that, without thinking overly far ahead, concerns only a "few years" (III.9, *F*751, *V*982) or even a few hours, then he puts into practice "that which today we call the principle of precaution, whereby to act is to abstain."[2] This is exactly the current meaning of *prudence*. For we have retained only two of the subparts of *prudentia*: to be prudent is to be cautious and circumspect.[3] One can certainly predict that Montaigne will use the word this way on numerous occasions, generally each time the modern editor attaches no note to the words *prudence* and *prudent*.[4] But from a conceptual point of view, the inquiry is finished if by Montaigne's "prudence" we mean that Montaigne is . . . prudent, in the very sense in which we use this word today. There is more at stake than this falsely simple result leads us to believe. Montaigne's conservatism is itself viewed as the result of his skepticism. Since André Tournon, a whole segment of critical interpretation has radicalized the Pyrrhonism of the *Essays*, and from this it rigorously deduces the impossibility of action in the strongest sense of the term, with regard to the world as well as the self. The skeptic "lets himself roll with the wind"[5]; there is no teleology of action and thus no *providentia*. As Quint emphasizes, the link to post-modernism is evident: starting in 1982, Starobinski associated Montaigne with the refusal of any projection of the self into the future, in order to better destroy the modern myth of Progress, which immolates the present on behalf of the future.[6] Prudence being one of the highest forms of human reason, along with *sophia* or the "contemplation" of eternal truths (fixed stars) by the *savant*, it is logical that we find here the whole debate on reason deriving from the "Apology for Raymond Sebond" (II.12). The dividing line between the post-modernists and Quint reproduces the one separating those for whom Pyrrhonism is Montaigne's ultimate truth and those for whom Pyrrhonism functions as an instrument, as a means at the service of an end that goes beyond it.

For his part Quint is equally unaware of the ancient notion of prudence. His fundamental presupposition is that nature and the natural take precedence, while *prudentia* comes entirely from acquired knowledge and work, or – if one prefers – from the cultural. One can reconstruct his reasoning as follows. He begins by identifying valor, ethos, or "virtue" exclusively with military valor. He continues by pointing out the disastrous consequences of military valor. Conclusion: it is necessary to abandon any idea of valor, since it produces such catastrophic results. By suppressing the notion of virtue, Quint can speak endlessly about ethics while never citing a single work on ethics. Indeed such works only address the question of virtues, with prudence at their summit. Thus he would have it that Montaigne opposes the naturalness of his own conduct to all philosophies of ethics. On the one hand, there is the overly stringent and virile mastery of the warrior who, in Stoic fashion, is cruel with others because he is hard on himself. On the other hand, Montaigne affirms that passivity is not a flaw, contrary to Stoicism which condemned *mollesse* (softness) or effeminate *mollitia*. When, at the other end of the *Essays* (III.12), Montaigne recounts how his non-Stoicism saved him from the troops that occupied his castle, Quint considers that this is the pinnacle of his naturalness and that such conduct expresses "the essence of human nature itself [i.e.,] the essence as well of noble conduct, to the extent that nobility itself is a gift of nature, nature in its noblest form" (*Montaigne and the Quality of Mercy*, p. 137). In a manner that is at once logical and successful, Quint becomes that which Tournon fears we will see in Montaigne, a dogmatic preacher. But a "soft" preacher: Montaigne's ideal ultimately stems from a form of common sense that is itself natural and within everyone's reach.

It seems to me that Quint only goes halfway. It is in any case possible to propose another conclusion to his reasoning. Instead of suppressing the notion of valor, it is sufficient to distinguish between false and "true" valor. The disastrous consequences of Military Stoicism thereby permit one to criticize Stoic virtue as an appearance of virtue. Glorious bravery is not "true" courage; it is either an excess of courage or an act of self-deception, or rather the two together. Now, the discernment of true courage (like that of true justice, etc.) is the work *par excellence* of prudence, which has the particularity of being both a moral and an intellectual virtue. To aptly judge one's own bravery, one must have both good judgment – this is the intellectual dimension – *and* a form of moral courage, or rectitude with regard to oneself. The "true" *mollitia* or cowardice is the aforementioned self-deception. "Cowardice, mother of cruelty" (title of II.27): the warrior's excess is like the too violent noise of his impetuous nature, which prohibits him from hearing the voice of wisdom, of humanity. One does not escape this naturally, but rather through working on oneself. Just as art or technique (Greek *technē*, Latin *ars*) is an *ergon*, work that transforms the material world through production, *poiēsis* or *operatio*, the virtues in general – and thus prudence which governs them – are *erga* that transform the human world (myself and others) through action – *praxis* or *actio*. The non-Stoic face presented to the invaders can thereby be described as the culminating point of artifice, as the result of a whole life of training. By controlling himself, he controls them. Certainly, Montaigne aligns himself with those who follow nature, or "naturalists" (III.12, F809, V1056). But when he says, "[to] naturalize art," in context this means to forget the artificial, the opposite of "true" art (III.5, F666, V874). Work, like God's grace, does not contradict nature or the innate. It fulfills it; it perfects it in and by an act of doing, an activity.

This overview has permitted us to flesh out the themes implied by the notion of prudence. (1) It is closely tied to nobility and exemplariness: ancient ethics are addressed only to those who are well born. (2) Since the former seek praise, the notion is also tied to the question of appropriate, indeed just pride, that is to say with the question of knowing what makes "true" valor, true control, true excellence. (3) Finally, the notion is tied to the problem of art and nature, of work done on an innately good inner foundation, the noble work of a character that is hypothetically noble. Montaigne presents himself therefore as a nobleman, as a *prudens*, and as an "artist." He is certainly conservative in politics, but not as a writer, where he is truly innovative. It is in the *Essays* that his least cautious prudence unfolds – not of a preacher but of a sort of director of conscience.

Like Marc Fumaroli, I conclude that Montaigne is fairly Jesuit, *pace* Tournon and Quint.

## MONTAIGNE AS NOBLEMAN: THE *MESTIS*

Quint has made it clearly understood that there was a malaise within the noble class of the time. But to restrict it as he does to the nobility of the sword is reductive, even if we readily acknowledge that military valor is paradigmatic of all noble virtue.

The question of prudence in the sixteenth century passes inevitably through the question of Machiavellianism, using the term very loosely to mean any form of political realism. Yet Montaigne has a complicated relationship with Machiavellianism. This is immediately felt by virtue of the fact that it is difficult to take from the *Essays* an unequivocal meaning of the word *prudence*. On the one hand, it is pejorative and often refers to cleverness and almost to deceitfulness: III.1 (*F*603, *V*795) translates it as "subtlety," deceitful skillfulness or *panourgia*[7]; II.26 (*F*473, *V*625) criticizes the "worldly-wise" ("prudans mondains") or those who are prudent by worldly standards, with their suppleness and readiness to be turncoats. On the other hand, and just as frequently, the word is charged with the noble meanings of the ancient *prudentia* (for example, in 1.25 [*F*99, *V*136] it is associated with "wise"). This ambivalence, which was already present in both Thomas Aquinas and the language of the period, is of course related to the highly problematic articulation of politics and morality. But this conflict itself reveals another. There is within the nobility of the time a truly existential malaise, a profound doubt with regard to their most fundamental values: in short, a moral crisis. The wars of religion exacerbated this; they did not create it.

The whole matter would be simple if Montaigne categorically rejected Machiavellianism (Friedrich has already demonstrated that this is not the case).[8] This would bring us back to the preferred portrait of the author as drawn by many current presentations. Having resigned from his office as counselor in the *Parlement* of Bordeaux at the age of thirty-eight (1571), Montaigne supposedly retired to his domain. Quite far from being "engaged" in the Sartrian sense, even as mayor he was allegedly, so to speak, disengaged, as Zen as a Chinese sage. If this portrait were accurate, then his relationship to Machiavellianism would not be problematic: a refusal of any intrigue based on a refusal of any participation in active life other than through lip service, out of a mere sense of inescapable duty. This is the portrait of Montaigne as an intellectual follower of the contemplative life, like a wise neo-Stoic. It is false.

Montaigne was one of those "political professionals"[9] who populated all the chancelleries and courts of the sixteenth century. The year of his resignation he was made a knight of the Order of Saint Michel, an entirely incongruous promotion for a nobleman of such low extraction and small renown. In an equally exceptional manner, he rose to the position of *gentilhomme* (gentleman-in-ordinary of the king's chamber in 1573). He left the *Parlement* in order to make himself available for another task. As Jean Balsamo and George Hoffmann have shown, he was aligned with the Foix clan. He was their *cliens* or loyal agent, and his *patronus* was Louis de Foix, for whom he was suspected in Bordeaux of being the straw man (see Villey's remarks for III.8 and 1.26). In the 1570s he was prepared, if not programmed, by the Foix to play a very precise political role in Guyenne: namely, that of go-between for the very Catholic Foix clan and their enemy Henri de Navarre, not to mention all the other factions concerned. His term as mayor of Bordeaux is the most salient moment of this role, but his responsibilities did not end after his mayoralty, and they probably began before it. Montaigne is thus not neutral.[10] Nor is he "wavering and half-and-half" ("chancelant et mestis"): he is not an opportunist (III.1, F601, V793). He firmly states his allegiance to the Catholic side, and all the more so since, as any go-between, he was surely suspected of playing a double game, of nevertheless being "two-faced" (*mestis*) (II.16, F473, V625) – that is, prudent by worldly standards. Likewise, it is because of his "negotiating . . . between our princes" (III.1, F600, V791) that he forcefully affirms in III.1 that he has always been without "perfidy," that we can "trust" him (F602, V794). Well placed at the start of book III, this chapter, just as the note "To the Reader," is a prologue reaffirming his ethos, his "good faith." This faith is like the *fides* that the *cliens* owes to his *patronus*, or the vassal to his clan. To betray it would be like losing one's soul.

One can therefore specify the type of nobility that forms his audience. This role of go-between was not a heroic, visible role at the forefront. Montaigne was simply, in a purely political fashion, the right man in the right place, and he never neglects to portray himself as such. Here one can generalize Hoffmann's views.[11] Montaigne was a careerist through and through, a political man who professionally managed his acts and deeds, the foremost of which were his writings. The very audience at which he aims is that of professionals like himself. It is not necessarily this or that class of noblemen, of the sword or of the robe. More supplely and openly, his audience encompasses *a priori* all those "well born" men who "serve": the obscure servants engaged in political or military tasks, the "private" men who have responsibilities yet are not leaders.[12] The essential point is that they live like Montaigne by virtue of being "born to a middle rank" (III.13, F826, V1078) and not "of prodigious fortune" (III.8, F715, V936). This word *middle* ("moyen") is crucial. It determines the audience less sociologically than psychologically, less objectively than subjectively. The "we" is defined by the opening words of III.7: "we cannot attain" the greatness of kings – and we take our revenge by making a virtue of our mediocrity. The *Essays* are hardly addressed to the *Grands* (the highest old nobility) or to princes, and they even construct their audience against them (see the link between III.7 and III.8). In short, this audience is in the social and psychological situation of Joachim Du Bellay when he was in Rome in the service of his uncle the cardinal: he was charged with managing important affairs, was a noble member of a clan, but was far from holding one of its foremost positions.[13] Proximity does not prevent an insurmountable distance from remaining. Therein lies the heart of the malaise. This whole noble class shares the noble values of the *Grands* they serve. Yet the very idea of nobility rests on an exaltation of superiority, of excellence. Being mediocre, in a middle rank (*moyen*), is not a conceivable part of the program; it amounts to denying the idea that any nobleman holds of himself, his identity as a nobleman.

Thus the relationship to Machiavellianism occurs in the form of a split. The *Essays* respond to it through a wisdom or a synthesis, that is, by the possibility of reconciling what was experienced as irreconcilable. To reconcile politics and morality, but also superiority and mediocrity, would be to reconcile this whole noble class – that is far from and near to the *Grands* – with itself.

Politics and morality: to be caught between different sides or parties, means to be torn between two equally inescapable necessities.

On one side there is the concern for skillfulness, and on the other there is the concern that an action be moral and worthy of praise, in a word, "beautiful," i.e., noble. To overcome this split, it is necessary to reconcile the "skillful man" and the "honest man," in other words the two meanings of *prudence*, the pejorative and the positive: "The men whose society and intimacy I seek are those who are called *honest and skillful men*" ("honnestes et habils homes") (III.3, F625, V824, my emphasis). To do so would be to reconcile Machiavelli with the French ideals of "virtue." The same would be true with regards to Guicciardini, who was praised for his knowledge in business but blamed for his incapacity to imagine that a noble deed could have anything other than a doubtful origin (II.10, F305, V418–19). Certainly, the nostalgia for a virtue like that of the ancients hardly ever leaves Montaigne, and he designates the latter – through a sort of play on the word *prud*-ence – as "prud'hommie"[14] or integrity. But he well knows that nostalgia is not a solution. Machiavellianism has its part of truth and necessity, which is worth keeping. Montaigne works therefore to construct an ethical configuration favorable to the reappearance of the ancients' *prudence*, favorable to its dialectic reappropriation, so to speak, which would integrate Machiavellianism. His father was a *prud'homme*, like the giant fathers in Rabelais. He and his readers will be *prudent*, in the ancient *and* modern manner.

Superiority and mediocrity: Montaigne sees himself "and so many others" with "the rear-end between two saddles" (I.54, F227, V313). This vigorous image of a split is connected to a habitual hierarchy in the *Essays*. At the bottom, there are "the simple peasants," i.e., the masses; at the top, there are "the philosophers," i.e., "strong and clear natures, enriched by a broad education in useful knowledge." Between the two are those in the middle, or "the half-breeds" (*mestis*) – a third and remarkable use of this term *mestis*. Montaigne and his readers are in the intermediary category, "we." One has here, in a very subjective fashion, an average man comparing himself to all moral greatness, and not only to the social grandeur of the *Grands*. Sometimes, as here, it is to bring "us" back to a bit more humility. But sometimes, through a stupefying reversal, it is to sing the praises of mediocrity. Indeed, Montaigne achieves the miracle desired by his whole audience: to pass off mediocrity and its absence of glory as the highest superiority or "virtue." The paradigmatic mechanism is put into place at the beginning of II.11. The man of quality seems to be *a priori* Cato committing suicide with "lustiness and verdancy," but above him is the sweet acceptance of the hemlock by Socrates. The death of the first is grandiose, "more tragic and tense," but that of the second "is still, I know not how, more beautiful" (*F*309–10, *V*424–5). Socrates is the non-hero's hero. According to this model, glorious actions can be praised and at the same time rejected in favor of the "quiet and obscure qualities" of "goodness, moderation, equability, constancy" (III.10, *F*782, *V*1021), in other words all the virtues cherished by Montaigne (it's the same game in III.2, *F*614, *V*809, where Alexander is vanquished by Socrates). One again finds the same dialectic and integrating structure. It is not a matter of refusing in the slightest his admiration for greatness, which too has its truth and necessity – Montaigne has a definite sense of admiration and a taste for the excessive.[15]

Quint has described this astonishing solution very well, but he does not indicate that it comes entirely from the logic of prudence. At the start of *NE*, VII, the in-between state Montaigne describes between philosopher and peasant, between the angel (or Cato: *F*617, *V*813) and the beast, is described by Aristotle as that between the divine man and the brute.[16] Next one finds the opposition that Montaigne establishes between the Stoics and Socrates: *egkrateia* vs. *sōphrosynē*. To be *egkratēs*, is to be strong in Stoic fashion, as master over oneself and over one's bad instincts. This force or *krateia* is the opposite of *akrasia* (*akrateia*) or the incapacity to master one's passions (*NE*, VII.1.1). Just as the absence of mastery is not exactly vice but rather an open door to all vices, likewise, strained mastery is not exactly virtue but rather the path that leads to it. The self-mastery characteristic of the Stoics is thus not the absolute summit. Above it is *sōphrosynē* or moderation. He who is moderate has acquired the habit of good without effort; he no longer, or barely, feels the movement of passions (see the very beginning of II.11, *F*307, *V*422): the Socrateses are superior to the Catos.

Yet, in Aristotle, *sōphrōn* is nearly the equivalent of *prudens*: *sōphrosynē* is so tied to *phronēsis* that it is described using a play on words as "preserving prudence" (*NE*, VI.5.5). More massively still, if there is a philosophy in which *mediocritas* is thought of as an *extremitas*, it is surely that of the famous golden mean, found in Aristotle but also in all of antiquity.[17] What gives force and authority to the

paradigmatic mechanism Cato/Socrates is the whole ancient theory of *prudentia*. Therein are the conceptual tools that will allow
the average nobleman to reconquer his dignity, by coupling admiration for superhuman virtues (i.e., for the inaccessible glory of the
*Grands*) *and* extreme valorization of the nearly professional qualities
of obscure servants. Alongside the glorious prudence still reserved
a short while ago for the prince, there is henceforth room for a new
type of "prudent" man, more modest, but no less proud of himself,
and proud of his modesty itself.

MONTAIGNE AS *PRUDENS*: THE ROYAL POSITION

Montaigne spends his time judging; he is part of "those who make a
practice of comparing human actions" (incipit of book II, F239, V331).
In so doing he imitates Plutarch, whom he qualifies as "so perfect
and excellent a judge of human actions" (II.2, F250, V346; *idem* in
II.31, F539, V714). One of his own readers will in fact return the
compliment by qualifying Montaigne himself as an "excellent judge
of human actions."[18] The fundamental contribution of the work on
skepticism has been to underline the importance of "judgment," the
critical mind or faculty of judging: Pyrrhonism proposes a hygiene
that aims to avoid troubling this faculty. And assuredly, each of the
judgments that Montaigne makes is a *trial* (an *essai*) or, as the incipit
of book II puts it, a means of *exercising* his faculty of judgment.
But this work on Montaigne's skepticism has not paid attention to
the content itself of his judgments, to what the "actions" designate.
Tournon contented himself with attributing the faculty of judgment
to the fact that Montaigne himself had been a judge.[19] After the nobility of the sword, here we are with the nobility of the robe. As with
Quint, though not false, this is an oversimplification. The role of a
judge who condemns does not interest Montaigne. He prefers glorious actions to criminal actions. His justice is not the commutative
kind that punishes misdeeds independent of each individual's merit,
but rather the distributive kind that rewards the beautiful actions
of noblemen: not survey and punish, but compare and praise. This
position is strictly speaking the position of the king, who thought-
fully distributes praise on the battlefield. This is eminently related
to *prudentia*, which alone knows what constitutes "true" valor, true
excellence or virtue. Human actions, present and past, my own and

those of others, can only be "judged" or evaluated by he who has good discernment. And only he who is familiar with affairs of the state has it: he who is a great *prudens*. In evaluating to what extent Alexander the Great merits praise (1.1), or why a certain page of Virgil is worthy of admiration (III.8, F715, V936–7), Montaigne shows himself to be an excellent evaluator, himself worthy of praise. "King of the matter" he treats (III.8, F720, V943), like the king, he knows how to thoroughly penetrate the value of each action he considers. Behind preparations for the battle of Pharsalia or for an amorous conquest, he knows how to see into the very "mind" of Caesar (1.50, F219, V302).[20] Moreover, he asks his readers to do the same with him. In exercising his faculty of judgment, he continually submits himself to the judgment of his readers, who are themselves constituted as *prudentes*. There is no modesty here.[21] Montaigne calls for recognition from his equals and not from the ignorant masses, that crowd of small minds who "fix their admiration with so bad a choice that . . . they teach us their own ignorance" (III.8, F715, V936–7).

What is at stake in the *Essays* is thus as simple as it is capital. It is particularly clear in the first edition (books I–II). It is a question of showing to what extent their author is a good judge of human actions, and therefore to what extent he is, royally, a *prudens*. Montaigne presents himself as occupying what is the central position of all ancient ethics by taking as a model the prudence of the prince.

Indeed, what was available in that period was the sublime portrait of the prudent prince. It is at once grandiose and frightening, in that it leads logically to the *raison d'État*.[22] The basis for it all is the theory of knowledge at work in a world in motion (Aristotelian *kinēsis*). From the moment that future outcomes are contingent, all rests on the fine point of discernment or judgment, which in political terms is the will of the prince. He must on each occasion, and at his own risk and peril, discern very exactly what course of action is appropriate: it is the famous "golden mean" ("juste milieu"). As Aristotle specifies, this mean or *mediocritas* is in fact an extreme, *akrotēs* in Greek and *extremitas* in Latin (*NE*, II.6.17). It is the fine line of the crest between two abysses: one false step, and excellence is missed. The helmsman who barely passes between two reefs is not allowed an error; likewise for the doctor who makes a diagnosis, or the chief general who decides *hic et nunc* to adopt a tactic. An error in judgment is similarly sufficient to make courage into a false courage. Given that we are not in the fixity of the supra-lunar realm, there can be no science of the particular case or *casus*. In certain technical domains, one is able to determine fixed rules (but even here rules are anything but laws: see Quintilian, *Institutio oratoria*, II.3.3). For cases that are simply recurring, it is already more difficult. The height of difficulty and motion are the raging sea or the battlefield, and obviously politics. A world in motion calls for rules that are not predetermined. This movement to the limits of instability pushes to the limit the weight that rests on discernment.

Hence the sublimity of the prince, whose prudence is our sole fixed point in a radically changing world. Hence also the canonicity of the *prudens*: he is himself the rule or *kanōn* on which to govern our actions. To act prudently we must act as a *prudens* would on the same occasion (*NE*, II.6.15; cf. II.4.4). The reason is that all men do not have the same worth. Only the *prudens* "sees the truth in each kind [of situation], being himself as it were the standard and measure of the noble and pleasant" (*NE*, III.4.4; cf. IX.4.2). Just as the judge is justice incarnate (*NE*, V.4.7), the *prudens* is the rule incarnate, in Greek *kanōn kai metron*, in Latin *norma et mensura*. It is the eye of the master, the absolute eye, so to speak. The healthy eye sees clearly; it sees things as they are: the theme of a healthy judgment is capital, starting with healthy tastes – one does not require the palate of a sick man to judge if a wine is good (*NE*, X.5.9–11). Montaigne makes this double movement to the limits his own. On the one hand, the more he shows the world as a radical instability, the more he praises the *constantia* of judgment, and of his in particular, although he sometimes says the contrary: all is wobbling around me, except my own judgment. On the other hand, it is not gratuitous if a healthy judgment and clairvoyant vision ("voir clair") are also constant themes with him, and even more so the idea of a rule or regulation. *Mens sana in corpore sano*: these are the marks of a "truly" strong mind, as are hardy judgments on the most delicate political or religious subjects.

Since we are in a world where there is no escape from judgment, the crucial question therefore becomes knowing what will guarantee the quality of the prince's judgment. The response is classic.

Good judgment is formed over the course of a long process. True worth comes with time; this is what constitutes the *senex*, i.e., the man who has become expert through experiences or *essais*. One can discern three chronologies, each of which refers to working on the self.

The first is the trio of concepts by which Thomas Aquinas resumes the chronology of decision-making according to the *Nicomachean Ethics*: (1) the *consilium* or deliberation; (2) the *iudicium* or decision; (3) the *imperium* or taking of action (the executive power). The essential point is that all three are needed to constitute prudence. *Consilium* or "counsel": it is necessary to weigh the pros and cons, as Montaigne does in very demonstrative fashion at the end of 1.47 – should François I have taken the offensive initiative in attacking Charles V in Italy or, on the contrary, waited for him in France? *Iudicium* or "resolution": one must reach a decision by following a *logos* or *ratio*, which Montaigne calls a "discourse" ("our reason and foresight" ["nostre discours et prudence"] at the end of 1.47). *Imperium*: once the decision is made, one must hold to it. To correctly judge what ought to be done *and* not do it would be a major moral flaw, a flaw against *prudentia*: "I see the better and approve it, but I follow the worse" (Ovid, *Metamorphoses*, VII.20). This is again a fundamental theme in Montaigne: to see clearly and live badly is impossible. Those who taste the beauty of moral treatises without for all that changing their lives do not have as penetrating a judgment as they imagine.

The second chronology describes the formation of any leader or of any master in his art. It also follows a trio of concepts: (1) *natura* or innate talents; (2) *ars* or *doctrina*, theoretical knowledge of the subject; (3) *usus* or constant practice. *Fit fabricando faber*: in art it is through forging that one becomes a blacksmith, or more generally a *homo faber*, not by instinctive routine but by a constantly alert intelligence, first awakened in the apprentice by the master then maintained by the fecund and permanent dialogue between theory and practice. Likewise in ethics, it is through forging that one forges oneself. By practicing courage (or justice) one truly becomes more and more courageous. One understands better and better what true courage is, enlightened first by a master in the subject, then by permanent reflection on one's practice: training and debriefing (an idea again rendered by "discourse," a decidedly important word in

Montaigne because it designates the prudential *logos*). The *Essays*
derive their principles of education – that of "well born" children
exclusively – from this concept by violently contrasting it to the
scholarly or the professorial, i.e., theory without practice. In this trio
as well the essential point is that all three are necessary. The visible
result will be the *habitus*, or in Greek the *hexis*, which defines any
virtue and thus prudence. The *habitus* is like a second nature, an
acquired ease that one can no longer destabilize, in short, a *firma
facilitas* (Quintilian, x.1.1). It is a "constant and definitive perfection . . . not given at birth but obtained thanks to unremitting work"
(Cicero, *De inventione*, 1.36). In Montaigne, the *habitus* is called
"habit" (*habitude*) and justifies the fact that one can no longer reform
oneself or change shapes.[23] It is strictly speaking a professional skill,
an expertise: the result of professional training that has shaped you
and even deformed you.

After the limited chronology of decision-making and the broader
one of years of training, there is the final chronology that covers
an entire life. What ultimately guarantees the quality of *prudens* is
expressed by the Thomist and Aristotelian theme of the connection
between virtues. Gradually, "a wise and just man" ("un homme prudent et juste") will acquire all virtues; if he remained "intemperate
and incontinent," he would be less worthy of incarnating *prudens*
(ii.11, *F*313, *V*429).[24] The point is once again that all are needed.
The slightest deficiency is a reason for taking away the first-place
position from one who claims to possess *prudentia*. Yet, if there is a
constant in the *Essays*, it is surely the affirmation of the total unity
of him who says "I" in the text: the affirmation of his living coherence, of his stability. Totality is similarly the rule that makes it
possible to judge "a particular action": "we must consider many circumstances and the *whole* man who performed it" before being able
to qualify it as praiseworthy (iii.11, *F*311A, *V*427A; my emphasis).
An immediate addition to the text shows that his own acquaintances
have in this way made mistaken judgments about him: "I have sometimes seen my friends call prudence in me what was merely fortune"
(*F*311B, *V*427B).

Read hastily, this last phrase could lead one to believe that Montaigne is not a *prudens*. But the "diligent" reader who wants to sound
out his soul must, in order to do so, consider him too in his entirety
and by using good discernment. In his entirety, i.e., not only in what

he says about himself but also, and perhaps above all, in all of the judgments regarding human actions conveyed by the *Essays*. One will then see that, in total, the author of these judgments corresponds point by point to all of the elements that constitute *prudentia*, elements that are merely outlined here.[25] Montaigne portrays himself as the rule and the measure. As much as the sublime prince and perhaps even more than him, he is the incarnation of the *prudens*. The man who "in all matters ha[s] worshiped that *golden mean [ariston metron]* of the past" (III.13, F845, V1102), the man who endlessly vaunts "moderation," is thus the man of excellence, of extremes and of the summit. The *metron* refers back to the *ariston*, to the excellence that is properly aristocratic, in a type of culture where being normal signifies being superior. Did you say: modesty?

## MONTAIGNE AS ARTIST: ART AND NATURE

Nature means: it is necessary to take into account what exists. Art: it is not a question of stopping there. Conservation vs. innovation. Montaigne criticizes all the "Masters of Arts," but he himself aims for a superior art, an "artificial excellence" (III.8, F707, V927): the art of living according to what is good, the very Ciceronian *ars bene vivendi*.[26]

Certainly, he radically demolishes "human prudence"[27] by separating action from its outcome.[28] No outcome is guaranteed; "events" depend not on us but on *Fortuna*, who disturbs our very deliberations, our "counsels" or "reason" (F209, V286; F712, V932–5). These ideas are taken from Pyrrho[29] as well as the apostle Paul: "[God] will bring to nothing the understanding of the prudent" (F370, V500; F415, V553 = 1 Cor. 1:19). To have faith in fortune is to have faith in God, in "divine . . . [prudence]" (III.13, F835, V1089), almost in his Providence. Outcomes occur by the grace of God: "All that we undertake without his assistance, all that we see without the lamp of his grace, is only vanity and folly" (F415, V553); "*Non nobis, Domine, non nobis*" [Not unto us, O Lord, not unto us] (F782, V1022). Hence his violent criticism of all arts and techniques, i.e., of their pretensions of guaranteeing outcomes (above all medicine, II.37 and III.13).

However, this is neither fatalism nor quietism. Montaigne wants to be a skillful man; he too aims for a successful outcome. His very

Machiavellian reminder that outcomes do not depend on us aims at those who assimilate prudence into a technique or *ars*. His target is "they," the brother and rival of "we," they who are always in sight, who instruct you "by flight" rather than "by pursuit" (III.8, F703, V922). Not so much the deceitful courtier as the overly self-confident professional, the old austere stager who is proud of his mastery of political workings. It is the classic sixteenth-century criticism of pride in one's *habitus* or trade. Infatuated with his capacities or "competence" (*suffisance*), the professional forgets about God.[30] This is seen in his choice of means. Because he is devoid of "moderation," he is ready to act forcefully, with "violent, and even reckless" decisions, for the right cause, i.e., the Catholic cause (II.19, F506, V668). Ethical autonomy at its highest produced a monster, the authoritarian autocrat, who sees himself only too much according to the model of the sublime prince.

"True" prudence will be the one that redefines action and mastery by suppressing the obsession with obtaining results at all costs. Montaigne describes himself in terms of the three arts where human reason is authorized to foresee the future by means of a modest rationality (papal bull of 1585)[31]: helmsman, doctor, and farmer. The first two fall under the rubric of prudence as caution. As mayor, he knew how to act in order to prevent problems. At the end of III.10, he is the helmsman Palinurus from the *Aeneid*: the sole member of the fleet not to sleep, and to be suspicious of the sudden calm. His inaction is only an absence of visible action and of *prudentia* in the eyes of those who do not know how to see "clearly," who are not *prudentes*. There is a remarkably ethical equivalence between the end and the means, between the salvation aimed for and the non-violence of the technique used, which moreover is related to the "*ne nos inducas in tentationem*" [lead us not into temptation] (III.10, F777, V1016). This non-prideful prudence conjoins self-interest and morality, "the useful and the honorable" (title of III.1). It is called *mesnagerie*, or management: of one's formidable neighbors (III.9, F738–9, V966–7) or of one's own internal passions, for which it is also necessary to avoid the storm before it becomes wild and carries you away (III.10, F778, V1017).[32] Essay III.10 ties together in classical fashion the idea of "managing" oneself and of "managing" the state: only he who knows how to govern or steer himself can govern others. The second *ars* is equally preventative. To treat an illness means to intervene as little as possible, and the goal of the doctor is not to wish the pest upon his patient in order to parade his art (F783, V1023). Just like Palinurus, the doctor must know how to decrypt what exists, the nature of things, the idiosyncratic constitution of the patient or of the state – a major theme for Montaigne and for Machiavelli before him. Thus, "conserve and endure" rather than rush headlong toward "innovation" (F783, V1023).

But it is not because "innovation" is the key word in *The Prince* that one can ignore it. For the purpose of politics is double, and unavoidably so: *conservatio et amplificatio*, the conservation but also the amelioration of the state (Cicero, *De imperio Cn. Pompei*, 49).[33] The defensive is not everything in politics. The problem after Machiavelli is to demarcate a domain where innovation remains legitimately possible. Montaigne's solution is to act on the hearts and minds of his readers. The latter are probably sick and require a doctor of the soul who will take their state into account. But that does not prevent one from going on the offensive, from attempting an operation, with the audacity of a strong mind. Montaigne's non-conservative action is the *Essays*. While he describes conservatism in terms of frustration and constraint, since the exterior world obliges him to steer with the utmost precision, through writing he can at last go "full sail" (III.3, F623, V821) and give the full measure of himself as a man of action in full possession of his talents.

The sole constraint is not to force or impose an *ars* or technique upon the innate: therefore, to combine art and nature. The clearest paradigm of this is the idealized colonization of America of which he dreams. The noblemen who are to be transformed have, like the Indians, an innate foundation of goodness, "such fine natural beginnings" (III.6, F695, V910). What remains is the need and obligation to work on this generous nature. Montaigne rejects the Catholic reformation (Henri III and the processions in shirts), because it is a violence inflicted upon each person's nature, upon his "form."[34] This type of reformation is what we would today call a revolution. Montaigne designates moderate revolution (what we today call reform) using the agricultural metaphor of "amendment" or enrichment of the soil (III.2, F616, V811 and F617, V813).[35] One does not destroy the foundation, the soil; one improves it. This precisely is Joachim du Bellay's conception of the amelioration of the French language, reused by Montaigne: "forms of speech, like plants, improve (s'amendent) and grow stronger by being transplanted" (III.5, F665, V874 [see du Bellay's *Defense and Illustration of the French Language*, vol. I, p. 3]). The farmer moreover imitates Nature, herself an artist in this sense – in Montaigne, as soon as art does not contradict nature, it no longer signifies artificiality. Agriculture in turn relies, and has since antiquity, on sexual metaphor. When human labor co-operates with nature, it is not rape but marriage. Whereas in *The Prince* the advice is to rape Fortune, Montaigne finds the possibility of another "male" action. It is necessary to sow the minds of readers as one sows women and furrows, otherwise both will produce monsters (1.8). It is therefore out of the question to remain in a state of idleness, i.e., *otium*, the opposite of the *negotium* that defines a person with political responsibilities. The affirmation in III.2 that each person has his "form" serves only to raise the bar of interior reformation. Amendment is the "true" reform.

A farmer of souls: in other words, a rhetorician. Not a preacher, but "a director of conscience and one who is directed,"[36] and for that reason he says "we." Correction, but fraternal, according to the Jesuit method. The counselor too sows, with love (with charity). With God's help and the help of the soil, it will grow straight. The preacher roars against the sin in you that must be violently extirpated. The counselor, because he is loving, does not force things: "our conscience must reform by itself" (III.2, F620, V816). Thus Montaigne dissociates "they" from "you," saying, "They send their conscience to the brothel" (III.5, F643, V846), rather than, "You send...." If he speaks so little of sin, it is not because he is hardly Christian. It is that he aims to bring his audience back to the better path with gentleness, imperceptibly, by using "diversions" (III.4) or in speaking "by halves," or "confusedly" (III.9, F762, V996). As with the Jesuits, not all truths are good to say to all people nor at all times, "at any time and in any way" (III.13, F826, V1076): it is necessary to take the circumstances into account, in entirely prudential fashion (*cf. NE*). To a prince who wants to avenge himself, it "would be misunderstanding the world" (III.1, F604, V795) to tell him to turn the other cheek. One must "divert" him toward another idea, that of a beautiful and truly noble act of clemency. "That is how it is done," that is how Montaigne acted and wrote

(III.4, *F*634, *V*835). The rhetorical *insinuatio* (and ethos) continually leads to a lesson of conduct (to a pathos): here to the prince, there to husbands overly concerned with being cuckolded (III.5), who are discreetly accused under the guise of excusing the other sex (at the very end of the chapter). Here again, to marry does not mean to bully. Husbands must take into account their wives' "nature," i.e., their sexual appetite; they should cease to impose a yoke of "laws" upon them in order to enter with them into the happy world of rules – the autonomy of the subject and the sharing of a modest rationality.

The line that separates Quint and the post-modernists is blurred yet again. For the question of prudence applies not only to Montaigne's "real" actions, i.e., on the exterior, as a politician. The act of writing and of publishing the *Essays* is no less real, or effective, in short prudential. The debate therefore logically reappears in the discussion about the book's organization. Here too the post-modernists deny any teleology, citing the remark, "I take the first subject that chance offers" (1.50, *F*219, *V*302). Quint, on the contrary, affirms, "For all of its willed diversity, his book can be read as a book" (p. iii). Any analysis of the organization of the *Essays*, concerted or not, will be a demonstration of their author's prudence (or lack thereof) based on the evidence, whereas regarding his exterior actions we essentially know only what he wanted to tell us. We do not have the space here to provide such analyses. But they all lead us to think that in the organization of his book Montaigne demonstrates the supreme skillfulness of a *prudens*. The spontaneity and the fragmentation of his writing are myths. Only the post-modern *doxa* still believe in them, for reasons more ideological than scientific. The very concerted form itself goes hand in hand with a more fundamental project, which is the "[idea] of instructing the public" (II.18, *F*504, *V*665). If the intention to portray himself as a "true" *prudens* is particularly evident in 1580 (in books I and II), the intention to reform is glaring in book III. In the latter, Montaigne is rhetoric itself, the "true" reformer and educator, in the spirit of the Council of Trent.

\* \* \*

To conclude in the abrupt manner by which Baltazar Gracian ends his *Arte de Prudencia*, to be prudent is ultimately "to be a saint": "that is saying it all in a single word." In Thomist terms, the *Essays* dream of seeing the "prudence of the saints" triumph over worldly prudence or "prudence of the flesh." This conclusion joins that of Fumaroli, who sees Montaigne as the "Loyola of an order

without vows or ecclesiastic discipline" and the *Essays* as "the
*Spiritual Exercises* of the Christian nobleman,"[37] with a François
de Sales – also a spiritual counselor for laypersons – as a logical
successor.

An author who believes he sees, amidst present misfortunes,
"ways of saving ourselves" (III.9, *F*734, *V*961) is not in an ivory tower.
As a good Christian helmsman, he is on the contrary attentive to
discerning and assisting through his feeble means the mysterious
ways of Providence. This is a modest attentiveness but not desperate,
for despair itself would be prideful. It is not sad like the gray Peni-
tents, but voluptuous: "Virtue is a pleasant and gay quality" (III.5,
*F*641, *V*845). Pleasure and the flourishing of the individual are on the
program for this brand of Catholicism, from Montaigne (and before)
to the bishop Jean-Pierre Camus (and beyond). It is not a matter of
painfully doing good deeds in the manner of Cato. It is a matter, at
the ultimate end of working on oneself, of doing "beautiful," noble
deeds that have an allure and an ease about them. Moral beauty and
sensual beauty will go hand in hand. Montaigne not only has a sharp
sense of *ars*, of a skillfulness more effective and virtuosic than that
of all those who are half-skilled. He also has an extreme taste for
appearances, for the beauty of women and of words, as well as for
the beauty of a gesture. He proves that the happiness that will reconcile everything is already there, in the very euphoria that the *Essays*
arouse.

Transforming his audience was worth trying (*essayer*). The *Essays*
assay therefore a certain number of strategies on their audience, all
prudential and detailed, all carefully calculated. The author's inces-
sant activity has a name, *diligentia* (with its parts: Cicero, *Orator*,
150). This activity in turn has as its force an unshakeable optimism,
that of a sort of missionary. Finally, the optimism itself is founded
on an act of faith. It is a book "written in good faith" (*F*2, *V*3), in the
literal sense: faith in God, in his clan, in the nobility of the French
aristocracy.

NOTES

1.   David Quint, *Montaigne and the Quality of Mercy: Ethical and Politi-
     cal Themes in the* Essais (Princeton: Princeton University Press, 1998),
     p. 45.

2. Jean Céard, "Agir et prévoir selon Montaigne," in F. Brahami and E. Naya, eds., *Montaigne et l'action, Bulletin de la Société des Amis de Montaigne*, special issue 8/17–18 (2000), p. 30.

3. This is the first, broad meaning given by R. Cotgrave, *A Dictionarie of the French and English Tongues* (London: Iship, 1611, repr. University of Carolina Press, 1968) *s.v.* Prudent: "Prudent, warie, sage, discreet, circumspect, advised"; the other refers to skillfulness: "slye, cunning, skilfull, expert, experienced in many matters."

4. In the writings of Thomas Aquinas (who takes the ideas from Aristotle), *cautio* is the act of staying on one's guard; *circumspectio* means to examine attentively (to in-spect) all that surrounds (*circum-*) a situation, all of its circum-stances (a concept whose importance for Montaigne is well perceived by Bernard Sève in "L'action sur fond d'indifférence," *Bulletin de la Société des Amis de Montaigne*, special issue "Montaigne et l'action," 8/17–18 (2000), pp. 13–22; *cf. NE* II.9). See *F*94, *V*129, "Such tender and *circumspect* prudence"; *F*140, *V*190, where *prudence* is reinforced by "precaution"; see also *F*357, *V*485; *F*607, *V*800; *F*713, *V*934; *F*754, *V*986, and for *caution F*92, *V*127; *F*525, *V*695; *F*621, *V*817; *F*804, *V*1051.

5. See Giocanti playing on III.9, *F*760, *V*994, in "L'action sceptique, un art de 'se laisser rouler au vent'," *Bulletin de la Société des Amis de Montaigne*, special issue "Montaigne et l'action," 8/17–18 (2000), pp. 69–77.

6. See Jean Starobinski, *Montaigne en mouvement* (Paris: Gallimard, 1982).

7. See Goyet, "Prudence et panurgie: le machiavélisme est-il aristotélicien?" in Ullrich Langer, ed., *Au-delà de la* Poétique: *Beyond the* Poetics: *Aristotle and Early Modern Literature* (Geneva: Droz, 2002), pp. 13–34.

8. Hugo Friedrich, *Montaigne*, trans. Dawn Eng, ed. Philippe Desan (Berkeley: University of California Press, 1991), vol. 4, p. 9.

9. See Laurent Gerbier, "Médecine et politique dans l'art machiavélien de la prévision," *Nouvelle Revue du Seizième siècle*, 21/1 (2003), pp. 25–42.

10. See Daniel Ménager, "Montaigne et la philosophie de l'ambassade," *Bulletin de la Société des amis de Montaigne*, 8/17–18 (2000), pp. 55–67.

11. See George Hoffmann, *Montaigne's Career* (Oxford: Clarendon Press, 1998).

12. For the meaning of "private" man, see *F*195–6, *V*267 (Diocletian); *F*601, *V*792 (Atticus); *F*613, *V*807; *F*614, *V*809 regarding "retired lives" and "private" (taken from *NE* which opposes them to leaders), and finally

*F756*, "I love a private life" (*V988*). It suffices to read the harangue of 1587, in which the go-between Rabot sings the praises of *prudentia* before the *Parlement* of Grenoble, in order to understand that it perfectly reflects Montaigne's intended audience: see Ennemond Rabot d'Illins, *Harangues*, in Stéphane Gal, *Le Verbe et le Chaos* (Grenoble: Presses Universitaires de Grenoble, 2004).

13. Montaigne has the same rejection of professors, intellectuals, or "pedants" (1.25). He spares only Turnebus, because the latter seems to have "never practiced any other profession than war and affairs of state" (*F103, V139*).

14. *Preud'hommie* (integrity) is formed from *preux* (valiant). In 1.28 (*F142, V192*) it reinforces *prudence*. The *prud'hommie* in question is that of his family (*F311, V427* and *F782, V1021*), of Rome before its decadence (*F359, V488* and *F368, V498*), and of the simple, faithful love in the good old days (*F679, V890*). See Claire Couturas, "Repères médiévaux et renaissants vers la *prud'hommie* selon Montaigne," *Réforme, Humanisme, Renaissance*, 56 (June 2003), pp. 41–59.

15. See Daniel Ménager, "La culture héroïque de Montaigne," *Bulletin de la Société des Amis de Montaigne*, 8/9–10 (1998), pp. 39–52.

16. See the refusal of the divine man at the very end of the *Essays* ("instead of changing into angels, they change into beasts," *F856, V1115*; cf. *F612, V806*.)

17. Beyond appearances, which result from a difference in emphasis, the Stoic's *prudens* corresponds trait for trait with the Aristotelian *phronimos*: see Danielle Lories, *Le sens commun et le jugement du* phronimos. *Aristote et les Stoïciens* (Louvain-la-Neuve: Peeters, 1998).

18. Because he understood feminine sexuality, which cannot be bullied (in III.5, *F658–9, V865–6*), better than Tirésias. In Léonard de Marande, S. J., in a book itself entitled *Jugement des actions humaines [Judgment of Human Actions]*, 1624, cited by Olivier Millet, *La Première réception des Essais de Montaigne (1580–1640)* (Paris: Champion, 1995), p. 203. See *F311, V427* and *F458, V605* (to judge "of the assurance of other men in dying," the most noteworthy "action" of human life).

19. See André Tournon, *Montaigne: la glose et l'essai* (Lyon: Presses Universitaires, 1983).

20. Just as, continues the paragraph, one sees the value of a horse not only when it runs, but also at rest: the value of the horse is canonical; it is one of Aristotle's first examples used to explain what virtue is (*NE*, II.6.2).

21. See Francis Goyet, "Humilité de l'essai? (Réflexions sur Montaigne)," in P. Glaudes, ed., *L'essai: métamorphoses d'un genre* (Toulouse: Presses Universitaires du Mirail, 2002), pp. 201–15.

22. See Francis Goyet "La prudence: entre sublime et raison d'Etat," in Isabelle Cogitore and Francis Goyet, eds., *Devenir roi: Essais sur la littérature adressée au Prince* (Grenoble: Ellug, 2001), pp. 163–78.

23. See Francis Goyet, "La notion éthique d'*habitude* dans les *Essais*: articuler l'art et la nature," *Modern Language Notes*, 118 (2003), pp. 1070–191.

24. Here we are reconstituting what the whole ending of the *NE*, vi, if not Montaigne, says.

25. In the *NE* it is necessary to mention at a minimum both the magnanimous man and the legislator of the last chapter, that supreme *prudens* who, like the savant or *sophos*, observes the immutability not of the stars (Thales) but of laws.

26. III.3, *F*626, *V*824: "A wellborn mind that is practiced in dealing with men makes itself thoroughly agreeable by itself. *Art* is nothing else but the list and record of the productions of such minds."

27. *F*92, *V*127; *F*165, *V*222; *F*347, *V*473; *F*407, *V*544; *F*408, *V*545; *F*713, *V*934; *F*812, *V*1061.

28. See Marie-Dominique Couzinet, "Action naturelle, action humaine, action divine," *Bulletin de la Société des Amis de Montaigne*, 8/17–18 (2000), pp. 45–53.

29. See Emmanuel Naya, "De la *médiocrité* à la *mollesse*: prudence montaignienne," in E. Naya, ed., *Polysémie sur la médiocrité au XVIe siècle* (Paris: Presses de l'Ecole Normale Supérieure, forthcoming), and John O'Brien, "Aristotle's Prudence, and Pyrrho's," in *Au-delà de la* Poétique / *Beyond the* Poetics: *Aristotle and Early Modern Literature*, ed. Ullrich Langer (Geneva: Droz, 2002), pp. 35–45.

30. By constantly exhibiting his lack of memory, Montaigne shows that this type of pride is not a threat to him.

31. See Jean Céard, "Agir et prévoir selon Montaigne," *Bulletin de la Société des Amis de Montaigne*, special issue "Montaigne et l'action," 8/17–18 (2000), p. 24.

32. Neighbors: "economic" prudence; the self: "monastic" prudence. See Diane Desrosiers-Bonin, *Rabelais et l'humanisme civil* (Geneva: Droz, 1992).

33. Also Nizolio, quoted in Goyet, "Prudence et panurgie," p. 29.

34. See George Hoffmann, "Emond Auger et le contexte tridentin de l'essai 'Du repentir,'" *Bulletin de la Société des Amis de Montaigne*, 8/21–2, (2001), pp. 263–75.

35. Frame translates *amendement* as "reformation" (616) in the first of these two passages, then as "amendment" (617) in the second. See Jean-Marie Le Gall, "Réformer l'Eglise catholique aux XVᵉ–XVIIᵉ siècles: restaurer, rénover, innover?," *Réforme, Humanisme, Renaissance*, 56 (2003), pp. 61–75, on the idea of reform in the Catholic world.

36. Marc Fumaroli, preface to Michael A. Screech, *Montaigne et la mélancolie* (Paris: Presses Universitaires de France, 1992), p. ix.

37. Preface to Screech, *Montaigne et la mélancolie*, p. xi.

# 8   Montaigne and the truth of the schools

In this chapter I shall address two questions: what did Montaigne have to say about the truth claims and pretensions to knowledge of the philosophy of his day? And how does this relate to his own project in writing the *Essays*? Truth is, of course, a notoriously difficult term. For some it resides in the relationship of propositions to reality. If there is a correspondence between the two, then the conditions for the proposition being truthful are satisfied; as Montaigne says, "If you say 'it is fine weather' and you are speaking the truth, then it is fine weather."[1] But you may wish to specify how this correspondence is achieved: in other words, you may wish to associate truth with verifiability, and account for how it comes to be known to be true. Lorraine Daston has pointed out that this version of truth can vary over time, depending on which of several different "epistemological virtues" it is linked to, such as certainty, objectivity, universality, applicability (the "pragmatic" version of truth), or correlation with a whole body of beliefs (what came to be known as the "coherence" theory of truth).[2] Montaigne himself, from his wide reading in ancient writings, touches on all these criteria, and associates them with what he sees as the aim of philosophy, which is to seek truth, knowledge, and certainty;[3] he shows himself moreover to be very sensitive to the relationship of authoritative statements and truth, by warning us to dissociate hermeneutic questions ("is this a correct account of what a certain philosopher said?") from philosophical ones ("how valid is this proposition?");[4] and as a writer about the self, he evinces an understandable preoccupation with truth-telling and sincerity. We can therefore expect his reaction to the philosophy of his day in all these regards to be thoughtful; it is also, as we shall see, relatively well-informed.

142

He earns his place in histories of thought, however, not so much for his critique of these issues but rather for his popularization of skepticism, principally in the longest chapter of the *Essays* entitled "Apology for Raymond Sebond".[5] Raymond de Sabunde or Sebon(d) (d. 1436) was the author of a work of natural theology, which set out to prove the existence of God and the truth of the Christian religion by natural reasoning alone. Montaigne translated the text into French at the request of his father, and felt it incumbent upon him to defend it from the attacks of those who doubted either that Sebond had employed the right arguments or that his project was in any way achievable.[6] Montaigne used the recently translated works of the ancient Pyrrhonist skeptic Sextus Empiricus[7] to launch a broad attack on those who doubted the value of Sebond's text, ending with an exposition of radical relativism in which the essayist explicitly cuts the ground from under his own feet as a defender of natural theology by calling into doubt all the sources of human knowledge. In this chapter he accepts Sextus Empiricus' division of philosophers into those who believe they know (the dogmatists), those who claim not to know (the academics), and those who are still seeking knowledge (the Pyrrhonists or skeptics).[8] Montaigne avers that the dogmatic philosophy dominant in his day is Aristotelianism, and directs his most savage criticisms at this philosophical target, accusing Aristotle himself of deliberate word-spinning and obscurantism, and claiming sarcastically that if one does not know one's Aristotle, one can know nothing about oneself.[9]

While the "Apology for Raymond Sebond" is without doubt important, it cannot be said to encompass all of Montaigne's aims in writing. His innovative study of himself, his discussion of religious, political, social, and cultural issues, his reflections on both individual and collective human conduct, his humanist practice of reading and writing are all features not captured by that unusually technical and structured chapter of the *Essays*. In these other aspects of his work, Montaigne shows himself to be programmatically unphilosophical. He sets out to write not impersonally but personally, not comprehensively but partially and inconsistently, not supra-temporally but consciously immersed in the passage of time;[10] he relies on an unsystematic mixture of anecdote, quotation, and moral reflection, into which in the course of the last twelve years of his life he interpolated intermittently yet more thoughts and quotations; his text rarely takes on the character of a sustained argument that is explicit about its own forms of validation. He is even willing knowingly to breach the rule of non-contradiction, and yet claim not to breach truth-conditions: "so, all in all, [it may indeed happen that I] contradict myself now and then, but truth, as Demades said, I do not contradict".[11] It is safe to say that no professional philosopher of the late Renaissance would have recognized what Montaigne wrote as a contribution to his subject, except in the loose sense that it consisted in reflections on ethics, politics, and natural philosophy. One of the reasons for quoting the *Essays* at some length in this chapter is to give a flavour of their author's very unphilosophical manner of expression and textual development, and to show how informal the link is between Montaigne's writing and the philosophy of his day. The essayist does, however, come to acknowledge that he has come to make common cause with the very philosophy he professes so much to despise, as we shall see.

Montaigne famously declares that although he was schooled in ancient literature by humanist teachers, he never engaged in the technical study of any of the university disciplines:

For to sum up, I know that there is such a thing as medicine, jurisprudence, four parts in mathematics, and roughly what they aim at. And perhaps I also know the service that the [university disciplines] in general aim to contribute to life. But as for plunging in deeper, or gnawing my nails over the study of Aristotle, monarch of modern learning, or stubbornly pursuing some part of knowledge, I have never done it; nor is there any [one of the arts disciplines] of which I could sketch even the outlines. There is not a child halfway through school who cannot claim to be more learned than I, who have not even the equipment to examine him on his first lesson, at least [in terms of] that lesson. And if they force me to, I am constrained, rather ineptly, to draw from it some matter of universal scope, on which I test the boy's judgment: a lesson as strange to them as theirs is to me. I have not had regular dealings with any solid book, except Plutarch and Seneca.[12]

There are good reasons for doubting this claim, given the technical knowledge of the law on display in the *Essays*, which Montaigne may have acquired at the University of Toulouse;[13] a plausible motive for the author's silence about this period of his life is that he wanted as a writer to give himself the airs of a gentleman scholar, not a crabbed and dusty pedant.[14] It is even the case that he rarely, if ever,

admits to his long practice as a magistrate. But whether he under-
went a university education or not, he does not disguise the fact
that he is aware of what is going on in the intellectual world about
him; he refers to some of the most contentious publications of his
day (by figures such as Copernicus, Paracelsus, and Machiavelli); he
employs the vocabulary of contemporary philosophy, and engages
in sharply focused critiques of the higher disciplines of law and
medicine.[15]

The account I shall give here of Renaissance philosophy as this
was taught in institutions around Europe is selective; it is intended
to reveal Montaigne's awareness and critique of it, and suggest what
role this critique plays in his project in writing the *Essays*.[16] The
basic philosophy course (*cursus artium*) taught in most European
universities in Montaigne's time consisted principally in a training in
grammar and logic, set in the context of an Aristotelian classification
of knowledge. This separated speculative thinking ("sciences") from
goal-oriented disciplines ("arts"), setting the former above the latter,
and establishing a clear hierarchy inside both domains. "Science" is
said by some sources to be characterized by "the most secure and
certain knowledge" (*scientia*), "indubitable evidence," and "precise
reasoning."[17] It is pertinent to examine these features in turn. The
"certainty" of the knowledge is not primarily a subjective mental disposition, but rather its objective fixedness or reliability, in contrast
to the conjectural knowledge of the arts (this being *opinio* as opposed
to *scientia*). The highest discipline in the sciences is metaphysics,
because its subject matter is the most universal and most certain, followed by physics, psychology, mathematics, and logic (looked upon
in this instance not as an instrument but as a science). Among the
arts, ethics, politics, law, and medicine take precedence as practical disciplines. Certain disciplines provide the premises necessary
to the other disciplines; Montaigne himself notes this, but gives it a
negative slant by suggesting that the whole edifice of knowledge has
thereby no validation outside itself:

It is very easy, on accepted foundations, to build what you please; for according to the law and ordering of this beginning, the rest of the parts of the
building are easily done, without [having to go back on what you have
said]. By this path we find our reason well-founded, and we argue with
great ease. For our masters occupy and win beforehand as much room in

our belief as they need in order to conclude afterward whatever they wish, in the manner of geometricians with their axioms, the consent and approval that we lend them, giving us the wherewithal to drag us left and right, and to spin us around at their will. Whoever is believed in his presuppositions, he is our master and our God; he will plant his foundations so broad and easy, that by them he will be able to raise us, if he wants, up to the clouds.

In the trade and business of human knowledge, we have taken for ready money the statement of Pythagoras, that each expert is to be believed in his craft. The [dialectician] refers to the grammarian for the meaning of words; the rhetorician borrows from the [dialectician] the subjects of his arguments; the poet from the musician his measures; the geometrician from the arithmetician his proportions; the metaphysicians take as their foundations the conjectures of physics. For each science has its presupposed principles, by which the human judgment is [circumscribed] on all sides. If you happen to [attack] this barrier in which lies the principal error, they have this maxim in their mouth, that there is no arguing [with] people who deny first principles.[18]

What he shows here is his polemical intention to characterize principles as mere presuppositions; this is somewhat unfair, for he declares in this very passage that the principles of metaphysics are taken from natural philosophy's account of reality.

The "indubitable evidence" of the sciences include the products of *experientia* (that which constitutes a common body of knowledge derived from the senses), which can be presupposed;[19] this is consistent both with the thoroughgoing sense epistemology of Aristotelians, expressed in the maxim *nihil est in intellectu quod non fuerit in sensu* (there is nothing in the intellect which was not previously in the senses), and with their correspondence theory of truth usually expressed through the formula *adaequatio rei et intellectus* (the correspondence of the thing and the intellect), or an attenuated version of this, in which the correspondence is between rational discourse and perceptions (the sense impressions received by the mind), not with the thing itself.[20] In this, Montaigne follows the Aristotelian line; he never departs from the claim that the senses "act as the proper and primary judges for us,"[21] and one of his most important chapters ("Of Experience") is all about the value of common, everyday experience. His agreement is however qualified by his long demonstration in the "Apology" of the unreliability and incompleteness of our senses inspired by Sextus Empiricus and other ancient sources. Evidence from the animal world is adduced to show that man cannot detect what some animals are able to detect around them; man is shown to be unable visually to judge size, to be misled by his sense of touch, taste, and hearing, to be subject to illnesses of the senses (as when those suffering from jaundice see things as yellow), and to be unable to agree from one individual to another on the impressions left on the senses by given objects. This is shown to lead to circularity: "to judge the appearances we receive of objects, we would need an [instrument of judgement]; to verify this instrument, we need a [proof]; to verify this [proof], an instrument: there we are in a circle."[22] The epistemological virtue of certainty, insofar as this resides in the senses, is thus radically challenged by Montaigne.

The third criterion of scientific knowledge (which embodies the same epistemological virtue, but in a different location), "precise reasoning," also comes under attack. Like his near-contemporary Francis Bacon, Montaigne sees human reason, as well as the senses, as a source of error;[23] it is a "two-edged and dangerous sword," "an instrument of lead and of wax, stretchable, pliable and adaptable to all biases and all measures," a "miserable foundation for our rules [. . .] which is apt to represent to us a very false picture of things."[24] He associates this attack on the faculty of reason and reasoning with some of the favourite targets of the skeptics. In this attack, pride of place is given to the syllogism,[25] of which he gives the standard parodic example: "ham makes us drink; drinking quenches our thirst; therefore ham quenches thirst."[26] He also undermines the truth-claim of the syllogism in the example of the liar paradox ("if you say 'I lie' and if you are speaking the truth, then you lie"[27]), as well as mischievously pointing out that it is a form of reasoning we share with animals such as the fox and the dog.[28]

His attack on scientific definition is even more savage. This is connected to the attack on the syllogism, in that the middle proposition of the first figure of the syllogism (its highest form) includes a cause, and the essential property of scientific knowledge in an Aristotelian scheme is that it is causal: as the scholastic tag has it, *scire est rem per causas cognoscere* (knowledge is comprehension of things by their causes).[29] Playing on the words "cause/causer/chose" (*cause* in

French means both "cause," and "case" and in the form of a verb
means "to chat"), Montaigne writes:

I see ordinarily that men, when facts are put before them, are more ready
to [pass their time] by inquiring into their reasons than by inquiring into
their truth. They leave aside the [things themselves] (*choses*) and amuse
themselves treating the causes (*causes*). [What funny prattling causifiers
(*causeurs*)]. The knowledge of causes belongs only to Him who has the guidance of things, not to us who have only the enduring of them, and who have
the perfectly full use of them according to our nature, without penetrating
to their origin and essence. Nor is wine [more agreeable] to the man who
knows its primary principles. On the contrary, both the body and the soul
disturb and alter the right they have to enjoyment of the world by mixing
with it the [authority of science].[30]

"Scientific" definition by *genus* and *differentia* also embodies
causal knowledge, most usually in its formal and material modes.
Again Montaigne is consistently savage in his attack on this, and
resolute in his defence of man's access to knowledge of phenomena
through experience which does not need to have recourse to scientific definition: "[this] logical and Aristotelian [ordering of material]
is not to the point. I want a man to begin with the conclusion. I
understand well enough what death and pleasure are: let him not
waste his time anatomizing them";[31] or again:

Our disputes are purely verbal. I ask what is "nature", "pleasure," "circle", "substitution." The question is one of words, and is answered in the
same way. "A stone is a body." But you pressed on: "And what is a body" –
"Substance" – "And what is substance" and so on, you would finally drive
the respondent to the end of his lexicon. We exchange one word for another
word, often more unknown. I know better what is man than I know what is
animal, or mortal, or rational.[32]

Through this standard scholastic definition of the species man by
*genus* (animal) and *differentia* (mortal, rational), Montaigne attacks
here both the redundancy of the definition and its association with
word-spinning and obscurantism. This attack is found again in a passage on the medical use of the concept of occult properties used as
an explanatory device, where he ends up by concluding that "the
greatest part, and I believe, more than two-thirds of the medicinal
virtues, consists in the quintessence or occult property of simples,
[about which we can be informed in no other way than by] use;

for quintessence is nothing else than a quality of which we cannot by our reason find out the cause."[33] Montaigne replaces definition with a form of intuition which arises from our being in the
world, and does not need a detour through philosophical language
to imprint the intentional object on the intellect. He may not ask,
as subsequent philosophers have done, whether such a form of intuition is at all possible without recourse to some form of language:
but he does point to language's inexorable circularity, giving the
example of the law's attempt (and failure) to enshrine intention
in words:

Why is it that our [normal mode of speech], so easy for any other use, becomes
obscure and unintelligible in contracts and wills, and that a man who
expresses himself so clearly, whatever he says or writes, finds in this field
no way of speaking his mind that does not fall into doubt and contradiction?
Unless it is that the princes of this art [i.e. that of writing contracts and
wills], applying themselves with particular attention to picking out [legal
formulas] and contriving [technical] phrases, have so weighed every sylla-
ble, so minutely examined every sort of combination, that here they are at
last entangled and embroiled in the endless number of figures and in such
minutes [distinctions] that they can no longer fall under any rule or prescription or any certain interpretation . . . by subdividing these subtleties they
teach men to increase their doubts; they start us extending and diversifying
the difficulties, they lengthen them, they scatter them.[34]

While rejecting or modifying some parts of traditional "scientific"
logic, Montaigne makes direct use of others; if, as we shall see, he
develops the notion of logical difference in his own idiosyncratic
way, he none the less exploits the traditional logic of opposition
which is connected to it. According to this there are four versions
of opposition: correlative opposites (double/half; father/son); contraries, either admitting intermediate terms (black/grey/white) or
not (odd/even); privative opposites (sight/blindness); finally contradictories which relate only to propositions ("Peter is nice"/ "Peter is
not nice"). This last gives rise to the "square of contraries" and the
categories of sub-contraries which can be used to check the logical
correctness of propositions; contradictories can only be resolved by
time (Peter is nice in the morning, but not nice in the evening), the
relation to the subject (Peter is nice to his wife, but not to his cat), or
the relation to the object (Peter nice in comparison to John, but not

nice in comparison to Mary).[35] Montaigne is a thinker who is struck by the diversity and inconsistency in the world around him and in himself, and needs these logical tools to express his perception of this, even if they are not present in the form of technical language or analysis, as these examples show:

I give my soul now one face, now another, according to which directions I turn it. If I speak of myself in different ways, that is because I look at myself in different ways. All contradictions may be found in me, by some twist or in some fashion. Bashful, insolent; chaste, lascivious; talkative, taciturn; tough, delicate; clever, stupid; surly, affable; lying, truthful; learned, ignorant; liberal, miserly and prodigal: all this I see in myself [in some respect] and according to how I turn; and whoever studies himself really attentively, finds in himself, [indeed] even in his judgement, this gyration and discord. I have nothing to say about myself absolutely, simply, without confusion and without mixture, or in one word. "Distinguo" is the most universal member of my logic.[36]

This is the record of various and changeable occurrences, and of irresolute and when it so befalls, [contrary] ideas: whether I am different myself, or whether I take hold of my subjects in different circumstances and aspects.[37]

The *distinguo* to which Montaigne refers here is the logical technique of relating terms and separating the most general classes (*genera generalissima*) from lesser classes (*genera subalterna*) and species;[38] in these and other passages, he applies it however not to scientific classification but rather to the particulars of experience (inter alia, his own subjective experience). In doing so, he attacks another of the epistemological virtues he associates with traditional philosophy, namely universality.

The issue of truth as proposition arises most acutely for him in the issue of honesty to oneself and others. Here the logical falsity of a proposition is distinguished from its moral falsity. A Renaissance example is afforded by the "true" proposition "Jesus is the Messiah" uttered by a Christian and a Jew respectively. In the case of the Christian, who believes the "true" proposition to be indeed true, it possesses both *convenientia rei* (correspondence to reality, or factual truth), and *convenientia menti* (correspondence to an intentional mental state, or coincidence with truth-telling and sincerity); a Jew does not believe that Jesus is the Messiah, so although the proposition in his mouth "Jesus is not the Messiah" has *convenientia menti*, it does not have *convenientia rei*. If the Christian were to lie and assert this proposition, it would possess neither *convenientia rei* nor *convenientia menti*; and if the Jew were to propose that Jesus was the Messiah, his utterance would have *convenientia rei*, but not *convenientia menti*.[39] This form of analysis makes it possible to distinguish between sincerity or lying on the one hand and factual truth on the other. Montaigne is very interested in making this distinction, since his whole project of self-description appeals to the "principle of charity"[40] in the readers, who, for the text to have the right illocutionary force (that of uninhibited truth-telling), must accept that Montaigne never lies to them; "This book was written in good faith, reader"[41] is after all the first injunction Montaigne makes to his public. He later adduces social and political reasons for the need for language to record correctly the intentions of the speaker; but he accepts at the same time that there are political reasons for princes to lie and betray trust.[42] He shows himself to be aware of the fact that the language of sincerity, being rhetorical and therefore reproducible by a speaker without a moral commitment to truth-telling, can always misrepresent, as "truth and falsehood are alike in face, similar in bearing, taste, and movement; we look upon them with the same eye."[43] In these passages and in the essays "Of Liars" and "Of the Useful and the Honorable," he reveals his grimly realistic awareness of this aspect of human linguistic behaviour, which leads him to be one of the few of his generation to describe Machiavelli's recommendation of unscrupulous and deceitful political behaviour as "solid."[44]

I have so far spoken about truth in respect of propositions. Like the schools of his day, Montaigne characterizes truth as double: that is, it is a property of things, or their objective thingness (*veritas simplex*; that which is the object of *experientia*), and a property of propositions about things (*veritas complex*).[45] Objective truth is opposed not to falsity or lying (which are both properties of propositions) but to non-existence (such as the chimera) or fictional existence (the *ens rationis*[46]). Montaigne knows about these, and indeed relates them to the productivity of the human spirit, not only as seen in imaginative literature, but also in philosophical speculation, whose origin is said by Plato, as he recalls, to be poetic;[47] he is aware of ancient theories about plural and possible worlds,[48] and he places a positive value on thought experiments:

So in the study I am making of our behaviour and motives, fabulous testimonies, provided that they are possible, serve like true ones. Whether
they happened or no, in Paris or Rome, to John or Peter, they exemplify,
at all events, some human potentiality, and thus their telling imparts useful
information to me.[49]

The instances of his use of the word *vérité* in the meaning of objective existence reveal that Montaigne associates this (perhaps surprisingly for a relativist) with unity, consistency, universality, and
uniformity.[50] But in respect of *veritas simplex*, he also frequently
denies that men have access to things themselves: they only have
access to the representation of things in their perception and understanding of them: "now since our condition accommodates things
to itself and transforms them according to itself, we no longer know
what things are in truth; for nothing comes to us except falsified and
altered by our senses".[51] This attack on yet another epistemological virtue, the objectivity of knowledge, was certainly conceded by
some Aristotelians,[52] but Montaigne's further point, that man is the
measure of all things, was not, for philosophers of the time relied on
*experientia* as an infallible source of knowledge (see above, p. 146):
Montaigne on the other hand finds no difficulty in admitting that
"the opinion I give of [things] is to declare the measure of my [vision],
not the measure of things."[53] This claim was not new in Montaigne's
time, nor specific to skepticism: as well as its ancient attribution
to Protagoras, it had been made by the celebrated fifteenth-century
thinker Nicholas of Cusa.[54] From this claim, Montaigne draws the
alarming conclusion that "naturally nothing falls where everything
falls. Universal sickness is individual health."[55] This phrase encap-
sulates a nightmare version of the "coherence" theory of truth, in
which the coherence which validates propositions is associated not
with truth but with error. Montaigne's concluding passage from the
"Apology" is even more devastating, as it attributes unceasing flux
to man's environment:

Finally there is no existence that is constant, either of our being or of that of
objects. [Both] we, and our judgement, and all mortal things go on flowing
and rolling unceasingly. Thus nothing certain can be established about one
thing by another, both the [person making the judgement] and the judged
thing being in continual change and motion. We have no communication

with being, because every human nature is always midway between birth and death, offering only a dim semblance and shadow of itself, and an uncertain and feeble opinion.[56]

The higher "scientific" disciplines and their associated epistemological virtues thus do not come out well of Montaigne's critique of them; nor, apparently, do the less elevated disciplines of the arts; his use of the terms *artiste, artialiser* to refer to these disciplines is consistently negative.[57] But there is a greater degree of agreement here with his own thinking than Montaigne seems prepared to make explicit. The arts and "practical philosophy" (politics, ethics, and "economics" in the sense of domestic management), being goal-directed and not purely speculative, are characterized by their instrumental attitude to knowledge; they are more concerned with the usefulness than with the essence of things.[58] Montaigne supports this position wholeheartedly, and he alludes approvingly to a well-known passage from Cicero which makes the same point.[59] What he and those whom he quotes have to say in this regard seems very close to a pragmatic theory of truth in modern terms. Even skepticism, normally looked upon as a philosophy which does not promote action, is made into a practical philosophy by Montaigne:

There is nothing in man's invention that has so much verisimilitude and usefulness [as Pyrrhonism]. It presents man naked and empty, acknowledging his natural weakness, fit to receive from above some outside power; stripped of human knowledge, and all the more apt to lodge divine knowledge in himself, annihilating his judgement to make more room for faith; neither disbelieving, nor setting up any doctrine against the common observances; humble, obedient, teachable, zealous; a sworn enemy of heresy, and consequently free from the vain and irreligious opinions introduced by the false sects. He is a blank tablet prepared to take from the finger of God such forms as he shall be pleased to engrave on it.[60]

He also adopts the looser versions of identity, difference and definition which are current in the arts disciplines of his day, and most notably in the discipline of law. There are many echoes of jurisprudence in Montaigne's writing relevant to the theme of this essay (reflecting no doubt his practice as a magistrate), including the reduction of truth to the mere performative utterance of a legal sentence (what the judge decides passes for truth by dictat[61]) and the low status

accorded to definition, as expressed in the legal maxim "every definition in civil law is precarious: for it is rare to find one which could
not be subverted."[62] Montaigne's predilection for verbal caution and
reticence – "I like these words which soften and moderate the rashness of our propositions: 'perhaps,' 'to some extent,' 'some,' 'they
say,' 'I think,' and the like"[63] – may also be related to the approved
use of such formulas by jurists.[64] Even though he subjects the law to
a rigorous critique at the beginning of the essay "Of Experience",
its practical solutions to the problems of everyday existence and
the almost infinite diversity of human life can only be congenial
to him.

As can be seen from his passage about his own internal contradictions quoted above, he ironically espouses the *distinguo* of practical
(and legal) philosophy, but transforms it into something rather different. There is according to him no complete identity in nature which
would allow scientific definition;

As no event and no shape is entirely like another, so none is entirely different from another. An ingenious mixture on the part of nature. If our faces
were not similar, we could not distinguish man from beast; if they were not
dissimilar, we could not distinguish man from man, All things hold together
by some similarity; every example [falls down], and the comparison that is
drawn from experience is always faulty and imperfect; however we fasten
together our comparisons by some corner. Thus the laws serve, and thus
adapt themselves to each of our affairs, by some roundabout, forced and
biased interpretation.[65]

This seems at first sight to be a critique of laws, but is in fact a
grudging admission of their applicability, which can only be effected
if there is a less than perfect match between the relevant legislation, couched as it is in general terms, and the infinite variability of
human actions and circumstances. Another feature of Montaigne's
acceptance of this practical but philosophically imperfect approach
to things is the importance he accords to the resolution of contraries
by time; so much so that he can claim never to contradict himself
because his writing has the character of a chronicle or a "register,"
that is, a financial account under which a line is never drawn, whose
sum is never fully resolved, and whose figures never reconciled. The
*contrerolle* or *registre* becomes one of the favourite images for his
own writing; he links it to the infinite generativity of the project

of self-portraiture: "who does not see that I have taken a road along which I shall go, without stopping and without effort, as long as there is ink and paper in the world? I cannot keep a record of my life by my actions; fortune places them too low. I keep it by my thoughts."[66]

As well as having a looser conception of identity, difference, and definition, the arts are also characterized by a wider range of argumentative procedures, known as topics. These consist in a reservoir or arsenal of arguments (*loci*) which cannot be reduced to syllogistic form, and are often based on premises which are not more than plausible.[67] Such premises are often, in the words of Aristotle, "generally accepted opinions [. . .] those which commend themselves to all or to the majority or to the wise – that is to all of the wise or to the majority or to the most famous and distinguished of them."[68] The argument from authority, so rigorously excluded from philosophical discourse[69], regains entry into the arts disciplines by this route. As Montaigne's exhaustive practice of quotation reveals, he is himself very partial to this mode of argument (at least in this form), although he also goes out of his way to undermine it also in the "Apology for Raymond Sebond" and elsewhere (see above pp. 145–6).

Two of these looser forms of argument are worthy of mention. We have already encountered the *locus a simili* (argument from similarity) in passages quoted above (pp. 154, 161); the fact that the similarity is rough and ready obviates the need for scientific definition, and leaves a space for the operation of human intuition. Second, the *locus a circumstantiis* (argument from circumstances) is the mechanism by which the singulars of experience find their way into legal discussions. The "circumstances" are recorded in Boethius' mnemonic *quis? quid? ubi? quando? quomodo? quibus auxiliis?* (who, what, where, when, how, with whose help?). Through the use of these questions, the truth of individual events is recorded. Montaigne, who claims history is his favoured reading, goes to great length to use examples in the *Essays* to represent the diversity and variety of human experience.[70] His use of examples rarely leads to inductive reasoning; to draw premature conclusions in the "register of the essays of [his] life"[71] would be to betray the skeptical creed of never concluding, of which he expresses his approval: "[the] effect [of the teaching of the Pyrrhonists] is a pure, complete and very perfect postponement and suspension of judgment.

They use their reason to inquire and debate, but not to conclude and choose."[72]

Montaigne also argues for a sort of "natural reasoning," seen in the parodic form of the syllogistic musings of his fox and his dog, and more seriously in his praise for ordered debate, which he sees as an innate feature of the human mind: "it is not so much strength and subtlety that I ask for as order [in debates]: the order that we see every day in the altercations of shepherds and shop boys, never among us."[73] For him to make such a claim, he has to restore some value to human reason, which, as we have seen, took such a battering in the "Apology for Raymond Sebond," in which reason is described in negative terms as "an instrument of lead and of wax, stretchable, pliable and adaptable to all biases and all measures." Curiously, if this passage is put in the context of Aristotle's definition of equity, much-quoted by jurists and almost certainly known to Montaigne the magistrate, a quite different light is cast upon it:

The essential nature of the equitable . . . is a rectification of law where law is defective because of its generality . . . For what is itself indefinite can only be measured by an indefinite standard, like the leaden rule used by Lesbian builders; just as that rule is not rigid but can be bent to the shape of the stone, so a special ordinance is made to fit the circumstances of the case. (Nicomachean Ethics, v.10. 1137b)

The scornful tone of Montaigne's description of the faculty of reason disappears if reason is seen as flexible and subject to circumstance, and hence closer to the particulars of human lives.

Montaigne's objection to the universal claims of the sciences is also met in this passage by Aristotle, the very model, according to the essayist, of wrong thinking in this regard. These claims are explored most aggressively in the opening pages to the chapter "Of Experience," where, after apparently conceding that reason is a better path to truth and knowledge than experience, Montaigne ends up, through an ingenious textual development, by recommending his reader to adopt not a general science of supra-temporal reason linked to the particulars of contingent lived experience but a general science of experience which retains its temporal character, linked to a particular science of reason which is no longer as abstract or subtle as it is in the derided case of syllogistic logic. The "truth of experience," which had been subverted by the "certain" demonstrations of the highest sciences, is now restored to its rightful place;[74] the *veritas complex* is reunited with the *veritas simplex*; the facticity of human life has had its radical particularity and its subjection to change and time restored to it.

This lesser view of truth and knowledge represented by the arts is found to be commendable (or at least plausible) by Montaigne:

Theophrastus said that human knowledge, forwarded by the senses, could judge the causes of things to a certain extent; but that having reached the ultimate and original causes, it had to stop and be blunted, because of its weakness and the difficulty of things. It is a moderate and pleasant opinion that our capacity can lead us to the knowledge of some things, and that it has definite limits to its power, beyond which it is temerity to employ it. This opinion is plausible . . .[75]

We may be in a world of perpetual flux, armed only with imperfect tools of perception, both sensory and rational; but that does not prevent us from developing practical strategies for living our lives. Montaigne seems to claim at one point in the "Apology for Raymond Sebond" that we should forever suspend our judgment, which as a piece of advice is anything but practical; but he also translates Pyrrhonism (whether justifiably or not in historical terms) into a pragmatic philosophy of religious and political conformism which can provide guidance for the conduct of life (see above, p. 153).

The claims and modes of argument of university philosophy – its oversubtlety, abstraction, supra-temporality, pretensions to conclusiveness, to comprehensiveness and to the epistemological virtues of objectivity, certainty and universality – thus provided Montaigne with a useful foil against which to react; it also gave him some ammunition for his own enquiries into human existence in the form of the looser assumptions and argumentative procedures of the arts, notably of the law, and he was able to concur with the pragmatic version of truth espoused by practical philosophy. Even the much-reviled Aristotelianism of his day provided him with some useful doctrines (sense epistemology, the incorporated nature of human beings, the conventionality of language, a flexible notion of equity), and, as Edilia Traverso has shown, this savage critic of peripatetic philosophy came at the end of his life to quote Aristotle approvingly (mainly on ethical matters).[76] So the *Essays*, which Montaigne conceived of as a profoundly unphilosophical project of self-description, turn out to share common ground with philosophy, and their author himself becomes by his own admission what he thought he would never become:

My behaviour is natural: I have not called in the help of any teaching to build it. But feeble as it is, when the desire to tell it seized me, and when, to make it appear in public a little more decently, I set myself to support it with reasons and examples, it was a marvel to myself to find it, simply by chance, in conformity with so many philosophical examples and reasons. What rule my life belonged to, I did not learn until after it was completed and spent. A new figure: an unpremeditated and accidental philosopher![77]

## NOTES

1. II.12, F392, V527B. I have on occasion amended the translation by Donald M. Frame; these changes are placed in square brackets. I have also included the original French where this is necessary to my argument. I am grateful to Richard Scholar and Terence Cave, who kindly read an earlier draft of this chapter and made helpful suggestions.

2. See Lorraine Daston, "Can scientific objectivity have a history?", *Alexander von Humboldt Stiftung Mitteilungen*, 75 (2000), pp. 31–40.

3. II.12, F371, V502A; Montaigne quotes this as a prelude to his undermining of the syllogism through the liar paradox (see below, p. 147).

4. F403, V539A: "We do not ask whether this is true but whether it has been understood this way or that. We do not ask whether Galen said anything worth saying, but whether he said thus or otherwise". On this distinction see R. G. Collingwood, *An Autobiography* (Oxford: Clarendon Press, 1939), pp. 29–43.

5. R. H. Popkin, *The History of Scepticism from Savonarola to Bayle* (New York and Oxford: Oxford University Press, 2003).

6. The most helpful recent book on Montaigne's translation and his defence of Sebond is Claude Blum, ed., *Montaigne: Apologie de Raimond Sebond: de la Theologia à la Théologie* (Paris: Champion, 1990).

7. On Sextus Empiricus, see Popkin, *History of Scepticism*.

8. II.12, F371, V502A. See also Frédéric Brahami, *Le scepticisme de Montaigne* (Paris: Presses Universitaires de France, 1997).

9. II.12, F403, V539A; II.17, F498, V657C; I.26, F107, V146A; III.13, F817, V1067B; III.5, F666, V874B.

10. III.2, F611, V805B; III.9, F762, V995–6C. See also Ian Maclean, *Montaigne philosophe* (Paris: Presses Universitaires de France, 1996), p. 13.

11. III.2, *F611, V805*.

12. I.26, *F106–7, V146*.

13. See André Tournon, *Montaigne: la glose et l'essai* (Lyon: Presses Universitaires, 1983); Ian Maclean, "Montaigne et le droit civil romain", in John O'Brien, Malcolm Quainton and James J. Supple, eds, *Montaigne et la rhétorique* (Paris: Champion, 1995), pp. 163–75.

14. I.26, *F119, V161A*; Maclean, *Montaigne philosophe*, p. 8.

15. II.12, *F429, V571A*; II.17, *F497, V655A*; Jean Starobinski, *Montaigne en mouvement* (Paris: Gallimard, 1982), pp. 169–221; Tournon, *La glose et l'essai*; Maclean, "Montaigne et le droit civil romain."

16. For the relevant parts of the arts course here discussed, see Ian Maclean, *Logic, Signs and Nature in the Renaissance: The Case of Learned Medicine* (Cambridge: Cambridge University Press, 2001), pp. 101–204; Maclean, *Montaigne philosophe*, pp. 17–57.

17. See Maclean, *Logic, Signs and Nature*, pp. 114–17.

18. II.12, *F403–4, V540A*. Montaigne uses *dialecticien* (translated by Frame as "logician") here to encompass all who engage in logical argument, whether in syllogistic or other forms.

19. See Charles B. Schmitt, "Experience and Experiment: A Comparison of Zabarella's View with Galileo's in *De motu*," *Studies in the Renaissance*, 16 (1969), pp. 80–138; Peter Dear, *Discipline and Experience: The Mathematical Way in the Scientific Revolution* (Chicago and London: University of Chicago Press, 1995).

20. The sixteenth-century Aristotelian Julius Caesar Scaliger (of whose work Montaigne is aware: see III.13, *F833, V1087B*), adapts the Thomist formula to read *orationis adaequatio cum ipsis speciebus*: *Exotericae exercitationes de subtilitate contra Cardanum* (Frankfurt: Wechel, 1592), p. 8 (first edn., 1557). See also Ian Maclean, *Interpretation and Meaning in the Renaissance: The Case of Law* (Cambridge: Cambridge University Press, 1992), p. 74; Paul Cranefield, "On the Origin of the Phrase Nihil est in intellectu quod non prius fuerit in sensu," *Journal of the History of Medicine*, 25 (1970), pp. 77–80.

21. III.3.8, *F710, V930B*.

22. II.12, *F* 330–58, 443–55, *V452–86, 587–601*; II.12, *F454, V600–01B*; Sextus Empiricus, *Hypotyposes*, II.4.20.

23. Francis Bacon, *Novum organum*, ed. Thomas Fowler (Oxford: Clarendon Press, 1878), pp. 210–11 (1.41).

24. II.12, *F496, V645C*; II.12, *F425, V565A*; III.6, *F693, V908B*; see also Maclean, *Montaigne philosophe*, p. 74.

25. For a simple account of the syllogism, see Maclean, *Logic, Signs and Nature*, p. 124.

26. I.26, *F126, V171A*.

27. II.12, *F*392, *V*527B.

28. II.12, *F*392, *V*527B; *F*337–9, *V*460–63.

29. See Maclean, *Interpretation and Meaning*, p. 72.

30. III.11, *F*785, *V*1026B. The phrase "l'opinion de science" is an oxymoron in philosophical terms: see Maclean, *Montaigne philosophe*, p. 32.

31. II.10, *F*301, *V*414A.

32. III.13, *F*818–19, *V*1069B.

33. II.37, *F*594, *V*781–2A.

34. III.13, *F*816, *V*1066–7B. My changes to this passage have been made to render more accurately the terms of legal art in this passage, such as the *usus communis loquendi* and *verba solemna*, on which see Maclean, *Interpretation and Meaning*, pp. 132–5, 142.

35. See Maclean, *Montaigne philosophe*, pp. 33–4; *Logic, Signs and Nature*, pp. 118–19.

36. II.1, *F*242; *V*335B. On *distinguo*, see Daniel Ménager, "Montaigne et l'art du distingo," in *Montaigne et la rhétorique*, pp. 149–59.

37. III.2, *F*611, *V*805B.

38. See Maclean, *Logic, Signs and Nature*, pp. 121–4.

39. See Maclean, *Interpretation and Meaning*, pp. 158–60.

40. See N. L. Wilson, "Substance without Substrata," *Review of Metaphysics*, 12 (1959), pp. 521–39; W. V. Quine, *Word and Object* (Cambridge, MA: M.I.T. Press, 1960), p. 59; Donald Davidson, "Radical Interpretation" (1973), in *Inquiries into Truth and Interpretation* (Oxford: Oxford University Press, 1984), p. 136n; Ian Hacking, *Why does Language Matter to Philosophy?* (Cambridge: Cambridge University Press, 1975), p. 148.

41. "To the Reader," *F*2, *V*3A.

42. See III.1, *F*599–609, *V*789–803.

43. III.11, *F*785, *V*1027B. The same point is made in respect of linguistic signs and intention by Umberto Eco, *A Theory of Semiotics* (Bloomington: University of Indiana Press, 1976), p. 7: "if [a sign] cannot be used to tell a lie, conversely it cannot be used to tell the truth."

44. II.17, *F*497, *V*655A.

45. See Maclean, *Montaigne philosophe*, pp. 23–9

46. On the concept of *ens rationis* in Montaigne's time, see Marie-Luce Demonet, "Les êtres de raison ou les modes d'être de la littérature," in Eckhard Kessler and Ian Maclean, eds., *Res et verba in the Renaissance* (Wiesbaden: Harrassowitz, 2002), pp. 177–95.

47. II.12, *F*400–01, *V*536–7C.

48. II.12, *F*390, *V*525C: "Now if there are many worlds, as Democritus, Epicurus and almost all philosophy has thought, how do we know whether the principles and rules of this one apply similarly to the

others?" III.11, *F*385. *V*1027B: "Our reason is capable of filling out a hundred other worlds and finding their principles and contexture. It needs neither matter nor basis; let it run on; it builds as well on emptiness as on fullness, and with inanity as with matter."

49. 1.21, *F*75, *V*105C.

50. See Maclean, *Montaigne philosophe*, p. 28. The claim that "truth must have one face, the same and universal" (II.12, *F*436. *V*578–9A) is made to demonstrate that dogmatic philosophies cannot possess it, as they all disagree as to what it is.

51. II.12, *F*452–3, *V*600A.

52. See above, n. 20 (Julius Caesar Scaliger).

53. II.10, *F*298, *V*410A.

54. Nicholas of Cusa, *Idiota de mente*, ed. Renate Steiger, *Opera omnia*, vol. 5 (Hamburg: Meiner, 1983), p. 172: *sic omnis rei mensura vel terminus ex mente est; et ligna et lapides certam mensuram et terminos habent praeter mentem nostram, sed ex mente increata, a qua rerum omnis terminus descendit.* See also Maclean, *Logic, Signs, and Meaning*, p. 105; Sextus Empiricus, *Hypotyposes*, 1.32.216.

55. III.9, *F*734, *V*961B.

56. II.12, *F*455, *V*601A.

57. E.g. III. 8, *F*787, *V*926B; III.13. *F*817, 823, *V*1067B, 1076B; III.5, *F*666, *V*874C.

58. III.11, *F*785, *V*1026B, quoted above, p. 161.

59. III.10, *F*769, *V*1006B: "for it is not new for the sages to preach things as they serve, not as they are"; II.12, *F*374, *V*505B (*De divinatione*, 1.18); cf. III.3.5, *F*639–40, *V*842B: "my philosophy is in action, in natural and present practice, little in fancy."

60. II.12, *F*375, *V*506A. The reference to the Aristotelian view of the mind as a *tabula rasa* is to *De anima*, III.4.430a; see also Romans 2:15.

61. *Digest* 1.5.25: *res iudicata pro veritate accipitur.*

62. *Digest* 50.17 202: *omnis definitio in iure civili periculosa est: rarum est enim ut non subverti potest.*

63. III.11, *F*788, *V*1030B.

64. For a fuller account of the presence of legal thinking in the *Essays*, see Maclean, *Interpretation and Meaning*, pp. 104–13, and "Montaigne et le droit civil romain."

65. III.13, *F*819. *V*1070B; cf. II.12, *F*342, *V*466A: "I ordinarily maintain . . . that there is more difference between a given man and a given man that between a given animal and a given man."

66. III.9, *F*721, *V*945–6; see also Philippe Desan, "La rhétorique comptable des *Essais*," in *Montaigne et la rhétorique*, pp. 163–75.

67. See Maclean, *Interpretation and Meaning*, pp. 75–85.

68. *Topics*, I.I.I00a.

69. II.I2, *F*376, *V*507A: "for truth is not judged by the authority and on the testimony of another."

70. I.26, *F*107, *V*146A; II.10, *F*303, *V*416A; see also Maclean, *Montaigne philosophe*, pp. 53–6.

71. III.I3, *F*826, *V*1079B.

72. II.I2, *F*374, *V*505B.

73. III.8, *F*706, *V*925; also I.26, *F*117–22, *V*158–62.

74. II.I2, *F*430, *V*571A.

75. II.I2, *F*420–21, *V*560B.

76. *Montaigne e Aristotele* (Florence: Le Monnier, 1974).

77. II.I2, *F*409, *V*546C.

# 9   The investigation of nature

> We have our philosophical persons to make modern and
> familiar,
> Things supernatural and causeless.
>
> Shakespeare, *All's Well that Ends Well* (II.3.2–3)

Loath to identify himself with any school of thought (he never even
directly called himself a skeptic), Montaigne nonetheless does name
himself a "naturalist": "We naturalists judge that the honor of invention is greatly and incomparably preferable to the honor of quotation"
(III.12, F809, V1056C). Used in a literary instead of a philosophic context, as well as somewhat off-handedly, the label would nevertheless
have sent a specific signal to readers. Today, the term applies capa-
ciously to a diverse array of scholars working within what can be
described as a pre-scientific mentality, most notably empirical medical practitioners such as Ambroise Paré (1510–1590) and observers
of flora and fauna such as Pierre Belon (1517–1564) and Guillaume
Rondelet (1507–1566). But Montaigne's peers used it more pointedly
to designate the attempt to explain phenomena without recourse to
divine causation, or "first causes."[1] Naturalism, in brief, entailed a
search for secondary causes.

All explanatory claims depend upon the identification of a cause
(Aristotle, *Post. Anal.* 71b8–12); but prioritizing natural over supernatural ones diminished some of the most cherished commonplaces
of natural theology such as arguments from design, the principle
of plenitude, the great chain of being, and the distinction between
*natura naturans* and *natura naturata* (nature as creator or created) –
concepts which Montaigne famously dismisses as presumptuous
in his "Apology for Raymond Sebond." While many writers, like

Jean Bodin, Pierre Boaistuau, and Jacques Aubert sought to reconcile "local" causality with a larger sense of God's hand in events,[2] contemporaries more often attributed to the movement an effort to overturn teleological conceptions of the world. Guillaume du Vair complained of the man who "observed an order and continual course of regular causes, which are brought forth one of another, hath called it Nature, and hath believed this Nature did all."[3] Louis le Roy similarly criticized, "these things proceed (after the opinion of the *Naturalists*) from the fatal law of the world; and have their natural causes."[4] Montaigne's neighbor, François de Foix de Candale, decried this vision of an autonomous universe in which "all things proceed by order and succession, each according to its place, with neither author, director, nor creator."[5] Pierre Crespet discerned in the movement a powerful dissuader of belief in miracles, for "those that have learned the cause no longer wonder, as in the eclipse of the moon or sun which impresses only the stupid and unschooled, not those who understand the cause."[6] To speak of "natural causes" became so marked that René Lucinge felt the need to prudently disclaim, "We will merely speculate on natural causes . . . so as to avoid the confusion in speaking of distant, heavenly ones."[7] Apologists' unrelenting efforts to stigmatize this tendency no doubt contributed toward radicalizing a movement that, at its origin, considered its interest in the workings of nature entirely orthodox.

In such a climate, extreme expressions of the urge to explain things "naturally" quickly arose. One particularly unorthodox example consisted in attempts to account for how humans could have been created by spontaneous generation from the earth.[8] Bodin's refutation of these views at the end of his 1566 *Method for the Easy Comprehension of History* provides a gauge of their currency, or at least familiarity, among circles that would have been close to Montaigne's own; Bodin, himself, articulated these theories more open-mindedly in the mouth of his "naturalist" Toalbe in the (prudently) unpublished *Colloquium of the Seven About Secrets of the Sublime*.[9] Montaigne encountered them as early as his 1564 reading of Lucretius (*De rerum natura*, II.991–8); in his personal copy, he flatly rejects Denis Lambin's attempt to read the offending passage in a light more congenial to Christianity.[10] Although apologists of the time shuddered at atheists who "have dreamed up that they are born by chance and by themselves," it is possible that Montaigne entertained such a notion with respect to New World natives.[11]

But Montaigne's relationship to the naturalist movement proves more difficult to determine. For traditional natural philosophers, the universe had yearned toward a goal that could lend to any event, no matter how insignificant, teleological import. "Atheisticall naturalists," on the contrary, were thought to want to explain the world without invoking the hand of God;[12] as Pierre de La Primaudaye put it, these "hawtie spirits . . . seeke out the naturall causes of things so curiouslie, that in the end they strive to finde out another beginning of all things than GOD."[13] Haughty or hidden, efforts to erect alternative accounts of phenomena – weather, political change, the distribution of species – entailed a confidence in one's ability to determine causality, a confidence that Montaigne, as a skeptic, ultimately could not condone. Moreover, some of the more ingenious explanations devised by naturalists forestall inserting them too casually into a progressive history that would make of the tendency a prelude to the scientific revolution. In fact, much of it would strike the modern scientific sensibility as naively analogical, even at its most premonitory: for Bernard Palissy, fossils were created by salt (since it acts as a preservative); for Jean Bodin, saunas work best when humid since "the thickness of the air, excited the vapor of the water, keeps the heat, while earlier it could not because of its fineness."[14]

Nevertheless, this emphasis of efficient over final causes (in the language of Aristotle, *Post. Anal.* 94a20–23; *Physics*, 194b23–195a27) does qualify Montaigne as a kindred spirit of early naturalists, even if only by denegation, "I am not a good 'naturalist' (as they call it) and I hardly know by what springs fear acts in us" (1.18, *F*52, *V*75A). The enthusiasms of the amateur Renaissance naturalist often came into play around a *Wunderkammer*, or curiosity cabinet.[15] Although usually not considered in this context, Montaigne's tower library seems to have served such a function, housing a sizeable collection of objects, including family relics (II.18, *F*503, *V*664C), historical tokens dating back to the English occupation of Aquitania (II.12, *F*436, *V*579A), and artifacts from the New World (1.31, *F*154, *V*208A). Such *cabinets* extended the collecting and comparative impulses that underpinned humanist editorial enterprises to the great "book" of nature.

Drawing variously upon travel literature, natural histories from antiquity, Aristotelian physics, and the tradition of *problemata*, many early naturalists were by no accident medical practitioners.[16]

Montaigne studied Aristotle's *Physics* in his second year of arts
school in 1547–8 and, shortly thereafter, seems to have been reading
Melanchton's *Physicē*.[17] He attended lectures probably sometime in
1551–3 (II.2, F246–7, V342) by the Galenist doctor and leading expo-
nent of the Parisian school of anatomy, Jacques Dubois (1478 [1489?]–
1555), who practiced human dissections in his home (an activity
that was, strictly speaking, illegal) and published "commentaries
on Anatomy which we have gathered through the observation of
many bodies which we have painstakingly dissected in public and in
private."[18] Montaigne met the well-known doctor, Simon Thomas,
in Toulouse (1.21, F68, V98C, n. 4), most likely in the entourage of
Henri de Mesmes;[19] to another, the pre-eminent Jean Fernel (1485–
1558), he alludes knowingly (III.13, F833, V1087B) as well as to
Paracelsus (1493–1541, II.12, F429, V571A; II.37, F586, V772A; F580,
V765A;); and he would likely have been familiar with the Bordeaux
circles in which moved the scholar–doctors Antoine Valet (1546–
1610), Étienne Maniald (1535–1599), and Pierre Pichot (ca. 1520–after
1577).[20] He appears to have read the works of two Italian scholars of
the medical avant-garde, Leonardo Fioravanti (?–1588) and Giovanni
Argenterio (1513–1572), mentioned in the *Essays* (II.37, F586, V772A;
F580, V765A).[21] The former may well have inspired a number of the
dietary observations in "Of Experience."[22] During his later trip to
Switzerland and Italy, he seeks out the noted naturalist doctors, the
Montpellier-trained anatomist, Felix Platter (1536–1614), Theodor
Zwinger (1533–1588), and Girolamo Borro (1512–1592) (*Journal de
Voyage*, F877–8, 1011).[23] His first editor, in Bordeaux, printed the
best-selling medical vulgarization, *Erreurs populaires*, by Laurent
Joubert (1529–1583) who had studied with Argenterio, as well as
more erudite works: two medical treatises in Latin by Pichot and
a work translated by Maniald and written by Rondelet, Joubert's
predecessor at the University of Montpellier. A friend of Dubois,
Rondelet's similar obsession with anatomy led him to dissect one
of his own deceased children. Later in life, Montaigne's meticulous
annotations in the *Journal du voyage* on the effects of the various hot
springs he visited would not have been out of place among medical
accounts of the time.[24]

To what use did Montaigne put his early training and enduring adult interest in natural phenomena? Frame's translation of
the *Essays* frequently capitalizes "Nature," thereby lending it an

ontological inflection lacking in the French. Yet, few thinkers idealized nature less. If legal training might have inclined someone in his
profession to think in terms of "natural law," he places the notion
in a decidedly biological context: "If there is any truly natural law,
that is to say, any instinct . . . the care every animal has for its
own preservation" (II.8, F279, V386A). As for anyone claiming to
erect a society on natural law, "Let them show me just one law
of that sort – I'd like to see it" (II.12, F437, V580A). Whereas even
Ambroise Paré had condemned "naturalistes" [naturall and mate-
riate philosophers] who rejected man's superiority over animals,[25]
Montaigne considered that one might best study human nature by
studying animals (II.12, F803, V1050B). What they taught was the
great lesson of egotism: in man, the instinct for self-preservation
becomes the basic enmity that opposes person and person: "let
each man sound within himself, and he will find that our private
wishes are for the most part born and nourished at the expense
of others" (1.22, F77, V107A). Nothing is less natural, then, nor
more at odds with human nature, than the practice of Christian
charity.

   If not principles, then a method? The most remarkable early
expression of naturalists' inductive approach can be found in Pierre
Belon's 1553 *Observations*, "presenting in what I have written herein
nothing that I have not seen myself."[26] Singularly unmoved by popular biblical and mythological sites, he reveals a decided penchant for
demystification: the famous Labyrinth of Crete is but an abandoned
mine; inspection of entrails reveals that a fabled local fish does not
nourish itself on gold; a similar dissection proves that chameleons
live not on air but insects.[27] Belon may have been the first person
to use "observation" in this markedly empirical sense, opposed to
its more common religious meaning of obedience.[28] Montaigne, at
times, voices something close to such nascent empiricism: "They
ordinarily begin thus: 'How does this happen?' What they should say
is: 'But does it happen?'" (III.11, F785, V1026–7B). But one finds similar formulations in popular polemic owing little to the newly emerg-
ing zoological and medical sciences, such as Pierre Burin's rejoinder
to defenders of the St. Bartholomew's massacre, "Now if the question at hand could be debated by reasoning, I would be pleased to do
so, but since the matter lies in the facts . . . it can only be debated by
'it is,' 'is not,' 'if it is.'"[29]

Most simply, Montaigne learned from his medical studies to be suspicious of how philosophers project upon nature a *technē*, or art, "I do not recognize in Aristotle most of my ordinary actions . . . [C] I would naturalize art as much as they artify nature" (III.5, F666, V874BC). Unlike the old natural philosophy, which continued to discern in nature a teleology, and thus lent itself to natural theologians stretching from La Primaudaye to Bodin and from Georges Pacard to Philippe du Plessis de Mornay, Montaigne seems particularly attentive to the confusion of effects for ends, and of results for goals. His book opens on this problem, initially appearing to address itself to means-end analysis, "By diverse means we arrive at the same end," which he famously complicates in three distinct stages. First, he finds against common wisdom that courage, and not just submissiveness, can serve to elicit a victor's mercy. Next, he overturns a distinction which would claim that submissiveness succeeds when addressed to weak adversaries, courage to strong ones. Finally, he shows that courage can provoke ire instead of mercy, completely reversing the direction of the essay.[30] More than rehearsing the old adage, "every rule has its exceptions,"[31] what is fundamental in this inaugural chapter is how the language of multiple "effects" gradually replaces the announced subject of multiple "means." In shifting the examination of behavior from a study of ends to one of causes, he displaces conscious intent in favor of more elusive motives, sometimes barely understood by their subjects. In other words, he moves from considering the narrow problem of how to incite clemency to a broader contemplation of how one type of human reaction unexpectedly provokes another – or, from a rhetorical to a psychological mode of analysis.

One might compare this shift to Protestantism's reformulation of works, or good acts, not as the means to salvation but as the effect of election; but Protestants' attachment to a starkly providential view of the world retained natural theology's teleological thrust.[32] For Montaigne, the question of effects derives most directly from medicine, and it is in that domain that he pursued most clearly his reflection on causality. Examining cases in which someone pretends to be blind, as a means of shirking duty, and, in fact, becomes blind, he embarks upon a detailed explanation, hypothesizing atrophy: "It is possible that the action of sight had become dulled through having been so long without exercise, and that the visual power had

wholly transferred itself to the other eye" (II.25, F521, V688A). In
another story about a man who dreamt he lost his sight and awoke
to find himself indeed blind, Montaigne foregoes the opportunity to
apply one of his favorite lessons, on the "force of the imagination";
instead, he exchanges cause for effect: "it is more likely that the
movements which the body felt within, of which the doctors may
find out the cause, if they will, and which deprived him of his sight,
were the occasion of the dream" (F522, V689A). A similar conjunction of medical semiology and etiology reappears in the essay that
closed the first edition, "Of the Resemblance of Children to Fathers."
Echoing debates of the status of the medical "sign," or symptom, in
which his old teacher, Dubois, had played a significant role, Montaigne reflects on the perplexing problem of hereditary illness and the
causal mechanism by which a drop of semen can, years later, transmit a paternal affliction: "If anyone will enlighten me about this
process, I will believe him about as many other miracles as he wants"
(F579, V764). He airs his principle grief against the medical profession, unsurprisingly its teleological pretensions: doctors claim
unpredictable outcomes as intended results. However, their diagnosis remains necessarily uncertain, as the same illness can cause
different symptoms and, conversely, different illnesses share similar symptoms: "how, for example, shall he find the proper symptom of the disease, each disease being capable of an infinite number of symptoms?" (F587, V773A).[33] Their prognosis risks equal
ineffectuality, since the same remedy can produce different effects
in different patients, while varying means can achieve the similar
ends: the doctor "needs too many details, considerations, and circumstances to adjust his plan" (F586, V773A). Even the various
doctrines by which each generation of doctors lays claim to the
power to cure are but the effect of evolving opinion and cultural
context.

His congenital antipathy toward medicine's proscriptive practices,
however, tends to obscure his very real affinity with its descrip-
tive function. He presents the *Essays* themselves as a sort of medical journal, "I want to represent the course of my humors" (II.37,
F574, V768A), and, as Jean Starobinski has shown, empirical medical categories inform the self-diagnosis with which he concludes
his work in "Of Experience."[34] Throughout the *Essays*, Montaigne
prefers to study cause and effects, over the analysis of means and

ends. If he resists an instrumental approach to empiricism, he does so because he considers causality too variegated and unpredictable to yield dependable rules, "different and contrary accidents, which often afflict us at the same time" (II.37, F587, V774A). "In natural things, the effects only half reflect their causes" (II.12, F396, V531B). Ultimately, for Montaigne, what one learns from experience cannot lead to positive empirical knowledge for "The inference that we try to draw from the resemblance of events is uncertain, because they are always dissimilar" (III.13, F815, V1065B). Once again, the medical influence upon Montaigne's thinking has been underestimated. He owes this critical assessment of empiricism to Galen's *Subfiguratio empirica*, an important, unidentified source for several key pages in the *Essays* (III.12, F793, V1037B and II.37, F594–5, V782A, where an anecdote about a serpent confirms the *Subfiguratio* as provenance, 10.77–8). His attendance of Dubois' lectures coincided with the period when Galen's works were replacing Avicenna's *Canon* in the medical curriculum throughout Europe. Galenism offered an attractive middle way between a theory-bound and stiffly institutional Aristotelianism on the one hand, and, on the other, the experimental practice of "low" sciences, like alchemy, typically misdirected into qualitative rather than quantitative approaches to nature. For an unbounded and indeterminate field, indexical methods (using measures, co-ordinates, and statistical analysis) need to supplant analogical reasoning;[35] but until one enjoyed access to a mathematics of probability, Galenism offered as likely a structure as any within which to attempt to make sense of recurring instances of particular natural phenomena.[36]

If not objective knowledge, what, then, does one learn from experience? A sense of one's own shortcomings, it would seem: "I do not regard the species and the individual, like a stone I have stumbled on; I learn to mistrust my gait throughout" (III.13, F822, V1074B). In other words, the accumulation of experience serves, for Montaigne, not an impartial, pre- or proto-scientific aim but the subjective, negative one of learning when to distrust oneself, "It is from my *experience* that I affirm human ignorance, which is, in my opinion, the most certain fact in the school of the world" (III.13, F817, V1075–6B, emphasis mine). Following a long critique of the inductive professions of medicine and law in "Of Experience," he devotes the last thirty pages of his book to the study of visceral sensations and impulses. This particular instance of "nature" earns its closing privilege insofar as it invokes only a minimal representation of sensory perception and slightest claim about exterior reality: "They must tell me whether what I think I feel, I therefore actually do feel" (II.12, F405, V541A). Hence his preference throughout the *Essays* for lessons drawn from internal sensations which are less easily falsified, such as nausea ("Of Cruelty"), vertigo ("Of Coaches"), abdominal pain ("Of the Resemblance of Children to Fathers" and "Of Experience"), and loss of consciousness ("Of Practice"). Whereas most thinkers "leave aside the cases and amuse themselves treating the causes" (III.11, F785, V1026B), Montaigne seems to have thoroughly assimilated Galen's suspicion of empiricism.[37] Hence, the search for a cause can even become a form of rationalization, hardly better than throws of the dice: "whatever direction I turn, I can always provide myself with enough causes and probabilities to keep me that way" (II.17, F496, V654A). Following Galen, the profusion of causes and effects leads to a confusion of consequentiality and to a "loosened" notion of causality. Such a state of affairs smiles upon assertions of individual freedom and suits Montaigne's dislike of determinism.

More unexpectedly, however, his critique of the knowledge of causes converges upon Lucretius' notion of random chance: "We cannot make sure of the master cause [i.e., the effectual one]; we pile up several of them, to see if by chance it will be found among them" (III.6, F685, V899B; *De rerum natura*, v.526–33 and vi.703–4 which he quotes following).[38] Contrary to the nonchalance with which Montaigne later maintained he approached reading, he studied *De rerum natura* as minutely as would have a professional scholar, and as carefully as specialists today pore over the *Essays*, comparing passages and compiling extensive lists of key notions on the flyleaves in a preliminary effort to organize the main ideas of Lucretius' system. The discovery of his personal copy allows one to rectify Hugo Friedrich's unfortunate conclusion that regarding Epicurean physics, "nature philosophy is missing, or rather Montaigne only considers it doxographically in order to dismiss it."[39] More recently, Ian Maclean has cast doubt on Epicurean influence, finding "no explicit trace of this anti-providentialism."[40] But Montaigne's interest in the Epicurean critique of causality may be partially obscured by his use of the old term, "fortune." Jacques Amyot translated Plutarch's critique of Epicurean fortuitousness as "Of Fortune," specifying within the text, "casuelle adventure" (causal randomness).[41] Du Vair concurred: "men attribute unto Fortune the accidents whose causes they comprehend not. And from thence it is come, that some being grown so brutish, as they observed no causes of the effects which they saw, they deemed all did happen by chance. So out of their ignorance and brutalitie, they have made themselves a Goddesse, which they call Fortune."[42] So frequent as to catch even the distracted eye of his Vatican censor, Montaigne's use of "fortune" seems to designate a rather similar appreciation of the haphazard nature of human events.

That the universe depended upon mere accident was not an unheard-of idea. Alvise Capuano in 1580 and Girolamo Grazoni in 1586 both were to have claimed that "the world was created by chance."[43] The notion seems accessible in the Middle Ages as well; Peter of Cornwall (1197–1221), wrote of many who did not believe in god, "They consider that the universe has always been as it is now and is ruled by chance rather than Providence."[44] But Montaigne's sense of fortune, or fortuitousness, is not identical with the modern notion of contingency, since he distinguishes the ordinary course of "natural" causality from chance occurrences: "All things, says Plato, are produced by nature, by fortune, or by art" (1.31, F153, V206C).[45] Or, again: "the good and health that fortune, nature, or some other extraneous cause (of which the number is infinite) produces in us, it is the privilege of medicine to attribute to itself" (II.37, F582, V768A). He sees both knowledge and action not as contingent (which can be or can not be), but simply as circumstantial (effected by context): "when we judge a particular action we must consider many circumstances and the whole man who performed it" (II.11, F311, V427A). In a very general way, his attention to circumstance and chance places him close in spirit to historians, from antiquity's Diodorus of Sicily to his contemporary, Jacques-Auguste de Thou. Medical practice, as we have seen, also stands to have exerted an influence through the ways that case studies took account of various dietary and environmental factors. It is no coincidence that the most vivid and detailed account of Henri III's assassination comes from his doctor, Marc Miron des Archiâtres, who noted not only the king's failing bodily functions but also the minutiae of court relations and political speculation that swirled about the tragedy.[46]

On a philosophical level, Montaigne appeals to chance against the Stoic notion of "fate," according to which nothing was supposed to occur by accident.[47] This priority awarded to chance leads both to a moral perspectivism and to the claim of a "random" style, "Musical fancies are guided by art, mine by chance" (III.2, F611, V805B).

Montaigne's thinking about randomness generally follows Epicurean arguments instead of the skeptical modes from Sextus Empiricus that one might have expected.[48] In particular, Montaigne's very use of the term "accident" often retains its original Latin meaning (from *cadere*, "to fall"). Speaking of the vertigo one feels facing climatic historical change and the "fall" of civilizations, he turns on its head a somber conclusion, "everything is crumbling about us," so as to derive a peculiarly Epicurean consolation: "naturally nothing falls where everything falls" (III.9, F734, V961B). This notion of events *befalling* one lies close to Epicurus' vision of the world as composed of transitory aggregates of atoms in free-fall: "All things in it are in constant motion – the earth, the rocks of the Caucasus, the pyramids of Egypt – both with the common motion and with their own. Stability itself is nothing but a more languid motion. I cannot keep my subject still. It goes along befuddled and staggering, with a natural drunkenness" (III.2, F610, V804B). Montaigne's interest clearly tends toward the personal and existential consequences of an unstable universe, "Our life is nothing but movement" (III.13, F840, V1095B), "Every movement reveals us" (I.50, F219, V302C), or "we, and our judgment, and all mortal things go on flowing and rolling unceasingly. Thus nothing certain can be established about one thing by another, both the judging and the judged being in continual change and motion" (II.12, F455, V601A).

Montaigne's Epicurean naturalism applied itself not so much to nature as humans' nature, not so much to the physical world, then, as to the mental one. Here lies a key to understanding his adaptation of the materialist system laid out in Lucretius, whose appeal lay in the parsimony of its premises: atoms, movement, and a unpredictable swerve in the fall of those atoms.[49] Little does it matter that Montaigne considers this swerve, or *clinamen*, as "very slight and ridiculous," preferring to regard it as aesthetic invention "as had at least a pleasant a subtle appearance" (II.12, F379, V511; Screech, [120] 259). Or that, elsewhere, he reproduces a criticism from Cicero (*De natura deorum,* 11.37) playing on the fact that *elementa* in Latin designates both atoms and the alphabet: "If the atoms have, by chance, formed so many sorts of figures, why have they never happened to meet to make a house, or a shoe? Why do we not believe likewise that an infinite number of Greek letters scattered about the place would be capable of forming the web of the *Iliad*?" (11.12, *F*407, *V*544–5). Montaigne has adopted Epicurean physics only as a hypothetical model (as perhaps it had already functioned for Lucretius). What interested Montaigne in this explanatory scheme was its simplicity and the possibility of investigating humans with as few presuppositions as possible concerning a "human nature" – a phrase notably rare in the *Essays* despite hundreds of occurrences of the word "nature" and "natural." Individuals possess a "nature" in the sense that everyone exhibits a temperament, but Montaigne avoids implying a fixed definition of what makes one human. Among the only times he does raise the problem, he denies that language distinguishes us from beasts since the only universal element of human communication concerns hand gestures, "this one must rather be judged the one proper to [defining characteristic of] human nature" (11.12, *F*332, *V*454C). Elsewhere, it appears ironically when his colleagues experience difficulty recognizing the humanity of visiting New World natives simply because they do not understand French, "human nature . . . ? Everything that seems strange to us we condemn" (11.12, *F*343, *V*467A). And it occurs often precisely where Montaigne seeks to blur the boundaries between humankind and the animal kingdom, "And there are half-breed and ambiguous forms between human and brutish nature" (11.12, *F*391, *V*525B), or the divine realm, "There are . . . some midway between divine and human nature, mediators and go-betweens between us and God" (11.12, *F*399, *V*534C).

Epicurean physics offered Montaigne a model for how one might account meaningfully for the vagaries of behavior without ascribing *a priori* a character to humans. One traditional attack on Epicurean materialism targeted its inability to account for thought; Montaigne overturns this objection by explaining the operations of thought as a dynamic system operating after the fashion of Epicurean physics. Such an approach to psychology projects a materialist schema onto the non-material, mental realm. Galen's theory of the humors had already implied psychological materialism, of course, but within a narrower, more causally deterministic framework aimed at specifying character. Montaigne found a system more congenial to his open-ended investigation of human nature in Epicurean physics. Just as Lucretius' *inclinatio* – the Latin term for *clinamen*, the unpredictable sideways moment of atoms – is without cause and thus can admit of no explanation, so, too, does the mysterious "inclination," that brought La Boétie and Montaigne together in a swerving-together-in-freedom, remain unexplainable since it is not impelled by anything external to the two friends: "I feel that this cannot be expressed, except by answering: Because it was he, because it was I" (1.28, *F*139, *V*188AC).[50] Unlike Aristotle and Cicero's notion of friendship motivated by willful choice and reasoned judgment of virtue, Montaigne and La Boétie find each other by "chance." To achieve such a rare fit "many coincidences are needed," judges Montaigne, playing upon the various meanings of *rencontre* in French, a coincidence, a collision, or a social encounter (1.28, *F*136, *V*184A).

More generally, the kinetic nature of such an "inclination" illustrates Montaigne's view that the mind is comprised not of states but of *movement*. Although he retains the categories of older faculty-based approaches to psychology, wisdom, for him, little resembles immobility and immutability; hence the premium he places on traveling in one's education (1.26, *F*112, *V*153A). Insofar as mental activity is identified with "reflexion" [reflexive movement] (III.10, *F*773, *V*1011B) – a turning back on oneself – thinking presupposes a dynamism that recalls Lucretius' natural world. Opinion is the name that people commonly give to the *clinamen* of the mind, denoting its haphazard swings in predilection. On the subject of historians: "they give themselves the right to judge, and consequently, to slant (*incliner*) history to their fancy; for once judgment leans to one side, one cannot help turning and twisting the narrative to that bias" (II.10, *F*304, *V*417A). Randomness can explain the production of thoughts themselves: "A frivolous cause, you will tell me. What do you mean, a cause? None is needed to agitate our soul: a daydream without body or subject dominates and agitates it" (III.4, *F*637, *V*839B).

One of the most striking examples of Montaigne's transformation of Lucretius' physical theories into psychological intuitions occurs when, in "Of Vanity," the generative *inanité*, or vacuum needed for movement in the Epicurean system, becomes a mental restlessness felt with regard to the tasks of house-holding that propels Montaigne's urge to travel. A sense of emptiness at home incites travel in a way that anticipates the modern notion of "vacation," derived from the Latin *vacare*, to make empty. As Montaigne notes in his copy of Lucretius, "There is emptiness in everything, thus movement" (Screech, 92), a notion which characteristically assumes anthropomorphic expression in the *Essays*, "We are all hollow and empty" (II.16, F468, V618A). Emptiness transcends the Aristotelian category of privation to take on a productive, positive value: "humility, fear, obedience, and amenability (which are the principal qualities for the preservation of human society) require a soul that is open (*vide*, empty), docile and with little presumption (II.12, F368, V498A). He introjects the hypothesis of a plurality of worlds in order to stress the fecundity of the imagination: "Our reason is capable of filling out a hundred other worlds . . . it builds as well on emptiness as on fullness, and with inanity as with matter" (III.11, F785, V1027B). One might also see the residue of Epicurus' "aggregate," or cluster of atoms into an apprehensible form, in Montaigne's conception of "custom" as social cement: "It is for habit (*coustume*) to give form to our life" (III.13, F827, V1080B).[51] The exploration of humans' nature takes on the playfully scientific quality of a sort of *Fantastic Voyage*.

At one point, Montaigne even admits that his study of the mind's inner workings can pass as a sort of physics, jokingly comparing himself to Aristotle, "I study myself . . . That is my metaphysics, that is my physics" (III.13, F821, V1072B – the essay opened by quoting the first line of Aristotle's *Metaphysics*). Linking physics to psychology was, in itself, hardly new. Philosophers from antiquity had elaborated their vision of the cosmos with respect to therapeutic ends: eliminating fear and bringing tranquility to the spirits of their adherents.[52] In one sense, then, Montaigne re-establishes the Platonic homology between physics and ethics,[53] but instead of appealing to a higher order and the ways in which it inscribes itself in the human soul, he suggests instead that Epicurus' universal *disorder* writes itself there. Epicurus' physics had addressed itself to the uneasy mind through its dual rejection of divine intervention and natural determinism: blind chance, which one could not possibly be expected to anticipate, nor to appease, need not therefore further trouble one. But Montaigne's relationship to the old microcosm–macrocosm equation seems even more complicated by the fact that he maintains a skeptical attitude toward the truth value of Epicurean physics, and his use of it to elaborate a purely human psychology that does not invoke theology seems heuristic rather than metaphysical.

Dubious, mild, yet inquisitive, Montaigne situated himself with respect to a developing philosophic tradition which sought explanations for natural phenomena without recourse to the teleological appeals frequent in medieval discussion and still persistent in the practice of natural theology of his day. While not yet scientific, nor even necessarily proto-scientific, this movement shifted the grounds of natural inquiry from an analysis of means and ends to one of cause and effect. Montaigne's originality within such a shift may well come from how he used Lucretius' *De rerum natura* to undermine naturalists' assumptions concerning causality while nevertheless retaining their anti-teleological thrust. With these simple tools, this most congenial of writers of philosophy and least seriously regarded philosopher in his own right initiated the first recognizably psychological study of human nature. Allowing for differences in personal inclination, such might easily sum up Descartes' aim in the *Discours* and *Meditations*: the extension of the naturalist program to an empirical investigation of discernment and the process of judgment.[54]

NOTES

1.  For a typical illustration of this distinction in the mouth of Jean Bodin's fictional "naturalist," see his *Colloque entre sept scavans qui sont de differens sentiments*, ed. François Berriot (Geneva: Droz, 1984), pp. 40–41, trans. Marion Leathers Daniels Kuntz, *Colloquium of the Seven about Secrets of the Sublime* (Princeton, NJ: Princeton University Press, 1975), pp. 33–4. See, also, Henri Busson, *Le Rationalisme dans la littérature française de la Renaissance, 1533–1601*, 2nd edn. (1922; Paris: Vrin, 1957), pp. 230–33; see also Jean Céard, *La Nature des prodiges: L'insolite au XVIe siècle, en France* (Geneva: Droz, 1977), pp. 489–93. Pomponazzi's 1520 *De naturalium effectuum admirandorum causis* constitutes a significant source for this movement (Basel: H. Petri, 1556, 1567), ed. and trans. Henri Busson, *Les Causes des merveilles de la nature* (Paris: Reider, 1930); for classical antecedents, see Robert Lenoble, *Esquisse d'une histoire de l'idée de la nature* (Paris: A. Michel, 1969).

2. Bodin, *Universae naturae theatrum* (Frankfurt: A. Wechel, 1597); Boaistuau, *Histoires prodigieuses* (Paris: C. Macé, 1560); and Aubert, *Institutiones physicae* (Lyon: A. de Harsy, 1584).

3. Guillaume du Vair, *De la constance et consolation és calamitez publiques* (Paris: M. Patisson, 1594), ed. Jacques Flach, *Traité de la constance et consolation* (Paris: Recueil Sirey, 1915), pp. 128–9; trans. Andrew Court, *A Buckler against Adversitie, or a Treatise of Constancie* (London: B. Alsop, 1622), p. 65.

4. *De la vicissitude ou varieté des choses en l'univers* (Paris: P. l'Huillier, 1575), ed. Philippe Desan (Paris: Fayard, 1988), p. 427, trans. Robert Ashley, *Of the Interchangeable Course, or Variety of Things in the Whole World* (London: C. Yetsweirt, 1594), fol. 126$^v$.

5. *Le Pimandre de Mercure Trismegiste de la philosophie chrestienne* (Bordeaux: S. Millanges, 1579), p. 713 (commentary to 16.9).

6. *Deux livres de la hayne de Sathan et malins esprits contre l'homme et de l'homme contre eux*, (Paris: G. de la Noüe, 1590), p. 85.

7. *De la naissance, durée et chute des estats*, ed. Michael J. Heath (Geneva: Droz, 1984), p. 201.

8. Andrea Cesalpino, *Quaestionum peripateticarum* (1571; Venice: Juntas, 1593), fols. 104$^v$–109$^v$; Giuliano Gliozzi, *Adamo e il nuovo mondo. La nascita dell'antropologia come ideologia coloniale: dalle genealogie bibliche alle teorie razziali (1500–1700)* (Florence: La Nuova Italia, 1977), pp. 306–21, 331–47, trans. Arlette Estève and Pascal Gabellone, *Adam et le Nouveau Monde. La naissance de l'anthropologie comme idéologie coloniale: des généologies bibliques aux théories raciales (1500–1700)*, preface by Frank Lestringant (Lecques: Théétète, 2000), pp. 253–61, 268–77.

9. *Methodus ad facilem historiarum cognitionem* (Paris: M. Le Jeune, 1566), trans. Beatrice Reynolds, *Method for the Easy Comprehension of History* (New York: Columbia University Press, 1945), pp. 334–64; *Colloque entre sept scavans*, pp. 338–9, *Colloquium of the Seven*, pp. 282–3.

10. Michael A. Screech, *Montaigne's Annotated Copy of Lucretius: A Transcription and Study of the Manuscript, Notes and Pen-Marks* (Geneva: Droz, 1998), p. 114.

11. Baruch Canephius (pseud.), *Atheomachie, ou refutation des erreurs et detestables impietez des atheistes, libertins, et autres esprits profanes de ces derniers temps* (Paris: J. Durant, 1582), p. 20; George Hoffmann, "Anatomy of the Mass: Montaigne's 'Of cannibals,'" *Publications of the Modern Language Association of America*, 117/2 (2002), pp. 207–21.

12. Richard Carpenter, *The Soules Sentinel, discovering the sicke-mans devout resolution, grounded upon the unavoydablenesse of death, and the certaintie of the resurrection* (London: W. Hall and J. Beale for A. Garbrand, 1612), p. 76.

13. *L'Academie françoise* (1577), trans. T[homas] B[owes], *The French Academie* (1586; London: G. Bishop, 1594), p. 39; see also Martin Fotherby, "those acute Naturalists, who hold it a servility to be led with brutish-beleeving, and will therefore entertaine no more of Religion then they find to be consenant unto Reason," *Atheomastix: Clearing Foure Truthes, Against Atheists and Infidels* (London: N. Okes, 1622), fol. B2ʳ.

14. Palissy, *La Recepte véritable* (La Rochelle: B. Berton, 1563) and "Des sels divers," *Discours admirables* (Paris: M. Le Jeune, 1580), in *Œuvres complètes de Palissy*, ed. Marie-Madeleine Fragonard et al., 2 vols. (Mont-de-Marsan: Editions Inter Universitaires, 1996), vol. 1, pp. 74–5, vol. 2, pp. 189–92; Bodin, *Universae naturae theatrum*, p. 212, quoted from the translation by Ann Blair, "Annotating and Indexing Natural Philosophy," *Books and the Sciences in History*, ed. Marina Frasca-Spada and Nicholas Jardine (Cambridge, Cambridge University Press, 2000), pp. 69–89, esp. p. 74; and her *The Theater of Nature: Jean Bodin and Renaissance Science* (Princeton: Princeton University Press, 1997).

15. Krzysztof Pomian, *Collectionneurs, amateurs et curieux* (Paris: Gallimard, 1987), trans. Elizabeth Wiles-Portier, *Collectors and Curiosities: Paris and Venice, 1500–1800* (Cambridge: Polity, 1990), pp. 45–9.

16. William A. Wallace, "Traditional Natural Philosophy," *The Cambridge History of Renaissance Philosophy*, ed. Charles B. Schmitt (Cambridge: Cambridge University Press, 1988), pp. 205, 231–3; Harold J. Cook, "Physicians and Natural History," *Cultures of Natural History*, ed. Nicholas Jardine, James A. Secord, and Emma C. Spary (Cambridge: Cambridge University Press, 1996), pp. 91–105.

17. Roger Trinquet, *La Jeunesse de Montaigne: Ses origines familiales, son enfance et ses études* (Paris: Nizet, 1972), pp. 465, 480–87, 514–19, and 544–8; Alain Legros, "Michaelis Montani annotationes decem: Le *Giraldus* de Montaigne et autres livres annotés de sa main," *Journal de la Renaissance*, 1 (2000), pp. 13–88, esp. p. 43.

18. Jean Dupèbe, "Sylvius contre Vésale," *Prosateurs latins en France au XVIᵉ siècle*, ed. Stephen Bamforth et al. (Paris: CNRS, 1987), p. 600; Jacques Dubois, *Introduction sur l'Anatomique Partie de la Phisiologie d'Hippocras et Galien* (Paris: J. Hulpeau, 1555), fol. 1ʳ.

19. *Mémoires inédits de Henri de Mesmes*, ed. Édouard Fremy (Paris: E. Leroux, 1886; Geneva: Slatkine, 1970), p. 141.
20. Alain Legros, "La vie et l'œuvre d'un médecin contemporain de Montaigne, Pierre Pichot," *Revue Française d'Histoire du Livre*, 2nd ser., 92–3 (1996), pp. 361–74. On Fernel's Galenism, see Laurence Brockliss and Colin Jones, *The Medical World of Early Modern France* (Oxford: Oxford University Press, 1997), pp. 129–38.
21. Jean Céard, "Contributions italiennes aux mutations de la médecine selon Montaigne," *Montaigne e L'Italia*, ed. Enea Balmas and Emanuele Kanceff (Geneva: Slatkine, 1991), pp. 229–43.
22. Anna Bettoni, "Cibo e rimedio: I meloni di Montaigne," *Codici del Gusto*, ed. Maria Grazia Profeti (Verona: Francoangeli, 1992), pp. 265–74.
23. Ed. François Rigolot (Paris: Presses Universitaires de France, 1992), pp. 15, 192.
24. Katherine Park, "Natural Particulars: Medical Epistemology Practice, and the Literature of Healing Springs," *Natural Particulars: Nature and the Disciplines in Renaissance Europe*, ed. Anthony Grafton and Nancy G. Siraisi (Cambridge, MA: MIT Press, 1999), pp. 347–67.
25. *Livre des animaux*, in *Œuvres completes*, ed. J. F. Malgaigne, 3 vols. (Paris: J.-B. Ballière, 1840–41), vol. 3, p. 763, trans. Thomas Johnson, *Of Living Creatures*, in *The Workes of that Famous Chirurgion Ambrose Parey* (London: T. Cotes and R. Young, 1634), p. 74.
26. *Les Observations de plusieurs singularitiez et choses memorables* (1553; Anvers: C. Plantin, 1555), fol. πp5$^r$, ed. Alexandra Merle, *Voyage au Levant (1553): Les Observations de Pierre Belon du Mans* (Paris: Chandeigne, 2001), p. 54.
27. *Ibid.*, fol. 4$^r$, p. 75 (1: 6); fol. 86$^r$, p. 165 (1: 52); fol. 186$^v$, pp. 292–3 (2: 34); numbers in parentheses refer to the original edition.
28. For example, Belon remarks of Greek priests who eat no fresh fish during their Lent, "ils sont austeres à observer telles superstitions," *ibid.*, fol. 78$^r$, p. 154 (1: 48); George Huppert, *The Style of Paris: Renaissance Origins* (Bloomington: Indiana University Press, 1999), p. 9.
29. *Response à une epistre commenceant, Seigneur Elvide, où est traitté des massacres faits en France, en l'an 1572* (Basel: M. Cousin, 1574), p. 18.
30. Edwin M. Duval, "Le Début des *Essais* et la fin d'un livre," *Revue d'Histoire Littéraire de la France*, 88/5 (1988), pp. 896–907.
31. Estienne Pasquier, "il n'y a reigle si generale qui ne souffre ses exceptions," undated letter [ca. 1586–8] to Nicolas Brulart, *Les Lettres d'Estienne Pasquier* (Avignon: J. Bramerau, 1590), fol. 418$^r$, *Lettres*

*historiques pour les années 1556–1594,* ed. D[orothy] Thickett (Geneva: Droz, 1966), p. 236.

32. Sachiko Kusukawa, *The Transformation of Natural Philosophy: The Case of Philip Melanchthon* (Cambridge: Cambridge University Press, 1995).
33. See Ian Maclean's magnificent roadmap of Renaissance Galenism, *Logic, Signs and Nature in the Renaissance: The Case of Learned Medicine* (Cambridge: Cambridge University Press, 2002), pp. 276–332.
34. Jean Starobinski, "The Body's Moment," *Montaigne: Essays in Reading,* ed. Gérard Defaux, *Yale French Studies,* 64 (1983), pp. 273–305, revised in *Montaigne en mouvement* (Paris: Gallimard, 1982), pp. 169–222.
35. Ian Hacking, *The Emergence of Probability* (Cambridge: Cambridge University Press, 1995); Barbara J. Shapiro, *Probability and Certainty in Seventeenth-Century England: A Study in the Relationships between Natural Science, Religion, History, Law, and Literature* (Princeton: Princeton University Press, 1983).
36. Maclean, *Logic, Signs and Nature,* pp. 172–6, 335–7.
37. *Ibid.,* pp. 134–8, 146–7, and 246–51.
38. Marcel Conche, "L'unité du chapitre 'Des coches,'" in Claude Blum and François Moureau, eds., *Études montaignistes en hommage à Pierre Michel* (Geneva: Slatkine, 1984), pp. 89–94, reprinted in *Montaigne et la philosophie* (Villers-sur-Mer: Mégare, 1987), pp. 129–34.
39. *Montaigne* (Bern: A. Francke, 1949), p. 91; trans. Dawn Eng, ed. Philippe Desan (Berkeley: University of California Press, 1991), p. 69.
40. *Montaigne philosophe* (Paris: Presses Universitaires de France, 1996), p. 66.
41. *Les Œuvres morales et meslees* (Paris: M. de Vascosan, 1572), fol. 121$^v$.
42. *Traité de la constance et consolation,* p. 140; trans. *A Buckler against Adversitie,* p. 75.
43. Nicholas Davidson, "Atheism in Italy, 1500–1700," in Michael Hunter and David Wootton, eds., *Atheism from the Reformation to the Enlightenment* (Oxford: Oxford University Press, 1992), pp. 55–85, esp. pp. 59, 75.
44. Robert Bartlett, *England Under the Norman and Angevin Kings, 1075–1225* (Oxford: Oxford University Press, 2000), p. 478.
45. See, also, George Hoffmann, "Monsters and Modal Logic among French Naturalists of the Renaissance," in Ullrich Langer and Philippe Desan, eds., *Reason, Reasoning, and Literature in the Renaissance* (*South Central Review,* 10/2 (1993), pp. 32–48.
46. Collected in vol. 3 of Simon Goulart, *Mémoires de la Ligue, contenant les évenemens les plus remarquables depuis 1576, jusqu'à la*

*paix accordée entre le roi de France & le roi d'Espagne, en 1598*, 6 vols. (Amsterdam: Arkstée & Merkus, 1758). See Nancy G. Siraisi on the development of "medical narrative" in *The Clock and the Mirror: Girolamo Cardano and Renaissance Medicine* (Princeton: Princeton University Press, 1997), pp. 195–213.

47. Jules Vuillemin, *Nécessité ou contingence: l'Aporie de Diodore et les systèmes philosophiques* (Paris: Éditions de Minuit, 1984).

48. Sextus opposes causal explanation by arguments based on infinite regress (*Outlines of Pyrrhonism*, III.5.24; III.10.67), the inability to find independent confirmation of sensory perceptions (*Against the Logicians*, II.49–50; *Outlines of Pyrrhonism*, III.7.38), and relational paradoxes (*Against the Physicists*, I.207–67; *Outlines of Pyrrhonism*, I.17.180–85; III.5.25–9).

49. Hans Blumenberg, *Die Legitimität der Neuzeit* (1966; Frankfurt: Suhrkamp, 1973), trans. Robert M. Wallace, *The Legitimacy of the Modern Age* (Cambridge, MA: MIT Press, 1983), p. 170; on the swerve as a mathematical definition of the *minimum*, and Lucretian atomism as a sort of differential calculus, see Michel Serres, *La Naissance de la physique dans le texte de Lucrèce: fleuves et turbulences* (Paris: Éditions de Minuit, 1977).

50. Ullrich Langer, *Divine and Poetic Freedom in the Renaissance: Nominalist Theology and Literature in France and Italy* (Princeton: Princeton University Press, 1990), p. 187.

51. "Perhaps Montaigne's vaunted cultural relativism might be better known as cultural atomism," Eric MacPhail, "Montaigne's New Epicureanism," *Montaigne Studies*, 12/1–2 (2000), p. 98.

52. Blumenberg, *The Legitimacy of the Modern Age*, pp. 263–77; Pierre Hadot, *Qu'est-ce que la philosophie antique?* (Paris: Gallimard, 1995), trans. Michael Chase, *What Is Ancient Philosophy?* (Cambridge, MA: Harvard University Press, 2002).

53. Rémi Brague, *La Sagesse du monde: Histoire de l'expérience humaine de l'univers* (Paris: Fayard, 1999).

54. Stephen Gaukroger, *Descartes: An Intellectual Biography* (Oxford: Oxford University Press, 1995), pp. 158–72.

# 10   Montaigne and skepticism

Montaigne has been called the founder of modern skepticism. According to this view, he was the first to put forward in a compelling way the arguments of ancient skepticism that had been rediscovered in the sixteenth century. The "Apology for Raymond Sebond," Montaigne's longest and most explicitly philosophical essay, presents the skeptical case in a sympathetic way and that presentation has been taken to express Montaigne's own philosophical position. But is Montaigne a skeptic? Is his philosophical stance a reappropriation of ancient skepticism or is he rather a profoundly original philosopher who in some way incorporates a skeptical tone or "moment" within his own original thought?

## ANCIENT SKEPTICISM

The history of ancient skepticism spans five centuries, from the third century B.C. to approximately 200 A.D. Skepticism was not, however, one continuous philosophical movement or school. Rather, there were two forms of skepticism, the Pyrrhonian and the Academic. Pyrrho of Elis, the first skeptic, left no writings, so that what we know of him comes through his disciple Timon and Diogenes Laertius' *Life of Pyrrho*. Academic skepticism emerged out of Plato's Academy when Arcesilaus became head of the Academy in the third century B.C. The Academic skeptics were inspired by the Socratic dialectic of some of the earlier dialogues. Carneades became head of the Academy in the mid-second century B.C. and continued the skeptical tradition there. Aenesidemus broke away from the New Academy and founded a movement based on a revival of Pyrrhonism. The participants in this movement became known in the mid-first century A.D. as 'Skeptics' (searchers or inquirers) and the teachings of this later Pyrrhonism are presented by Sextus Empiricus in his *Outlines of Pyrrhonism*.[1] Our most important sources for knowledge of ancient scepticism are Cicero's *Academica*, Diogenes Laertius' *Life of Pyrrho*, and Sextus' *Outlines* and *Adversus mathematicos*. These works were practically unknown throughout the Latin Middle Ages, but were recovered in the Renaissance. In particular, Henri Estienne published a translation of Sextus' *Outlines* in 1562 and this title appears in the catalogue of Montaigne's books.[2]

Pyrrho expresses the skeptical position in terms of three teachings: we can know nothing of the nature of things; hence, the right attitude towards them is to withhold judgment; the necessary result of withholding judgment is imperturbability (*ataraxia*).[3] Academic skeptics engaged in the practice of argument in order to achieve suspension of judgment, whereas Pyrrho's tranquil indifference was not based on argument.[4] But differences such as these do not affect the more basic agreement on imperturbability as the goal and suspension of judgment as the means to that goal.[5]

Suspension of judgment involves especially judgments concerning good and evil because these are the kinds of judgments that give rise to torment and disturbance in the soul.[6] How, then, does the skeptic conduct his life? According to Sextus, "we live in an undogmatic way by following the laws, customs, and natural affections."[7] The skeptic, in other words, acquiesces in the customs and traditions of his society, not because he judges them to be inherently good but because he has abandoned any inquiry into what is good or bad by nature.

## MONTAIGNE'S SKEPTICISM

The claim that Montaigne is a skeptic does find support in the *Essays*, both in their form and in their content. The essay form itself is non-dogmatic and non-authoritative. There is also an undeniably skeptical tone, a "common sense" skepticism that is often made explicit in the *Essays*: "when some new doctrine is offered to us, we have great occasion to distrust it, and to consider that before it was produced its opposite was in vogue; and, as it was overthrown by this one, there may arise in the future a third invention that will likewise smash the second" (II.12, F429, V570). This kind of healthy commonsense skepticism also has important practical consequences especially evident in Montaigne's attitude toward accusations of sorcery and witchcraft: "To kill men, we should have sharp and luminous evidence; and our life is too real and essential to vouch for these supernatural and fantastic accidents" (III.11, F789, V1031).

Montaigne often recommends moderation based on past experience of one's mistaken beliefs. This skepticism is a version of the recognition of one's ignorance and it extends even to one's speech: "I like these words which soften and moderate the rashness of our propositions: 'perhaps,' 'to some extent,' 'some,' 'they say,' 'I think,' and the like." If he had children to educate, he would teach them to speak this way, preferring that they keep "the manner of learners at sixty than to represent learned doctors at ten" (III.11, F788, V1030).

The most important evidence for the claim that Montaigne is a skeptic is his longest, most famous, and most conventionally philosophical essay, the "Apology for Raymond Sebond." Sebond was a Spanish theologian of the fifteenth century whose book, entitled *Natural Theology* or *Book of Creatures*, was given to Montaigne's father who asked his son to translate it from Latin into French. Montaigne did so and then wrote the "Apology" as a response to two criticisms commonly made of this and other such works in natural theology.

In his prologue, Sebond claims that God has revealed himself clearly in two books: in the Bible and in Nature. Sebond holds that man can know the truth about God and himself, insofar as it is possible for natural reason to know it, by reading these truths in the book of Nature. In this book of Nature, each creature is like a letter, and man himself is the main, the capital letter. The two objections to Sebond that Montaigne addresses in the "Apology" are: first, that Christians do themselves harm in trying to support their belief by human reason (II.12, F321, V440); second, that Sebond's arguments are weak and unfit to prove what he proposes (II.12, F327, V448).

Montaigne tells us at the beginning of the "Apology" that Sebond's *Natural Theology* was given to his father at the time "when the innovations of Luther were beginning to gain favor and to shake our old belief in many places" (II.12, F320, V439). The intellectual crisis brought on by the Reformation coincided, then, with the rediscovery and revival of the arguments of the ancient skeptics, and so skepticism was available as a means for combating the innovations of the

reformers.[8] Since the reformers combat established theological arguments with their own counter-arguments, reason shows itself to be
powerless to settle theological disputes. Therefore, the traditional,
i.e., Catholic, side finds an ally in skepticism, especially in the skeptical determination to submit to custom. This solution might be
characterized as "conformist fideism" or "skeptical fideism."[9] The
skeptic may either truly believe (without reasons) or he may simply
conform for the sake of tranquility. Montaigne has been interpreted
in both ways.

In the reply to the second objection, Montaigne answers the attack
on Sebond's reasons with an attack on reason itself. Human reason is "so lame and so blind that there is nothing so clear and
easy as to be clear enough to her . . . that all subjects alike, and
nature in general, disavow her jurisdiction and mediation" (II.12,
F328, V449). The reply moves through several increasingly skeptical
stages. First, Montaigne attacks man's presumption that he is "master and emperor of the universe" by comparing him to the animals
with respect to the intellectual capacities that are supposed to prove
his superiority (II.12, F329, V450). This detailed examination of animal behavior (derived mostly from ancient sources) establishes the
fact of animal intelligence, especially through the principle "from
like effects, we must infer like causes." Man wants to equal himself
to God on account of his reason: the comparison with the animals
shows that he is really no better than the brutes.

Second, Montaigne deepens the attack on human presumption
and vanity by showing that philosophy and learning do not make us
either happy or good. "We have strangely overpaid for this fine reason that we glory in, and this capacity to judge and know, if we have
bought it at the price of this infinite number of passions to which
we are incessantly prey" (II.12, F358, V486). Ignorance and simplicity
actually succeed better than reason in producing tranquility of soul
and virtuous conduct. This praise of ignorance and simplicity leads
Montaigne into the third stage of his attack on reason, a stage that is
more explicitly skeptical than the preceding ones. He turns to consider "man in his highest estate," the philosophers who, more than
anyone else, ought to be able to assure us of the power of human
reason. Montaigne identifies three types of philosophers: the dogmatists (Peripatetics, Epicureans, and Stoics) who believe they have
found knowledge; the Academic skeptics (such as Clitomachus and

Carneades) who despair of the quest for knowledge; and Pyrrho and the other skeptics who say they are still in search of the truth.

It is here at this third stage of the attack on reason that we find Montaigne's detailed and sympathetic account of Pyrrho and of the teachings of Pyrrhonian skepticism.[10] Montaigne's own personal emblem, a scale with the motto "What do I know?" suggests the skeptical suspension of judgment and is meant to capture the desirability of the skeptical mode of speech, best expressed by the interrogative rather than the affirmative (II.12, F393, V527). The way he concludes his full and sympathetic account of skepticism lends itself to the view that he is a skeptic and even a Christian skeptic:

There is nothing of man's invention that has so much verisimilitude and usefulness [as Pyrrhonism]. It presents man naked and empty, acknowledging his natural weakness, fit to receive from above some outside power; stripped of human knowledge, and all the more apt to lodge divine knowledge in himself, annihilating his judgment to make more room for faith; neither disbelieving nor setting up any doctrine against the common observances; humble, obedient, teachable, zealous; a sworn enemy of heresy, and consequently free from the vain and irreligious opinions introduced by false sects. He is a blank tablet prepared to take from the finger of God such forms as he shall be pleased to engrave on it. (II.12, F375, V506)

Montaigne's strategy at this stage of the attack on reason is the skeptical practice of showing the variety and contradiction of philosophical opinion. He begins by considering "divine things," especially philosophical opinion on the nature of the divinity. At one point, he presents a list of more than twenty-seven different opinions on what the divine must be. "The clatter of so many philosophical brains" shows that man has attained no knowledge in the sphere of divine things (II.12, F383, V516). He then turns to consider philosophical opinion on "human and natural things," especially the human body and soul. The display of the variety of opinions – some of them plausible and some bizarre – leads to the same conclusion: man has attained no knowledge, not even about what is closest to him, his own self.

Now Montaigne enters the fourth and most devastating stage of his attack on reason, an attack which he refers to as a "final fencer's trick," an "extreme remedy," and a "desperate stroke." An attack on the very foundations of knowledge is an attack on the possibility of knowledge as such and not simply a denial of all existing claims to knowledge based on philosophical disagreement. At this extreme, Montaigne says, one must ruin oneself in order to ruin one's opponent (II.12, F418–19, V558). Before initiating this final and fatal skirmish, Montaigne again praises the Pyrrhonian skeptics: their position is both "bolder and more plausible" than that of the skeptics who admit the authority of probability and allow the judgment to incline toward one probability rather than another (II.12, F422, V561). He is setting the scene for the most thorough-going doubt that leaves standing no criterion for the distinction between true and false.

The soul has no way to distinguish between truth and falsehood because error is received into the soul by the same road and in the same manner as truth. Things do not lodge in us in their own form and essence: if they did, we would all receive them in the same way. For example, wine would taste the same to the healthy and the sick man. In fact, however, there is nothing in the world that is believed by all men with universal consent. Even within one and the same man, opinions change, sometimes because the judgment is affected by the changing condition of the body and of the passions of the soul itself. "If my touchstone is found to be ordinarily false, and my scales uneven and incorrect," what possible assurance can I have that what I believe so firmly at this moment is actually true? (II.12, F423, V563). What is chiefly at issue here is the veracity of the senses. "The schools that dispute man's knowledge dispute it principally because of the uncertainty and weakness of our senses; for since all knowledge comes to us by their means and mediation, if they err in the report they make to us . . . we have nothing left to go by" (II.12, F446, V590–91).

Montaigne presents at least six arguments which radically undermine the claim that the senses are the reliable foundations of knowledge. First, it is not certain, nor can it be established, that man is provided with all of the senses that would be necessary to know the world. "For if any one sense is lacking, our reason cannot discover its absence. It is the privilege of the senses to be the extreme limit of our perception. There is nothing beyond them that can help us to discover them; no, nor can one sense discover the other" (II.12, F444, V588). Second, we have no warrant to believe that our senses alone need to be consulted, for the animals also have senses and often keener ones than ours. Third, in order to base our judgments on the senses, we ought to be in agreement first with the animals and then among ourselves. But this is never the case: some people, for example, have senses that are dim while others have sharp senses. Fourth, our senses interfere with each other, e.g., sight and touch can give contrary impressions. Fifth, there can be no judge in disputes about the senses. "To judge the appearances that we receive of objects, we would need a judicatory instrument; to verify this instrument, we need a demonstration; to verify the demonstration, an instrument: there we are in a circle" (II.12, F454, V600–01). Finally, our senses do not comprehend the objects but only their own impressions: the impressions and the objects are different things. Therefore, we cannot claim that the impressions resemble the objects for we have no way to verify this resemblance. "How can the soul and understanding make sure of this resemblance, having of itself no communication with foreign objects?" (II.12, F454, V601).

This series of arguments attacking the reliability of the senses as the foundation of knowledge culminates in the metaphysical claim that all things – both ourselves and the objects we seek to know – are constantly changing. "Thus nothing certain can be established about one thing by another, both the judging and the judged being in continual change and motion" (II.12, F455, V601). The "Apology" concludes with the assertion that only faith can raise man above his humanity to communication with the eternal. This turn from skepticism to faith is the principal ground for the view that Montaigne is a skeptic–fideist.

The skeptical features of the reply to the second objection, especially the arguments based on the variety and contradiction of philosophical opinion and the arguments undermining the reliability of the senses, are standard skeptical strategies. Many of the arguments attacking the senses as the foundation of knowledge appear, implicitly or explicitly, in Descartes' Meditations, and so Montaigne has been seen as the predecessor of Descartes, providing the skeptical challenge that Descartes meets by shifting the ground of certitude from the senses to the mind.

Most of those who regard Montaigne as a skeptic do, however, acknowledge that there are decidedly non-skeptical features of his thought which are at least difficult to reconcile with a thoroughgoing self-conscious skepticism. First, within the "Apology" itself, we find instances of what appears to be an astonishing credulity. In their introduction to the "Apology," the editors Villey and Saulnier assure us that this essay contains numerous borrowings from the skeptics and presents unequivocal statements of Montaigne's adherence to Pyrrhonism. But then they must try to explain Montaigne's comparison between man and the animals in the reply to the second objection. Here he presents numerous stories, many of which appear to be fabulous and he seems to simply accept these stories. Villey and Saulnier attempt to account for this credulity:

> If in . . . (the comparison of man with the animals) one is astonished at finding so little of that critical sense, of which Montaigne shows so much in other parts of the same essay, one should not forget that these stories were guaranteed by the authority of Plutarch, from whom they are borrowed often almost verbatim, and that most of these legends were accepted without reserve by the scholars of the 16<sup>th</sup> century. (V437)

So, Montaigne's uncritical reporting of these stories, his apparent credulity, cannot really be reconciled with the otherwise overwhelmingly skeptical tone of the essay. Montaigne's credulity, his openness to the testimony of both the learned and the simple, is one of the most pervasive features of the essays. Certainly, he is not entirely uncritical and he occasionally rejects judgments made by historians. Nevertheless, he admits into the realm of the possible many reports that are at best highly improbable.

Second, Montaigne does make judgments whereas one of the fundamental teachings of the skeptical school is the suspension of judgment. In fact, this point was made not long after Montaigne's death by Guillaume Béranger in response to the claim that Montaigne was a Pyrrhonist, a claim which appeared in the 1662 Port-Royal *Logique*. Béranger observes that the *Essays* contain extensive discussions of *forming* the judgment.[11]

Third, Montaigne does not pursue the skeptical goal of imperturbability. On the contrary, he emphasizes and seems graciously to accept his changeability and mutability. Not only is he affected and moved by circumstances, he is inherently unstable and immersed in the flow of time.

Fourth, Montaigne's project in the *Essays* can be properly described as the project of self-knowledge. In that respect, he appears to be Socratic rather than skeptical. For Socrates, the examined life is the only fully human life. As the often-cited example of Pyrrho's unperturbed pig suggests, "the Skeptic way of life is the deliberately unexamined life."[12]

Fifth, Montaigne does appear at least to profess the Catholic faith. Indeed, the "Apology for Sebond" is ostensibly a defense of the Catholic faith against the attacks of atheists. But the very nature of that defense has given rise to widely divergent interpretations concerning Montaigne's sincerity in matters of faith, for the attack on reason carried out in the reply to the second objection is in fact a double-edged sword: at the same time that it destroys the presumption of the atheists, it undercuts Sebond's project of a rational defense of the faith. On account of this apparently ambiguous stance toward reason and theology, Montaigne has been described as an atheist or agnostic who veils his atheism so as to avoid persecution or because he recognizes the value of religion for social stability, as a skeptic–fideist who accepts the impotence of reason on the philosophical level and who therefore believes without reasons, and as a conformist skeptic–fideist who "argues that faith is best understood as one form of the undogmatic participation recommended by the classical Pyrrhonists."[13] The view that Montaigne is a skeptic–fideist is, of course, an attempt to reconcile his presumed skepticism with his apparently sincere expressions of religious belief.

### SKEPTICISM TRANSFORMED

Either Montaigne is an inconsistent thinker, incorporating contradictory and incompatible philosophical views within an ultimately incoherent and ill-defined literary work, or he is an original philosopher, transcending the boundaries of the classical–Christian tradition. In fact, Montaigne anticipated the learned reaction to what looks like a jumble of borrowings from ancient authors: "And I let fly my caprices all the more freely in public, inasmuch as, although they are born with me and without a model, I know that they will find their relation to some ancient humor; and someone will not fail to say: 'That is where he got it!' " It is here also that we find Montaigne's own characterization of himself as an original philosopher:

My *mœurs*[14] are natural; I have not called in the help of any teaching to build them. But feeble as they are, when the desire to tell them seized me, and when, to make them appear in public a little more decently, I set myself to support them with reasons and examples, it was a marvel to myself to find them, simply by chance, in conformity with so many philosophical examples and reasons. What rule my life belonged to, I did not learn until after it was completed and spent. A new figure: an unpremeditated and accidental philosopher! (II.12, F409, V546)

Within this account of his moment of self-discovery, Montaigne displays the very movement of thought that is the essence of his unpremeditated and accidental philosophy. That movement of thought is dialectical, beginning in pre-philosophical consciousness, ascending to philosophical articulation, and returning in amazement to its beginnings. It is within this dialectical movement of thought that the skeptical aspects of the *Essays* can be seen as both integral and transformed. I will go through the five non-skeptical features of Montaigne's thought discussed above so as to set out the dialectic that is at work in the *Essays* with respect to each. In this way, the skeptical moment and its transformation will become visible.

First, then, how are we to reconcile Montaigne's skepticism with his credulity? As he does in the "Apology," so also in "Of the Power of the Imagination," Montaigne repeats many stories that are or at least may be fabulous. But at the end of that essay, he says quite plainly that he is well aware of what he is doing and he gives some hints as to why he does it. After reporting stories about a cat who, by its gaze alone, caused a bird to fall from a tree and about a falconer who brought down a bird from the air by the power of his gaze, Montaigne writes: "At least, so they say, – for I refer the stories that I borrow to the conscience of those from whom I take them" (I.21, F75, V105). In spite of the fact that he himself is not certain of the truth of the stories, he reports them and even uses them as material on which to reflect and as examples from which to draw conclusions. Montaigne provides this explanation:

In the study that I am making of our *mœurs* and motions of the soul, fabulous testimonies, provided they are possible, serve like true ones. Whether they have happened or not, in Paris or Rome, to John or Peter, this is always some human potentiality of which I am usefully advised by the telling. I see it and profit from it equally in shadow as in substance . . . There are authors whose end is to tell what has happened. Mine, if I knew how to attain it, would be to talk about what is possible to happen. (I.21, F75, V105–6)

In the "Defense of Seneca and Plutarch," Montaigne defends Plutarch against an accusation that Jean Bodin makes in his *Method of History*. Bodin accuses Plutarch of "writing incredible and entirely fabulous things" (II.32, F546, V722). Montaigne concludes his defense of Plutarch against Bodin's accusation in this way:

We must not judge what is possible and what is not, according to what is credible and incredible to our sense . . . It is a great error and yet one into which most men fall . . . to balk at believing about others what they themselves could not do – or would not do. It seems to each man that the ruling pattern of nature is in himself; to this he refers all other forms as to a touchstone. The ways that do not square with his are counterfeit and artificial. What brutish stupidity! (II.32, F548, V725)

The skeptical act with respect to human testimony is the initial suspension of the judgment that what I am hearing is impossible because it is incredible, and incredible because unfamiliar. It is an act of openness to the possible, to the unfamiliar. Montaigne's credulity *is*, in this sense, his skepticism.

Montaigne refers to our presumption as "our first and original malady" (II.12, F330, V452). Our presumption is the first and most persistent obstacle to wisdom. Thus, it is presumption with which the activity of philosophy must first come to terms and where its skeptical moment must occur. The skeptical moment is not immediate disbelief but precisely the refusal simply to dismiss what is not familiar, what is not immediately recognized as being like us. Montaigne's skepticism, then, is not the doubt of the ancient skeptics but rather an openness to what is possible and an overcoming of presumption at the deepest level. Montaigne incorporates the transformed skeptical act into his own mode of thought. With respect to the animal stories which occur in the most skeptical part of the "Apology," Montaigne tells us that he would not have spent so much time on the long list of stories if it were not for the fact that we prefer, in some sense, what is foreign and strange. He would not need to go collecting stories from foreign lands and centuries, for he says: "in my opinion, whoever would observe up close what we see ordinarily of the animals who live among us, would find there facts just as wonderful as those we go collecting in remote countries and centuries." In the course of the list of animal stories from Chrysippus, Plutarch, and others, he mentions the astonishing tricks that mountebanks teach their dogs. Then he says:

but I observe with more amazement the behavior, which is nevertheless quite common, of the dogs that blind men use both in the fields and in town; I have noticed how they stop at certain doors where they have been accustomed to receive alms, how they avoid being hit by coaches and carts . . . I have seen one, along a town ditch, leave a smooth flat path and take a worse one, to keep his master away from the ditch. (II.12, F340, V463)

The movement of Montaigne's thought is first to open us to the possibility of the strange and foreign, then lead us back to the familiar and let us see the extraordinary in the ordinary, in the familiar and the common.

The second non-skeptical aspect of the *Essays* concerns the fact that Montaigne makes definitive moral judgments throughout the *Essays*, whereas the skeptics seek to suspend judgment. The passage in which Montaigne describes himself as an accidental philosopher reveals something of the dialectical movement of thought as it pertains to moral judgment. He desires to express his pre-philosophical *mœurs* or ways of being. In order to do this, he turns to philosophy and then discovers that his life conforms to many philosophical examples and discourses. Thus, he is a new figure. The dialectic is circular: he returns to his pre-philosophical starting points. Yet something new has been introduced, something philosophical. The transformed skeptical moment, an openness to possibility, allows for the moral innovation that is one of the most important purposes of the *Essays*.

On the one hand, Montaigne often insists that his *mœurs* are just what he learned in the nursery. His judgments thus seem to affirm simply what was there from the beginning. On the other hand, the *Essays* introduce a new possibility of moral character. In "Of Vanity," Montaigne says that his *mœurs* are "a bit new and unusual" (III.9, F749, V980). And in "Of Drunkenness," he complains about the traditional ranking of vices:

Confusion about the order and measurement of sins is dangerous. Murderers, traitors, tyrants, gain too much by it. It is not right that their conscience should be relieved because some other man is indolent, or lascivious, or less assiduous in his devotions. Each man lays weight on his neighbor's sin and

lightens his own. Even our teachers often rank sins badly, in my opinion.
(II.2, *F*244–5, *V*340)

The very passages in which he affirms his beginnings are the passages which reveal his innovations, the way in which his *mœurs*
are "a bit new and unusual," and the way he reorders the virtues
and vices. Cruelty is the extreme of all the vices (II.11, *F*313, *V*429).
Truth is the foundation of virtue (II.17, *F*491, *V*647–8). Montaigne
does not make a radical break with the moral tradition of the virtues
but neither does he simply acquiesce in the authority of custom.

The same can be said of his political views. There is indeed an
inherently conservative tendency in skepticism. Because the skeptic
has abandoned any hope of discovering what is truly good or evil, he
submits undogmatically to the customs and institutions of society.
Attempts at radical reform are actually dangerous because

nothing presses a state hard except innovation; change alone lends shape to
injustice and tyranny. When some part is dislocated, we can prop it up; we
can fight against letting the alteration and corruption natural to all things
carry us too far from our beginnings and principles. But to undertake to recast
so great a mass, to change the foundations of so great a structure, that is a
job for those who wipe out a picture in order to clean it, who want to reform
defects of detail by universal confusion and cure illness by death. (III.9, *F*731,
*V*958)

On the other hand, he also reveals an openness to change. In the
very place where he says that the best thing he could do as mayor was
"to conserve and endure," he qualifies this by adding that innovation
"is forbidden in these times, when we are hard pressed and have to
defend ourselves mainly against innovations" (III.10, *F*783, *V*1023).
That is, he implies that there are times when innovation is not to be
feared. In "Of Custom," there is the suggestion that habit can work
against change that is beneficial:

Nations brought up to liberty and to ruling themselves consider any other
form of government monstrous and contrary to nature. Those who are accustomed to monarchy do the same. And whatever easy chance fortune offers
them to change, even when with great difficulties they have rid themselves
of the importunity of one master, they run to supplant him with another,
with similar difficulties, because they cannot make up their minds to hate
domination itself. (I.23, *F*83–4, *V*116)

The change that is described approvingly is in the direction of liberty. In the course of discussing the license that he takes in his new form of writing, Montaigne provides a remarkable formulation of his intention: "God grant that this excessive license of mine may encourage our men to attain freedom, rising above these cowardly and hypocritical virtues born of our imperfections" (III.5, F642, V845). Montaigne is keeping open the possibility of something like the Roman republic. He is highly skeptical of projects of rational reform, but the transformed skeptical moment is this openness to the possibility of the unpredictable chance for freedom. The seizing of the chance moment is the object of his accidental philosophy.

The third non-skeptical feature of the *Essays* that must be accounted for in terms of circular dialectic is the way in which Montaigne's goal differs from the skeptical goal of imperturbability. All three forms of Hellenistic philosophy share the same goal, although each strives to achieve it in a different way. Stoic immovability, Epicurean apathy, and skeptical imperturbability are all versions of the divine *stasis* and thus are attempts to escape the temporality and changeability that are integral to the human condition.

Montaigne explicitly rejects the Epicurean version of the divine *stasis:*

Crantor was quite right to combat the apathy of Epicurus, if it was built so deep that even the approach and birth of evils were lacking. I have no praise for the insensibility that is neither possible nor desirable. I am glad not to be sick; but if I am, I want to know I am; and if they cauterize or incise me, I want to feel it. In truth, he who would eradicate the knowledge of evil would at the same time extirpate the knowledge of pleasure, and in fine would annihilate man: *this insensibility does not come without a great price: inhumanity of the soul, torpor of the body* [Cicero]. (II.12, F364, V493)

One of the ways in which Montaigne takes up the issue of imperturbability is in terms of the inconstancy of human action: the constancy and consistency that is the essence of philosophical unchangeability is an extremely rare and difficult achievement. Readers of the *Essays* have long recognized the similarity between the first essay of book I, "By Diverse Means we Arrive at the Same End," and the first essay of book II, "Of the Inconstancy of our Actions." Villey and Saulnier maintain that Montaigne places these essays first because the theme of inconstancy is especially important for him (V7). But the first essay of book III, "Of the Useful and the Honorable," does not seem to continue this pattern. There is, however, a dialectical movement that unites the first essays of all three books.

"By Diverse Means we Arrive at the Same End" begins with the observation that "the most common way of softening the hearts of those we have offended" when they have us at their mercy is to move them to pity by our submission. However, it has sometimes happened that defiance and steadfastness have achieved the same effect and have moved the avenger to mercy. He tells three stories of conquering princes whose hearts were softened by the spectacle of heroic resistance. Montaigne then turns to himself: "Either one of these two ways would easily win me, for I am wonderfully lax in the direction of mercy and gentleness. As a matter of fact, I believe I should be likely to surrender more naturally to compassion than to esteem. Yet to the Stoics pity is a vicious passion; they want us to succor the afflicted, but not to unbend and sympathize with them" (I.1, F4, V8). As the contrast with Stoic immovability emphasizes, Montaigne is easily moved. In this first essay, Montaigne also introduces the theme of inconstancy: "Truly man is a marvelously vain, diverse, and undulating object. It is hard to found any constant and uniform judgment on him" (I.1, F5, V9).

Inconsistency is the explicit theme of essay II.1. Montaigne finds it strange to see intelligent men trying to find consistency in human action since "irresolution seems to me the most common and apparent vice of our nature" and "nothing is harder for me than to believe in men's consistency, nothing easier than to believe in their inconsistency" (II.1, F239, V332). Montaigne concludes this essay on the same subject with which he began: "In view of this, a sound intellect will refuse to judge men simply by their outward actions; we must probe the inside and discover what springs (ressorts) set men in motion" (II.1, F244, V338).

Essay III.1, "Of the Useful and the Honorable," does not appear to take up the theme of inconstancy in the direct manner we find in I.1 and II.1. But in the course of his discussion of dishonorable actions, Montaigne tells us a good deal about himself, especially his conduct as negotiator between princes. "This whole procedure of mine is just a bit dissonant from our ways" (III.1, F603, V795). It is here that we see the third moment of the dialectical movement. "And if anyone follows and watches me closely, I will concede him the victory if he does not confess that there is no rule in their school that could reproduce this natural movement and maintain a picture of liberty and license so constant and inflexible on such tortuous and varied paths, and that all their attention and ingenuity could not bring them to it . . . The way of truth is one and simple . . ." (III.1, F600, V791). The standard of reason cannot capture Montaigne's lower kind of constancy which he describes as "the way of truth."

In essay I.1, we do find the theme of the inconstancy of men but we also find there Montaigne's marvelous laxity in the direction of mercy and gentleness. That is, the assertion that he is easily moved is, at the same time, the assertion that he is invariably merciful. His marvelous laxity is accidentally conformed to Stoic philosophical constancy. Thus, his constancy is there from the beginning and is brought out dialectically in the ascent to philosophical reason in essay II.1 and the descent to "the way of truth" in essay III.1.

Montaigne's moral consistency in some way resembles but is not the same as philosophical imperturbability. His consistency is compatible with being easily moved and with "liberty and license." Further, his kind of consistency is not achieved through skeptical suspension of judgment but through discovering the truth that was already there in his pre-philosophical starting points. His consistency, then, might be characterized as a kind of integrity that is simply and fully human, rather than as an attempt to achieve the divine *stasis*.

The fourth non-skeptical aspect of the *Essays* that must be explained dialectically is the search for self-knowledge. From the very beginning of the *Essays*, Montaigne makes it clear that the object of his study is himself, that whatever the title or topic of any given essay might be, it is really always himself that he seeks to understand. In this respect, he is more Socratic than skeptic. Montaigne's essay form can be located, in some sense, in the tradition of the dialogue, for the essay displays a kind of inner dialogue, bringing in many voices through quotation of the learned and expression of common opinion. But, in the end, it is always thought itself and the thinker himself that are the real focus of attention. It was said that Socrates brought philosophy down from the heavens and into the cities of men. Montaigne says: "I study myself more than any other subject. That is my metaphysics, that is my physics" (III.13, F821, V1072). What is more, "I dare not only to speak of myself, but to speak only of myself; I go astray when I write of anything else, and get away from my subject" (III.8, F720, V942).

The circular dialectic of accidental philosophy is the dialectic of self-knowledge. Thought returns to the most familiar: it is precisely the most familiar that is most difficult to see. The account of the essay form presented by Michael Oakeshott explains this mode of thought as a dialectical process involving ignorance and knowledge. The essay is the form taken by philosophical reflection that sees itself as "the adventure of one who seeks to understand in other terms what he already understands."[15] Philosophical thought springs from the paradox that we know and, at the same time, we are ignorant.

All reflection begins with something assumed to be known, but in reflection what is assumed to be known is assumed also not to be known. We begin with knowledge which is nevertheless assumed to be ignorance . . . In short, reflection presupposes doubt but not universal doubt . . . The process in reflection is *dialectical*, a process of considering something recognized as knowledge and supposed to be true, yet considering it with the assumption that it is not true.[16]

There is, indeed, a skeptical moment here, but it is a moment within a dialectical process that reveals the truth that was already present in the familiar starting points.

What is essential to the essay form, as invented and practiced by Montaigne, is that it allows for chance. Montaigne writes: "I take the first subject that chance offers. They are all equally good to me" (I.50, F219, V302). They are all equally good because they all lead back to himself, not according to a deliberate method but by accident: "This also happens to me: that I do not find myself in the place where I look; and I find myself more by chance encounter than by searching my judgment" (I.10, F26–7, V40). In "Of Prognostications," Montaigne refers to the daemon of Socrates as an impulse of the will that was instinctive and not dependent on reason. "Everyone feels within himself some likeness of such stirrings of a prompt, vehement, and accidental opinion. It is my business to give them some authority, since I give so little to our wisdom" (I.11, F29–30, V44). It is impossible to give authority to the accidental through a method since the accidental is unpredictable.

Thus, we have seen that in the passage where he tells us that he is an unpremeditated and accidental philosopher, this discovery is a surprise, an unexpected and unpredictable revelation of himself. Montaigne's "self" is not present in the *Essays* as "substance" or "subjectivity." It is present just as the most familiar. That is why the circular dialectic comes back to himself and why, in the end, he wonders most at himself: "I have seen no more evident monstrosity and miracle in the world than myself. We become accustomed to anything strange by custom and time; but the more I frequent myself and know myself, the more my deformity astonishes me, and the less I understand myself" (III.11, F787, V1029).

Merleau-Ponty notes that the words "strange," "absurd," "monster," and "miracle" are the words that recur most frequently when Montaigne speaks of man.[17] The self is, in the end, "the place of all obscurities, the mystery of all mysteries."[18] Montaigne, he says, puts "not self-satisfied understanding but a consciousness astonished at itself at the core of human existence."[19]

The fifth non-skeptical aspect of the *Essays* is Montaigne's Catholic faith. In addition to his many references to the content of faith, e.g., the resurrection of the body, Montaigne also professes obedience to the Church even in his thoughts and writings. As I noted above, many commentators hold that these professions of faith and obedience are insincere, that Montaigne is really an atheist or skeptic who hides his true beliefs for his own protection or for the sake of social stability. The evidence for the claim that he is an atheist or skeptic rests principally on his reply to the second objection against Sebond's natural theology. In general, those who believe that Montaigne is sincere in his professions of faith maintain that he is a fideist or a skeptic–fideist, i.e., that he is a skeptic on the philosophical level and a believer who believes simply, without any support from reason.

The first objection to Sebond's theology is put forward in the name of piety by those who think of themselves as believers. They say that "Christians do themselves harm in trying to support their belief by human reasons, since it is conceived only by faith and by a particular inspiration of divine grace" (II.12, F321, V440). The second objection is put forward by unbelievers and atheists. Sebond's arguments, they say, are "weak and unfit to prove what he proposes." And these unbelievers set out to shatter Sebond's arguments with ease (II.12, F327, V448). Those who see Montaigne as an atheist place him on the side of the second objection. Those who see him as a fideist place him

on the side of the first objection. Montaigne, however, refutes *both*
objections and he also finds something true in each objection, so that
any interpretation of the "Apology" that places him simply on either
side must be inadequate.

The two objections, as formulated by Montaigne, are usually
regarded as opposites, as the opposing and contradictory voices of
belief and unbelief. Frédéric Brahami, for example, says that "the
second objection is diametrically opposed to the first" and that
"these two radical positions, that of belief and that of unbelief undermine the synthesis of Sebond."[20] But when these objections are
exposed more fully, they show themselves to be related to each other
and even dependent on each other at a deeper level. The first objection defines faith in terms of its origin: faith is "belief that is conceived only by faith and by a particular inspiration of divine grace."
God inspires those whom it pleases him to inspire: that is why they
believe and others do not. There is a direct communication by God
to the mind of the believer. Faith, then, is taken to be private, inarticulate, and incommunicable. The second objection is a reaction
against the possibility of faith but it also accepts this understanding
of what faith is. Unbelief must see faith as a private experience, an
experience that it ultimately regards as illusory because it is publicly
indefensible.

Rationality prides itself in being both public and common. In the
first place, it is completely transparent and communicable: when
the demonstrations of Euclidian geometry are displayed, for example, they can be understood by any rational human being and they
receive universal assent. The truths of faith, of course, do not receive
universal assent. Second, rationality is universal, the defining characteristic of the human species, whereas particular inspiration is not
universal. Therefore, on this view of reason, faith (understood as
particular inspiration) cannot give a public account of itself. It is
defenseless before the court of reason. *The first and second objections, then, share the same understanding of the meaning of faith.* It
is this shared understanding that gives rise to the "dialectic" of the
two objections, and it is this shared understanding that Montaigne
is most deeply concerned to refute.

Montaigne's defense of the mind's place in the life of faith leads
him directly into the second objection. In the process of responding
to the understanding of faith in the first objection, he just suddenly

finds himself speaking in the voice of unbelief. He says: "I have already, without thinking about it, half involved myself in the second objection" (II.12, F327, V448). The way in which Montaigne falls into the second objection and the way he characterizes reason from the very beginning of his response suggest that once reason is invited in, it claims for itself an authority that ultimately admits no other authority. Now it must be said that this presumption of reason is very similar to the position taken by Sebond's natural theology: man is said to be in the image of God by virtue of his reason. This, of course, is why Montaigne's so-called "defense" of Sebond seems ambiguous or even ironic: an attack on reason is an attack on the second group of objectors but, at the same time, it is an attack on Sebond's entire project of natural theology. In attacking the arrogance of reason, Montaigne is acknowledging what is true in the first objection, namely, that Christians do themselves harm by seeking to support their faith by reason, if reason is presumed to be the autonomous reason of the second objection. So also, in demanding public evidence of faith, he acknowledges what is true in the second objection, namely, the indefensibility of claims to private inspiration.

Montaigne's response to the second objection leads to the conclusion that reason, to which we had turned for a common ground, to which we had turned as the universal and defining characteristic of the species, is so highly particularized that it cannot serve as the common, public ground we were seeking. The logic of his response to the first objection drove Montaigne to the common, public, universal ground of reason. But autonomous reason, instead of being the rock on which to build anything common, turns out to be a mere dream or, worse, a nightmare that dissolves into chaos. Where, then, does Montaigne himself stand on the question of the relation of faith and reason, at least insofar as his stand is revealed in the dialectic of the two objections? We can begin to answer this by returning to the issue of his sincerity in calling this essay a "defense" of Sebond. The tendency has been to see Montaigne's apology for Sebond as either completely ironic or as unselfconsciously ambiguous and self-contradictory because, if he is either an atheist or a skeptic–fideist, then he must deny any harmony or compatibility between faith and reason, and that compatibility is Sebond's most fundamental assumption.

If we see the two objections in their relation to each other and follow the movement of Montaigne's thought as he works his way through the objections and their shared understandings of reason and faith, we find that he is in fact defending a transformed version of Sebond's assumption. Montaigne calls this essay an apology for Sebond because he *does* affirm the harmony of faith and reason – but not faith as defined in the first objection and not reason as assumed in the second objection. Faith as defined in the first objection is incomplete, imperfect, and even presumptuous: it is unexamined belief and it must be completed and in some way transformed in its dialectic with reason. The autonomous reason of the second objection is proud and presumptuous: it must be reformed in its dialectic with faith.

The dialectic transforms unexamined belief and autonomous reason so as to bring them into harmony. In "Of Vain Subtleties," Montaigne refers to the error of those in the middle region (between the simple and the learned believers) who "regard our sticking to the old ways . . . as simplicity and stupidity." It turns out that Montaigne's sticking to the old ways is actually due to his having come through error to reach "the extreme limit of Christian intelligence" (1.54, F227, V312). We also find a similar change in "It is Folly to Measure the True and False by our own Capacity." The presumption of the simple consists in believing too easily whatever they are told, whereas the presumption of the learned is more insidious: they disdain as false whatever seems impossible to them. Montaigne says "I used to do [that] once . . . I felt compassion for the poor [simple] people who were taken in by these follies. And now I think that I was at least as much to be pitied myself" (1.27, F132, V178–9). Now Montaigne is subject neither to the unthinking credulity of the simple nor to the arrogant presumption of the learned.

That same circular movement of thought is just what occurs in the dialectic of the two objections in the "Apology": from simple inarticulate belief he ascends through doubt to autonomous rationality and then descends through doubt to the truth of faith. Of course, he cannot simply return to or deliberately adopt the stance of unthinking belief as if he had never ascended from it. He ends up in a kind of middle position that transcends both simple credulity and learned presumption, and that, in philosophical terms, would be called "learned ignorance." Perhaps this is what T. S. Eliot has in mind when he says that "what makes Montaigne a very great figure is that he succeeded . . . in giving expression to the scepticism of *every* human being. For every man who thinks and lives by thought must have his own scepticism, that which stops at the question, that which ends in denial, or that which leads to faith and which is somehow integrated into the faith which transcends it."[21] Montaigne's skepticism is integrated into the faith which transcends it. The faith that has transcended and transformed doubt is not an unthinking and inarticulate faith but Montaigne's way of living the examined life as a Christian.

At the beginning of his reply to the second objection Montaigne says that the means he will take to beat down the pride and presumption of the second objectors is "to make them feel the inanity, the vanity and the nothingness of man" (II.12, *F*327, *V*448). How will he do this? "Saint Augustine, arguing against these people, has good cause to reproach them for their injustice in that they hold those parts of our belief to be false which our reason fails to establish. And to show that there can have been plenty of things whose nature and causes our reason cannot possibly establish, he puts before his adversaries certain known and indubitable experiences into which man confesses he has no insight." Presumably Montaigne is referring to the *City of God* (especially book 21, ch. 5), where Augustine makes this argument and gives examples, mostly from Pliny, of natural marvels. But Montaigne does not propose to follow Augustine's procedure. Rather, he says, "*We must do more,* and teach them that to convict our reason of weakness, there is no need to go sifting out rare examples" (II.12, *F*328, *V*449; emphasis added). "Doing more than St. Augustine" might plausibly be understood to imply a defense of a thorough-going skepticism. But seen within the dialectic of faith and reason, "doing more than St. Augustine" means showing the ordinary to be extraordinary. Montaigne's circular dialectic reveals the strange in the familiar, the extraordinary in the ordinary. At the same time that the reply to the second objection destroys the common world for autonomous reason, it opens up the world for faith. The world is restored through true faith to its astonishing strangeness. A world created out of nothing, a world in which the Word was made flesh, is revealed as such in the philosophical activity that ends in wonder at the most familiar.

NOTES

1. This account of the history of ancient skepticism is based on E. Zeller, *The Stoics, Epicureans and Sceptics*, trans. Oswald J. Reichel (London: Longmans, Green, and Co., 1892), A. A. Long and D. N. Sedley, *The Hellenistic Philosophers*, vol. 1 (Cambridge: Cambridge University Press, 1987), and A. A. Long, *Hellenistic Philosophy: Stoics, Epicureans, Sceptics* (London: Duckworth, 1974).

2. C. B. Schmitt, "The Rediscovery of Ancient Skepticism in Modern Times," in Myles Burnyeat, ed., *The Skeptical Tradition* (Berkeley: University of California Press, 1983), pp. 226–37.

3. See Zeller, *Stoics, Epicureans, and Sceptics*, p. 521, and Long and Sedley, *Hellenistic Philosophy*, p. 14.

4. Long and Sedley, *Hellenistic Philosophy*, pp. 24 and 447.

5. David Sedley, "The Motivation of Greek Skepticism," in M. Burnyeat, ed., *The Skeptical Tradition* (Berkeley: University of California Press, 1983), pp. 9–10.

6. Sextus Empiricus, *Outlines of Pyrrhonism*, in Herman Shapiro and Edwin M. Curley, eds., *Hellenistic Philosophy* (New York: The Modern Library, 1965), pp. 163–4.

7. *Ibid.*, p. 213.

8. Richard Popkin, *The History of Scepticism from Erasmus to Spinoza* (Berkeley: University of California Press, 1979), p. xvi.

9. See Terence Penelhum, *God and Skepticism: A Study in Skepticism and Fideism* (Dordrecht: D. Reidel Publishing Company, 1983), pp. 15, 23.

10. Montaigne presents a somewhat different appraisal of Pyrrho in "Of Virtue" (II.29, V705–6, F533).

11. Craig Walton, "Montaigne on the Art of Judgment: The Trial of Montaigne," in Richard A. Watson and James E. Force, eds., *The Skeptical Mode in Modern Philosophy: Essays in Honor of Richard Popkin* (Dordrecht: Martinus Nijhoff Publishers, 1988), p. 89.

12. Terence Penelhum, "Skepticism and Fideism," in Myles Burnyeat, ed., *The Skeptical Tradition* (Berkeley: University of California Press, 1983), p. 291.

13. Terence Penelhum, *God and Skepticism*, p. 169.

14. I have left *mœurs* untranslated because no English translation that I am aware of captures precisely the scope of meaning that Montaigne wants to convey. Frame translates *mœurs* in this passage as "behavior" which seems to me too narrow. Screech's "ways of life" is better but does not necessarily convey the moral dimension that Montaigne intends.

15. Michael Oakeshott, *On Human Conduct* (Oxford: Oxford University Press, 1975), p. vii.

16. Michael Oakeshott, *Religion, Politics and the Moral Life*, ed. Timothy Fuller (New Haven: Yale University Press, 1993), pp. 138–9.

17. Maurice Merleau-Ponty, *Signs*, trans. Richard C. McCleary (Evanston: Northwestern University Press, 1964), p. 201.

18. *Ibid.*, p. 198.

19. *Ibid.*, p. 203.

20. Frédéric Brahami, *Le scepticisme de Montaigne* (Paris: Presses Universitaires de France, 1997), p. 23.

21. T. S. Eliot, "The *Pensées* of Pascal," *Selected Essays* (New York: Harcourt Brace, 1932), p. 363.

# 11 Montaigne on moral philosophy and the good life

Moral philosophy today is not what it was in the Athens of Socrates and Plato, nor what it was in Montaigne's France. Philosophers today tend to think their task is, as Alexander Nehamas puts it, "to offer systematically connected answers to a set of independently given problems."[1] Philosophy is understood, moreover, as a largely if not wholly theoretical enterprise. Montaigne did not see it that way; and if we want to understand his relation to moral philosophy we need to begin by asking what he could have taken it to be.[2] We must moreover include some consideration of how he saw the good life. With everyone else, he took it that in ancient philosophy – the philosophy he mainly studied – the pursuit of philosophy and the pursuit of the good life were inseparable.[3] In this chapter I examine his reactions to some views of moral philosophy that he scrutinized with great care. I then consider what bearing his responses had on the moral philosophy that came after him, which for convenience I will refer to as modern moral philosophy.

## MONTAIGNE'S READING OF HIS PREDECESSORS

Montaigne was aware of several versions of moral philosophy. Greek works were available to him in translations into Latin or French. By the time of the editions of the *Essays* of 1588 and 1595 he could draw a portrayal of Socrates from Xenophon's *Memorabilia* and Plato's early dialogues. He knew Plato's own systematic writings on ethics as well, the *Republic* and the *Laws*. Of Aristotle's work he read at least the *Nicomachean Ethics* with care. From Cicero, and more significantly from Plutarch and Seneca (1.26, F107, V146), he learned about Hellenistic philosophy, especially Stoicism and Epicureanism.

He had a translation of Epictetus' *Manual*, one of the classic Stoic texts. He took material from Diogenes Laertius' *Lives of the Philosophers*, and he learned about skepticism from him and from Sextus Empiricus.[4] He thought Lipsius might have given him much fuller knowledge of the ancients.[5] Even Lipsius, of course, could not have taught him what we now know of Hellenistic and later Roman thought. But Montaigne did not care about Stoic logic and physics, or about the finer variations of skeptical epistemology, or about the many different views held in antiquity about freedom of the will.[6] He cared about what the ancients said about the good life and how to live it; and what he knew of that was enough to elicit responses that set the problems that shaped the main directions taken by modern moral philosophy.[7]

Many Renaissance writers dealt in more or less philosophical ways with morality,[8] but Montaigne found them less useful than the ancients. He had probably read Jacques Tahureau's popular *Dialogues* of 1565 and he read and borrowed slightly from the 1557 *Dialogues* of Guy de Brués.[9] The second dialogue in the latter work is a superficial discussion of skeptical arguments aimed at showing that morality is no more than conventional. De Brués had not read Sextus Empiricus, and his main argument for skepticism is the variation of opinion on moral matters. He wished to refute the position, as Montaigne did not; and his anti-skeptical arguments are not very powerful. Neither of these philosophical authors would have taught Montaigne anything about the nature of moral philosophy beyond what he himself could get from the ancient sources. Nor had they anything fresh to say about the good life. But one author from the period of the Renaissance did give Montaigne a detailed vision of a different kind of moral philosophy, a Christian moral philosophy: Raymond Sebond, whose long treatise, the *Book of Creatures*, he translated and on which he commented at length in the "Apology" (II.12).[10] I begin by examining Sebond's view and considering very briefly some aspects of Montaigne's extensive response to it.

## SEBOND'S MORAL PHILOSOPHY

The "Apology for Raymond Sebond" is more argumentative and less tied to Montaigne's personal experience than any of the other essays. We would therefore consider it more purely philosophical than the others; and it gives us important pointers to Montaigne's views about moral philosophy. To see what they are we must begin with Sebond's own thought. His *Book of Creatures*, usually referred to as his *Natural Theology*, is indeed an extended and connected series of arguments on religious topics. It should nonetheless be considered philosophy. Sebond himself tells us that he never rests any of his conclusions on the Bible or on any other authority. He aims, in fact, to show that arguments from common experience support both the Bible and the teachings of the Roman Catholic Church.[11] By using philosophical argument to back up theological points Sebond was doing one of the things the Church held that the philosopher was supposed to do: serve as handmaiden to theology.[12] Montaigne would have seen him as one kind of philosopher.

At the outset, moreover, Sebond announces his concern with morality. His doctrine, he says, contains everything man needs to know about himself and his creator, not least "the rule of nature, by which also each is instructed about that to which each is naturally obliged toward God and toward his neighbor, and not only instructed but moved and urged to do from love and willingly" (*LC*, pref. pp. v–vi). His teaching is accessible to all. "It presupposes neither grammar nor logic nor any other liberal art, nor physics nor metaphysics." Morality presumably does not rely on those disciplines either, because even without them Sebond will teach his reader "to know what is his good, his ill, his duty, to whom and by whom he is obliged" (*ibid.*, p. vii). The doctrine, he claims, is not only certain but efficacious: "It makes man constant, humble, gracious, obedient, enemy of vice and of sin, loving of virtue" without making him proud of his self-sufficiency (*ibid.*, p. viii). Montaigne must have seen Sebond therefore as offering, among other things, a substantial moral philosophy, including – if only sketchily – a view of the human good. His arguments, Sebond says, are all to be drawn from the book of nature. The pagan philosophers could, of course, observe nature, but they were "not enlightened (*eclairé*) by God and purged of our original taint (*macule*)." Therefore they could not read the book properly (*ibid.*, p. xi). Sebond's moral philosophy will thus be far superior to theirs.[13]

What Sebond seeks first to show is the ways in which we differ from other creatures, since he assumes that our special characteristics are indicators of God's purpose in creating us. Our distinctive features will therefore show us how we ought to act. Experience shows that there are four kinds of things: some simply exist, some also live, some living beings feel and sense, and some – humans – also have intelligence, which includes both the ability to judge and free will (*liberal arbitre*) (*LC*, 1.4; xxxvi.55). The kinds form a scale of value, with possessors of mere being as the lowest and possessors of intelligence as the highest. Animals perceive, but since they cannot remember they can neither learn nor exercise prudence. Man has all the properties of the lower orders and more. He thinks, he remembers, he can master knowledge and doctrine, and he can assent or reject freely (*LC*, 1.6–7).

From the complex of beings we can infer that there must be one being who made all the rest. Since no part of what is natural could have made everything, there must be a being above nature who did. This being – God – has his own purposes for everything he created. (*LC*, ii–xvii.11–37) It follows that "the will of God being first and before all things, being the rule and justice itself, nothing can be good or just if it is not conformed to it" (*LC*, xxxviii.57). Unlike the rest of creation, man does not necessarily behave as the order of nature requires that he should. Consequently he needs instruction about what he ought to do. Experience amply shows that man shares existence, life, and sentience with many other things. The proper marks of man, the features that differentiate him from inferior beings, are his understanding and his free will. Hence "[for] whatever I wish to prove about man as man, I must necessarily draw my argument and my conclusion from one of these two powers, or from both" (lxv.113–14).

The first law we are to obey is to preserve ourselves and to develop our nature. The beings of lower rank all do this; and "since man is of the number of natural creatures, and the most noble among them, by so much the more is he obliged to obey and follow this commandment of nature" (*LC*, lxvi.114–15). Since we have the ability to affirm or deny any proposition presented to us, it follows that we should affirm those that it is most useful for us to believe, what is most noble, and what has the most power to console us and keep us from despair. For example, we can affirm or deny that God exists, but – since God is our infinite good – it is plainly better to affirm it (*LC*, lxvii–lxviii.116–19). Sebond goes on to argue that by this rule – believe what is most useful – we ought to accept all the main points of Christian faith (*LC*, LXXX.128f.).

Because we alone possess free will, we alone can choose to obey or disobey. Hence our actions, unlike those of animals, are imputed to us as meritorious or blameworthy (*LC*, LXXXII.130–31). Now nothing was given to creatures for their ill. Hence there must be some benefit to us from the fact that we can earn merit or fail to do so. Merit requires reward, demerit punishment. But man cannot adequately reward and punish man, so there must be a God who does. Otherwise our fitness for merit and demerit would be pointless. Just as the power of sight requires that there should be visible things, so the ability to acquire merit requires that there should be a rewarder. And as man is the peak of creation, "the whole structure of the universe would be useless, and everything would be confused and without order" if there were no punishment and reward. This enables us to infer that God is just, that he is in no hurry to punish, and that he allows time for repentance (*LC*, LXXXII–LXXXVII.136–40).[14]

We infer also that we must be immortal so that we can be duly rewarded and punished.[15] We can be rewarded for what is specific to us and distinguishes us from animals, our free will. And since this ability is intellectual and spiritual, the human good which is to be our reward must be intellectual and spiritual as well, and not bodily (LXXXIX.140–42). We can now see how important it is for us to reflect on the difference that experience shows there to be between us and the animals: the main things we need to know come from reflection on our free will (*LC*, XCII.149).

The next law after the one requiring self-preservation arises from God's generosity. He made all other things for our use and benefit, and we owe him gratitude in return (*LC*, XCVI.153–5). This is shown among other things by the fact that we alone in creation are able to give thanks to God (c.165). We should be especially grateful that he has made us the most valuable created beings in the universe and has shown his love toward us. We are obliged to repay him with love. The behavior of animals in serving us is a lesson in how we should serve God. They and we form one community held together by love. But although we are to love all other creatures, we are to love our fellow humans most because man is the image of God (*LC*, CX–CXXV.191–216).

Sebond then outlines a more or less Augustinian ethics of love. "Virtue," he says, "is nothing but good love, vice nothing but bad love." Love is totally in our own power, and it takes its moral character from the object loved. It is against nature to love inferior things more than we love what is superior to them in the scale of being. Hence we should love God above all else, and ourselves only after that. Perfect love of God is not only our first duty. It is also our first good. It makes us resemble God and brings lasting joy. Self-love, not surprisingly, is the cause of evil. It results at best in transient joys and more often in sadness. These two loves are the source of both our knowledge and our errors about good and evil. Love of God is a torch lighting up good, self-love obscures that light. Those who love rightly constitute one city and those who love badly another. Sebond adds that they must ultimately end up in different places, since like attracts like. And he reminds us again that "the will of God is manifested by the creatures and by their order, they neither signify nor advise us of anything that is not in accordance with his will" and that in this book he has "drawn conclusions only by arguments from the creatures and their comparison" (*LC*, CXXXII–CLXIX.223–98).

## MONTAIGNE'S REPLY TO SEBOND

The distinctive pattern of Sebond's systematic moral philosophy is clear. Once he has shown that God exists and created the world, he takes it that experience gives us the information we need to infer with certainty how we should act and what our good is. We can learn from experience what are the distinctive features of each kind of created being. These features are to be interpreted as signs of God's will for the behavior of that kind of creature. Our own most distinctive feature is our intelligence which includes our free will. This aspect of our nature enables us to resemble God and makes us the most valuable kind of creature in the universe. We must preserve our body because it carries our intelligence and free will, but our chief duties arise from the activities we alone are equipped by our nature to carry out: loving and thanking God, caring for our neighbor, choosing to do our duty and earning merit. Our good is spiritual, not bodily, and is to be expected rather in an after-life than in this one.

Montaigne's response to this way of doing moral philosophy is made clear in the early parts of the "Apology." It is striking that he is prepared – at least here – to accept the principle of Sebond's argument. "It is not credible," he says, "that this whole machine [i.e., the universe] should not have on it some marks imprinted by the hand of this great architect . . . He has left the stamp of his divinity on these lofty works . . . It is what he says himself, that his invisible operations he manifests to us by the visible" (II.12, F326, V446–7). But the conclusions he draws using this mode of argument differ drastically from Sebond's.

One of the conclusions is that "it is not by a true judgment, but by foolish pride and stubbornness, that we set ourselves before the other animals and sequester ourselves from their condition and society" (II.12, F359, V486). Montaigne provides more than thirty pages of argument to show that we share most of our properties with the animals (II.12, F327–58, V448–86). Animals communicate with one another as much as we do; they live with at least as much order as we; they reason as we do; they are capable of learning new ways of acting; they even show signs of religion; they are in many ways better equipped and cleverer than we are in matters of bare survival; they form friendships and families with as much loyalty as we; they repent and acknowledge faults; they can abstract from sensible qualities in responding to experience; they enjoy more of natural good than we do. Of course there are human doings which are not found among animals: making war, for instance. But is this something to be proud of? And on free will, the key to Sebond's account, Montaigne is scathing:

there is no apparent reason to judge that the beasts do by natural and obligatory instinct the same things we do by our choice and cleverness . . . Why do we imagine in them this compulsion of nature, we who feel no similar effect? Besides, it is more honorable, and closer to divinity, to be guided and obliged to act lawfully by a natural and inevitable condition, than to act lawfully by accidental and fortuitous liberty . . . (II.12, F336–7, V460)

Montaigne does not deny that we have this "accidental liberty": he casts doubt on it, but more importantly he denies that it is something to be proud of, something that gives us more nobility and value than anything else in the universe. He also doubts that there is any reason to think that we are of the highest value, and that the rest of the world was created to serve us (II.12, F329–30, V450–51). Montaigne seems to be suggesting here that we are as much a part of the natural world as the animals are. If there is anything that distinguishes us from them it is precisely our presumption in thinking we are better than they. Unlike the animals we cannot even keep order in our societies by ourselves. The only moral conclusion that can be drawn in Sebond's way is that

the first law that God ever gave to man was a law of pure obedience . . . to obey is the principal function of a reasonable soul, recognizing a heavenly superior and benefactor. From obeying and yielding spring all other virtues, as from presumption all sin. (II.12, *F*359, *V*488)

But Montaigne argues in much of the rest of the essay that natural reason alone will not suffice to obtain the practical knowledge we need. Sebond's way of doing moral philosophy cannot tell us either about our good or about the laws we are to obey. It ends in its own subversion.

## THE FAILURE OF PREVIOUS MORAL PHILOSOPHIES

Could the moral philosophies of Greece and Rome do better? Montaigne often writes as if he thought so. He tries to be, or finds himself being, an Epicurean, a Stoic, a skeptic.[16] His point in trying on these views is always the same. He treats them as offering ways of living. They matter less as *theories* of the good than as instructions for its attainment. In taking them in this way Montaigne is being true to the aims of ancient moral philosophy.[17] Aristotle was not alone in holding that in philosophical ethics, "the end aimed at is not knowledge but action."[18] Seneca would agree that we should test doctrine by its practicability. For our teachers, he says, "let us choose . . . not men who pour forth their words with greatest glibness . . . but men who teach us by their lives, men who tell us what we ought to do and then prove it by practice, who show us what we should avoid, and then are never caught doing that which they have ordered us to avoid."[19]

Montaigne sometimes talks as if he thinks that all the ancient philosophers took the good life, the life of *eudaimonia* or happiness or human flourishing, to be the life of pleasure. "All the opinions in the world agree on this – that pleasure is our goal . . . The dissensions of the philosophical sects in this matter are merely verbal . . . Whatever they say, in virtue itself the ultimate goal we seek is

voluptuousness" (1.20, F56–7, V81–2). But he knew this was too simple. He knew that even the Epicurean vision of the life of pleasure
called for an austere simplicity and for as much control of impulse
and feeling as the more famously difficult virtue of the Stoics. The
different schools of ancient moral thought offered specific visions of
the good life and definite versions of the training needed to stay on
the path toward it. For none of them was the good life constituted by
a surplus of pleasure over pain or by gratification of whatever desires
one happened to have. All of them called for the discipline of desire.

In 11.26, "Of the Education of Children," giving what Comte-
Sponville calls the finest praise of philosophy ever written, Montaigne makes it clear that he accepts this ancient view of its task.[20]
Philosophy "teaches us to live," he says, and it has lessons for us
at every age. It should be taught to children as well as studied by
the old. "The soul in which philosophy dwells should by its health
make even the body healthy. It should make tranquillity and gladness
shine out from within." As "the moulder of judgment and conduct"
it should be "everywhere at home." Philosophy is not a matter of
quibbles over logic, nor a quarrelsome discipline "of no use and no
value." On the contrary, "there is nothing more gay, more lusty, more
sprightly" (11.26, F118–22, V160–65).

Here as elsewhere, however, Montaigne does not leave things as
he finds them. Though the moral essays of Plutarch and Seneca's
moral letters are the best of ancient moral thought (11.10, F300, V413),
Montaigne is not simply a follower. There are three striking ways in
which he departs from ancient models.

First, Hellenistic philosophy was transmitted by schools, each of
which had a leader responsible for preserving the founder's teachings
and instructing new disciples in the methods he thought proper for
attaining the good life. Some schools charged fees; some admitted
women; all allowed for developments of doctrine but tried to maintain the traditions of the founder. Their organizations differed but all
had some definite structure and expected members to live within its
bounds.[21] Montaigne belongs to no school and accepts no leader. "I
dislike inculcation," he says,

even of useful things, as in Seneca; and I dislike the practice of his Stoical
school of repeating, in connection with every subject, in full length and
breadth, the principles and premises for general use, and restating ever anew
their common and universal arguments and reasons. (III.9, F734–5, V962)

He would not have accepted Seneca's admonition: "Do everything as if Epicurus were watching you."[22]

Second, Montaigne thinks that none of the ancients had given a convincing account of the highest good and the way to attain it. In the "Apology for Sebond," Montaigne frequently uses the standard skeptical tactic of pointing to disagreements among judges of equal competence – or incompetence – to show that we have no knowledge on a given point.[23] This kind of disagreement, he says, plainly exists about the good. As evidence he cites St. Augustine's account of Varro's claim that there were 288 sects of philosophers quarreling over the issue. "There is no combat so violent among the philosophers, and so bitter, as that which arises over the question of the sovereign good of man," he remarks, and he approvingly quotes Cicero saying that "he who disagrees about the supreme good, disagrees about the whole principle of philosophy" (II.12 F435, V577).[24] Insofar as the philosophical quest is for a good that will be the same for all men, Montaigne – perhaps reluctantly – abandons it. "Since philosophy has not been able to find a way to tranquillity that is suitable to all, let everyone seek it individually" (II.16, F471, V622).[25]

Third, the Hellenistic and Roman schools did not consider it a flaw in their teachings that most people could not live in accordance with them. Seneca put the point bluntly: "Many think that we Stoics are holding out expectations greater than our human lot admits of; and they have a right to think so. For they have regard to the body only. But let them turn back to the soul. They will measure man by the standard of God." Such critics think, he continues, "that whatever they themselves cannot do, is not done; they pass judgment on virtues in the light of their own weakness."[26]

Montaigne takes the opposite position. The issue is so central to his understanding of moral philosophy – and indeed of morality – that he must be allowed to state his position himself:

What is the use of these lofty points of philosophy on which no human being can settle, and these rules that exceed our use and our strength? I often see people propose to us patterns of life which neither the proposer nor his hearers have any hope of following, or . . . any desire to follow . . . It would be desirable that there should be more proportion between the command and the obedience; and a goal that we cannot reach seems unjust . . . Man . . .

is not very clever to cut out his own duty by the pattern of a different nature than his own. To whom does he prescribe what he expects no one to do? Is it wrong of him not to do what it is impossible for him to do? (III.9, $F756$–8, $V989$–91)

Montaigne tests theories of the good life by seeing whether or not he can live as they direct. Socrates and Cato, perhaps Epaminondas, come close to exemplifying the lofty Stoic life. Montaigne finds that he himself cannot, and he doubts that anyone else can either. The same is true of the Epicurean life and the skeptical life. (Montaigne seems to think it true even of the Christian life: see the acid comments in 1.56, $F230$–31, $V319$–20.) But it is a fatal flaw in a theory if it tells us that the good life is one that we cannot live. The well-taught student of philosophy "will not so much say his lesson as do it" (1.26, $F124$, $V168$). Seneca thinks that with his philosophy he can shape men's souls more easily than workmen can curve or straighten wood.[27] Montaigne says that "when straightness and composure are combined with constancy, then the soul attains its perfection" (II.2, $F249$, $V345$). But he can find no one, or almost no one, who is so constantly straight: certainly not himself (cf. III.2, $F610$–11, $V804$–5). Pyrrho the skeptic, "like all the others who were truly philosophers," tried to live according to his ideas. He may have succeeded. But for us to do so "with such perseverance and constancy as to establish them as our ordinary usage . . . it is almost incredible that it can be done" (II.29, $F533$, $V705$). It is not only Montaigne's test that classical moral philosophy fails. It is its own.

## THE VARIABILITY OF VALUES

Christian thinkers, building on Stoic philosophy and Roman law, developed a doctrine of laws of nature that would guide us as far as human reason could to the virtuous life in this world. That life is a prerequisite for attainment of heavenly blessedness. And obedience to the laws of nature would yield a decent life on earth for all. This is Sebond's basic teaching, and it is in accord with main-stream Catholic doctrine. But Montaigne doubts that there are any laws of nature which bind all humans alike. Sebond, he holds, had failed to prove that there are.[28] And the same sort of disagreement that Montaigne took to militate against classical claims concerning the highest good also destroys claims about universal laws of nature. If a law were imprinted on us by nature, Montaigne argues, we would all alike accept it and find it motivating us (1.14, F33, V51; 11.12, F422–3, V562). "For what nature had truly ordered for us we would without doubt follow by common consent . . . Let them show me just one law of that sort – I'd like to see it" (11.12, F437, V580).

Montaigne emphasizes the importance of early education and of custom in forming what we call conscience (1.23, F83, V115). The variation among customs shows that it is a mistake to think that they are laws binding on everyone. But if there are no such laws, the best we can do is to obey the laws of our own local authority (1.23, F86, V118; cf. 11.12, F437, V580). The skepticism and relativism implied by these remarks, and many others like them, posed one of the major problems for modern moral philosophy.[29]

Montaigne seems, moreover, to block any hope of a solution. Natural law was taken by Stoic and Christian alike to be warranted as showing the means to the attainment of the highest good. But as I have noted, Montaigne thinks that we cannot get any agreement on the highest good; and even if we could, most people could not realistically hope to obtain it. How were philosophers to find useable moral certainties to put in place of Montaigne's skeptical doubts?

The innumerable disagreements about the good are due, Montaigne thinks, to the variety and changeability of our desires and interests. We differ from one another in our tastes and likings. Nature provides no common standard of the good. This holds not only for particular enjoyments and satisfactions, but more generally. In his most striking statement on the topic, Montaigne gives a philosophical underpinning to his denial that we can find a universally acceptable idea of the good. "Each man," he says, "is as well or as badly off as he thinks he is. Not the man of whom it is thought, but the one who thinks it of himself, is happy" (1.14, F46C, V67). This radically subjectivist principle gets its punch by what Montaigne takes to be facts about human nature. First, "[v]ariety is the most general fashion that nature has followed, and more in minds than bodies . . . Their most universal quality is diversity" (11.37, F 598, V 786). Second, we are all constantly changing within ourselves. Montaigne finds himself to be in constant change; he can get no firm footing within himself. His evidence comes from himself, but that suffices because "You can tie up all moral philosophy with a common and private life . . . Each man bears the entire form of man's estate" (III.2, *F*610–11, *V*804–5; cf. II.12, *F*434, *V*576). If our nature is a clue to divine directives, as Sebond thought, then even God did not intend us all to pursue the same highest good, as the ancients thought we should.

Montaigne thus thinks that "men are diverse in inclination and strength; they must be led to their own good according to their nature and by diverse routes" (III.12, *F*805, *V*1052). From the first essay on, the theme of diverse ways to the same end appears again and again in Montaigne's book. But the ancients did not think there could be diverse routes to the same end. They thought that if we knew the end we would find that there is just one sure path to its attainment. Without a common end it would not be possible, on this view, for there to be common moral guidance. As long as morality is conceived in terms of means to an end, uncertainty or difference concerning the end brings the same uncertainty or disagreement about the means, whether they be moral virtues or moral rules. And when the view of morality becomes problematic so too does another ancient common-place. The idea that the sage or the hero could be an exemplary secular figure whose life could guide others was expressed frequently in Renaissance thought. Montaigne examined several such exemplary figures. He found none who could be his own guide, with the possible exception of Socrates – and even he had his flaws. Moreover there could be no direct way for Montaigne to present himself or his life as such an exemplar. I suggest below (p. 224) that he constructed an indirect and quite novel mode of exemplarity. Its key feature is that each person can and should find his own guidance within himself. The view undercuts claims that anyone might have to be an authoritative exemplar for others. Given Montaigne's radical subjectivism about the good and his skepticism about natural law, no other conclusion was possible for him.

## MORALS WITHOUT A HIGHEST GOOD

For the modern moral philosophers who give up on the ancient form of the search for the highest good – and that includes most of them – there is a new problem. If acting for one's own benefit and acting for the common good necessarily go together, an understandable desire for that good would move everyone to be virtuous. Without such a good to attract us, what motivating factor would be forceful and constant in all of us and also sufficient to bring us to a common morality that would benefit everyone? Here I can sketch only a few of the answers.

Hobbes, often taken to be the originator of modern moral philosophy, faces the issue directly. There is, he says, "no such *finis ultimus*, utmost aim, nor *summum bonum*, greatest good, as is spoken of in the books of the old moral philosophers."[30] But all men fear death more than anything else; and Hobbes derives laws of nature which will get a grip on everyone because of the urgent desire everyone has to stay alive.[31] These laws would prevent men from warring with one another and allow for the development of society; Hobbes could not claim that each person would be guaranteed the best human life possible.

Bentham takes pleasure as the ultimate end, claiming that all men always in fact seek their own. This does not express a disagreement with Hobbes on the highest good: "pleasure" is just a place-holder for "satisfaction of whatever desires you happen to have." The basic moral law, for Bentham – the only one he thinks capable of rational justification – requires us to act for the greatest happiness of everyone we affect. But if each of us necessarily pursues our own good, we can only be led to work for the good of all if society artificially rewards us for doing so or punishes us for failure. Bentham's utilitarian way of keeping a means–end view of morality while doing without the unifying force of the ancient conception of the highest good was profoundly influential.[32]

Kant accepts a most Montaignean picture of the instability of our desires. And because he holds that happiness consists in satisfaction of desires, he concludes that rules directing the search for happiness could never be certain. But he believes that we possess unshakeable practical certainty of the basic law of morality. Moreover our awareness of that basic law suffices necessarily to give us a motive to comply with it, a motive different in kind from the desire for our own happiness. Morality is therefore entirely different from self-interest. Aiming to replace the old means–end pattern of moral thinking, he presents a new way of obtaining moral directives. Among those directives is one that tells us to aid others in their pursuit of their happiness. Kant is emphatic in holding that we are to help them to achieve what they themselves take their own good to be. We are not to impose our own idea of the good on them. He thus builds a Montaignean view of the diversity of human aims squarely into morality. His theory was radically innovative. But he was driven to it in large part to cope with the problem Montaigne had made salient: how to obtain indubitable moral guidance without deriving it from any idea of a common highest good.[33]

## LATER RESPONSES TO MONTAIGNEAN CHALLENGES

Montaigne's attempt to show that there are no morally significant differences between human beings and animals raised a different question for modern moral philosophy. If we are like animals, we are simply one species of natural animate being. Our minds must be as wholly part of nature as the minds of animals. Montaigne puts with great forcefulness a question that arises from this position:

If nature enfolds within the bounds of her ordinary progress, like all other things, also the beliefs, judgments, and opinions of men; if they have their rotation, their season, their birth, their death, like cabbages . . . what magisterial and permanent authority are we attributing to them? (II.12, F433, V575)

If all of our opinions have causes, like all other occurrences, how can we say that we ought to accept some and not others? If all reasons for beliefs are equally caused by antecedent natural events, how can any reasons be better than any others? Most importantly for our purposes, if the authority of every opinion is doubtful then how if at all does a wholly naturalistic view of human beings allow room for morality?

David Hume, who is often thought to be a skeptic, accepts the naturalism that Montaigne suggests, and proposes an answer to his question about how we attribute authority to some beliefs but not to others. He also offers an account of how some kinds of reasoning can be better than other kinds even though both kinds are caused by antecedent events. He goes so far as to offer naturalistic accounts of religious belief. And he suggests that because religion arose initially from human fear and ignorance, the spread of better beliefs about how to control nature would lead to its subsidence.[34]

Hume thus goes far beyond anything Montaigne himself would have claimed. Montaigne is in fact not unambiguously committed to the naturalism suggested in the "Apology." Although he says that even animals show signs of religion he nonetheless expresses in the same essay, and in many other places, an anguished concern about man's dependence on divine aid that singles us out from all other creatures. Hume's philosophy seemed at the time to be so outrageous that it could not to be taken seriously. But Montaigne's criticisms of Sebond did not convince most people that there are no major differences between humans and animals.

There were in fact many writers who used arguments like those by Sebond that Montaigne had ridiculed. Samuel Pufendorf was the most widely read. He rests much of his theory on such arguments in his massive Latin treatise of 1672, *The Law of Nature and of Nations*.[35] Sebond suggested that moral laws emanate from God's will. Pufendorf is far clearer and more elaborate in presenting just such a view. Like Montaigne, he held that God's mind and purposes are wholly inscrutable.[36] But he also holds, as does Sebond, that God has given us empirically discoverable clues to the laws that he commands us to obey. We find them by discovering the most important ways in which we differ from other created beings. Our capacity to think and to use language, Pufendorf thinks, is one major difference between us and the animals. Because of these abilities we are capable of understanding laws and making contracts, which the animals are not. We need the help of other humans to survive and to improve our lives. We also tend to want more than a fair share of goods and to be generally difficult in society. These features of our nature show that God intended us to live together under laws backed by threats of punishment and offers of reward. We can discover the laws of nature by finding out empirically what it takes for us to live peaceably together. And we can be as certain of the results here as we can in any other empirical study. Montaigne's long polemic against this kind of argument led Pufendorf at most to be more careful in distinguishing us from animals than Sebond had been.

For Kant the naturalistic view of the universe is only half the story. We are indeed causally enmeshed in a deterministic natural world. But the fact that we can know this to be true is evidence that there is more to the human mind than a Humean chain of necessitated ideas. And free will makes a decisive difference between animals and us. It enables us to become aware of our desires and impulses and freely to decide whether or not to act on them. Moreover morality gives us grounds for belief in God and immortality: without these beliefs we cannot think it reasonable to be held to the obligations morality imposes on us. There is no reason to think that Kant had read Sebond; but the issues raised by the naturalistic strain in Montaigne's thought were very much alive for him, as they are for us.[37]

## MONTAIGNE'S AFFIRMATIVE HUMANISM

It would be a mistake to take the "Apology for Raymond Sebond" as giving the whole of Montaigne's approach to moral philosophy. The deep skepticism about knowledge which that essay expresses in innumerable places is contradicted in the essay itself (II.12, F343, V457) and elsewhere (I.28, F140). The conviction that no one is constant about anything is belied by Montaigne's accounts of the constancy of his own deepest convictions and habits (e.g., I.26, F122, V165; II.12, F428, V569; III.2, F615, 619, V811, 815). In the closing peroration of the "Apology" he quotes Seneca as saying "Oh what a vile and abject thing is man if he does not raise himself above humanity." But he promptly adds an important qualification to this condemnation: it is "impossible and unnatural" to be more than human – at least by our own effort, and without divine aid. Only Christian faith can bring about such a "divine and miraculous metamorphosis" (II.12, F457, V604). Recalling Montaigne's frequent criticisms of philosophers who aspire to be more than human in their control of their passions and desires, we must wonder how seriously he took the Senecan claim that we are "vile and abject" if we stay in the human condition.

The late essays make it clear that he had at least had second thoughts on the matter. "What a monstrous animal," he exclaims, "to be a horror to himself, to be burdened by his pleasures, to regard himself as a misfortune!" (III.5, F670, V879). This is not the cry of one who sees us as Seneca did. If the late Montaigne does not accept Sebond's naive exaltation of mankind as the most valuable of all creatures, he also refuses to be ashamed of himself just because he is human. "I rarely repent," he says, "and . . . my conscience is content with itself – not as the conscience of an angel or a horse, but as the conscience of a man" (III.2, F612, V806). We are neither animals nor angels. We might wish to be better than we are. But to feel like this is not to repent for our nature, nor to consider it as flawed by inherited sin. "Repentance does not properly apply to the things that are not in our power; rather does regret" (III.2 *F617*, *V813*). And Montaigne does not regret being human. His lengthy discussion of love in III.5, "On Some Verses of Virgil," strikingly parts company with Sebond's ascetic view of the good. He expresses no puritanical dismay about the many ways in which women and men enjoy their sexuality. Nor does he treat himself as a fallen being because of the pleasure he gets from sex. "Each one of my parts makes me myself just as much as every other one," he says, referring to his private parts, "And no other makes me more properly a man than this one" (III.5, *F677*, *V887*).

From his trials of the visions of the good life proposed by ancient philosophers Montaigne concludes that they could not give him adequate guidance. He bows in the direction of Christian morality but aside from doubting that people live according to it he does not discuss it (see 1.56, *F234*, *V323*). He is not left bewildered, however, because he finds direction from within himself. We have, he says, "a pattern established within us by which to test our actions, and according to this pattern, now to pat ourselves on the back, now punish ourselves." This voice accusing or excusing us, as St. Paul puts it (Rom. 2:14–15), is his own court applying his own laws (III.2, *F613*, *V807*). And he is not alone in having such an "essential pattern" (III.3, *F625*, *V823*). "There is no one who, if he listens to himself, does not discover in himself a pattern all his own, a ruling pattern ["une forme maitresse"]" which suffices as a guide (III.2, *F615*, *V811*). He does not say that only the better born or better educated are capable of self-governance. Anyone can find a *forme maitresse* within. If Montaigne can claim to be an exemplar in no other way, then at least he can be one in seeking his own distinctive form and trying to live as it directs.

Montaigne is not a philosopher if to be one means working out systematically connected answers to independently given questions. He does not elaborate a philosophical morality of self-governance. But what is perhaps his most important philosophical legacy is the deep ambivalence that appears when we compare these late remarks about the possibility of a morality of self-governance with the abject morality of religious obedience dominating the "Apology for Raymond Sebond." Pufendorf and many other modern thinkers spelled out versions of morality as obedience in philosophical terms. But starting in the early seventeenth century a whole series of writers began to work out what a morality of self-governance would look like. That line of thought reached its culmination in Kant – a long-time admirer of Montaigne. His vision of morality as obedience to a law we each give to ourselves was the most radical version of self-governance proposed during the Enlightenment. Its influence is strong today. And religious moralists today still propound versions of morality as obedience. If Montaigne did not create a philosopher's answers to the questions of ethics, he did more. He shaped the questions we are still asking.

NOTES

1. Alexander Nehamas, *The Art of Living* (Berkeley: University of California Press, 1998), p. 104.
2. Cesare Vasoli gives a useful survey of Renaissance understandings of philosophy in general, without saying much about moral philosophy as such: "The Renaissance concept of philosophy," in Charles B. Schmitt and Quentin Skinner, eds., *The Cambridge History of Renaissance Philosophy* (Cambridge: Cambridge University Press, 1988), pp. 57–74.
3. "From antiquity to the Renaissance, the enquiry into man's supreme good . . . was generally accepted as the defining characteristic of ethics": Jill Kraye, "Moral Philosophy," in Schmitt and Skinner, *Cambridge History of Renaissance Philosophy*, p. 316.
4. For details see Pierre Villey, *Les Sources et l'évolution des "Essais" de Montaigne* (Paris: Hachette, 1933), vol. 1, pp. 59ff. Skepticism for Montaigne, as for the ancient philosophers on whom he drew, was as closely connected to the conduct of life as were Epicureanism and Stoicism. The skeptic hoped that his arguments for and against any proposition whatever would end by producing suspension of belief. One would simply not know what to think about the proposition, and consequently one would have no belief about it. If one had no settled belief about what is good and what is bad, one would remain calm in the face of whatever fortune produced. And this calm was for the skeptic the most desirable state of mind.
5. *Essays*, II.12, F436, V578.
6. For a fine overview of modern scholarship on Hellenistic philosophy, see *The Cambridge History of Hellenistic Philosophy*, eds. Keimpe Algra, Jonathan Barnes, Jaap Mansfield, and Malcolm Schofield (Cambridge: Cambridge University Press, 1999).
7. I raise no questions about the accuracy of Montaigne's understanding of those he read. For a reassessment of some common views of Greek

ethics, see Nicholas White, *Individual and Conflict in Greek Ethics* (Oxford: Oxford University Press, 2002).

8. See Kraye, "Moral Philosophy", in Schmitt and Skinner, *Cambridge History of Renaissance Philosophy*, pp. 303–86, for a thorough survey.

9. Villey, *Sources*, vol. 1, pp. 34–40 on Tahureau, and pp. 95–6 on de Brués. See Jacques Tahureau, *Les Dialogues*, ed. Max Gauna (Geneva: Droz, 1981), and *The Dialogues of Guy de Brués*, ed. Panos Paul Morphos (Baltimore: Johns Hopkins Press, 1953).

10. Sebond was born toward the end of the fourteenth century in Gerona or Barcelona and died in 1436. The *Liber creaturarum (seu naturae) seu Liber de homine* was written in the last two years of his life and published in 1484. A second printing entitled *Theologia naturalis* was published in 1485. In the sixteenth century there were several reprintings of it under the latter title, and an abridgement also had several printings. There was one French translation prior to Montaigne's. See Joseph Coppin, *Montaigne traducteur de Raymond Sebond* (Lille: Morel, 1925), and especially Hans-Peter Bippus, *In der Theologie nicht bewandert: Montaigne und die Theologie* (Tübingen and Basel: Francke, 2000), for details. Bippus, p. 175n.11, notes the paucity of literature about Sebond and comments on some of what there is. He gives at pp. 176–211 the fullest discussion of Sebond that I have found in the Montaigne literature. He finds the title *Theologia naturalis* misleading, and notes that the phrase is not used in the book itself. We should see it, he suggests, as a version of physico-theology: Bippus, p. 179. I follow him in using Sebond's original title.

11. References to Sebond are to Montaigne's translation of the *Liber creaturarum* as reprinted in *Oeuvres complètes de Michel de Montaigne*, vols. 9–10, ed. M. A. Armaingaud (Paris: L. Conard, 1932). For this point see the preface, pp. ix–x. Future references are identified as *LC* (*Livre des créatures*) and are given in the text, by chapter and page. The preface and chapters I–CCI are in vol. 1, Chapters CCII–CCCXXX in vol. 2.

12. Perhaps not a very good one. "Philosophy, says St. Chrysostom, has long been banished from the holy schools as a useless handmaid." (1.56, *F*234, *V*323).

13. Sebond does not explain how his claim to give an account of the world which leads to all the truths taught by the Catholic Church can be wholly independent of religion and theology and therefore support it while also implying that his philosophy is only possible because he has received grace and knows he has received it. It was presumably because of the claim to be able to demonstrate all the doctrines of the Church by natural reason that the preface was put on the Index, at least for a

while. Montaigne's translation softened some of these audacious claims. See Coppin, *Montaigne traducteur*, pp. 67–70, and Philip Hendrick, *Montaigne et Sebond: L'art de la traduction* (Paris: Champion, 1996), ch. 5.

14. In vol. 2 Sebond adds a lengthy section on repentance, *LC*, CCXCIV–CCCXXX.

15. Later Sebond argues that because our obligation to God is infinite we must be able to suffer infinite torment if we do not fulfill it. So, again, we must be immortal (*LC*, CCXXVII).

16. See André Comte-Sponville, *"Je ne suis pas philosophe": Montaigne et la philosophie* (Paris: Champion, 1993).

17. Pierre Hadot, *What is Ancient Philosophy?*, trans. Michael Chase (Cambridge, MA: Harvard University Press, 2002), has expounded this aim of ancient philosophy quite powerfully, as has Alexander Nehamas. See in particular Nehamas, *Art of Living*, ch. 4 on Montaigne and Socrates.

18. Aristotle, *Nicomachean Ethics*, trans. Ross (Oxford: Oxford University Press, 1980), 1095a6.

19. Seneca, *Epistles*, trans. Richard M. Gummere (Cambridge, MA: Harvard University Press, 1920), Loeb Classical Library, *Ep.* LII.8. Hereafter cited as Seneca, *Ep.*

20. Comte-Sponville, *"Je ne suis pas philosophe,"* p. 32: an essay to which I am much indebted. Comte-Sponville makes clear the central place Montaigne gives to moral philosophy, while acknowledging the importance for him of epistemological questions.

21. See Tiziano Dorandi's two chapters on the schools in *The Cambridge History of Hellenistic Philosophy*, eds. Keimpe Algra, et al., pp. 31–64, on which I rely.

22. Seneca, *Ep.* XXV.5, cited in Michael Erler and Malcolm Schofield, "Epicurean Ethics," in Keimpe Algra, et al., *The Cambridge History of Hellenistic Philosophy*, pp. 642–74 (p. 674).

23. See Julia Annas and Jonathan Barnes, *The Modes of Scepticism* (Cambridge: Cambridge University Press, 1985), ch. 3 for a good survey of the standard modes of skeptical argument.

24. St. Augustine discusses Varro's view in *The City of God*, XIX.1.

25. In *Art of Living*, ch. 4 Nehamas stresses the individualism of Montaigne's search for the good.

26. Seneca, *Ep.* LXXI.6, 23.

27. Seneca, *Ep.* L.6.

28. Sebond's *Book of Creatures* is not the "quintessence extracted from St. Thomas Aquinas" that Turnebus told Montaigne it was (II.12, *F*321, *V*440). But action-guiding laws of nature as Aquinas thought of them

were ordained by God as suitable to beings with our specific nature. Sebond's views are close enough to those of Aquinas on the relation between natural law and human nature for Montaigne's critique of the former to make unnecessary a separate examination of the latter.

29. See Comte-Sponville, *"Je ne suis pas philosophe,"* for an insightful account of the politically and religiously urgent anti-dogmatism that is what Montaigne's so-called skepticism really amounted to.

30. Thomas Hobbes, *Leviathan*, ed. Richard Tuck (Cambridge: Cambridge University Press, 1991), I.XI, p. 70.

31. *Leviathan*, I.xv. Cf. John Locke, *An Essay concerning Human Understanding*, ed. Peter H. Nidditch (Oxford: Oxford University Press, 1975): "The Mind has a different relish, as well as the Palate; and you will as fruitlessly endeavor to delight all Men with Riches or Glory (which yet some men place their Happiness in) as you would to satisfy all Men's Hunger with Cheese or Lobsters . . . Hence it was, I think, that the Philosophers of old did in vain enquire, whether the *Summum Bonum* consisted in Riches, or bodily Delights, or Virtue, or Contemplation: And they might have as reasonably disputed, whether the best Relish were to be found in Apples, Plumbs, or Nuts" (II.xxi, p. 269).

32. Bentham's theory is set out in his *Introduction to the Principles of Morals and Legislation* (1789), of which there are many editions.

33. For Kant, see J. B. Schneewind, *The Invention of Autonomy* (Cambridge: Cambridge University Press, 1998), ch. 25 and references. In the present chapter I rely heavily on the material I present in the book.

34. Hume's general view is given in his *Treatise of Human Nature*, (1739–40). He discusses the origins of religion in his *Natural History of Religion* (1757), and analyzes arguments about God in the *Dialogues concerning Natural Religion* (1779).

35. See Schneewind, *Invention of Autonomy*, ch. 7 for discussion of and references to Pufendorf.

36. For Montaigne on this point see 1.32, *F*160, *V*216; II.12, *F*369, 389–90, 392–3, *V*499, 523–4, 527–8.

37. For Kant's views see Schneewind, *Invention of Autonomy*, chs. 22–3.

# BIBLIOGRAPHY

## WORKS BY MONTAIGNE

*The Complete Essays of Montaigne*, trans. Donald M. Frame (Stanford: Stanford University Press, 1958).

*The Complete Works of Montaigne*, trans. Donald M. Frame (Stanford: Stanford University Press, 1957).

*An Apology for Raymond Sebond*, trans. and ed. Michael A. Screech. (London: Penguin, 1987).

*Essais*, ed. Pierre Villey, rev. Verdun-L. Saulnier (Paris: Presses Universitaires de France, 1965); repr. in the series Quadrige.

*The Essays of Michel de Montaigne*, trans. Michael A. Screech (London: Allen Lane, 1991).

*Journal de voyage*, ed. François Rigolot (Paris: Presses Universitaires de France, 1992).

## SELECTIVE CRITICAL BIBLIOGRAPHY

Abel, Günter, *Stoizismus und frühe Neuzeit* (Berlin: De Gruyter, 1978).

Algra, Keimpe, Jonathan Barnes, Jaap Mansfield, and Malcolm Schofield, eds., *The Cambridge History of Hellenistic Philosophy* (Cambridge: Cambridge University Press, 1999).

Annas, Julia, and Jonathan Barnes, *The Modes of Scepticism* (Cambridge: Cambridge University Press, 1985).

Annas, Julia, "Plato the Sceptic," in James C. Klagge and Nicholas D. Smith, eds., *Methods of Interpreting Plato and his Dialogues* (Oxford: Oxford University Press, 1992), pp. 43–72.

Arnould, Jean-Claude, ed., *Montaigne: La justice*, special issue of the *Bulletin de la Société des Amis de Montaigne* (2001).

Aulotte, Robert, *Amyot et Plutarque* (Geneva: Droz, 1965).

*Plutarque en France au XVIe siècle* (Paris: Klincksieck, 1971).

Balmas, Enea, ed., *Montaigne e L'Italia: Atti del Congresso Internazionale di studi di Milano-Lecco, 26–30 ottobre 1988* (Geneva: Slatkine, 1991).

Bettoni, Anna, "Cibo e rimedio: I meloni di Montaigne," in Maria Grazia Profeti, ed., *Codici del Gusto* (Verona: Francoangeli, 1992).

Bippus, Hans-Peter, *In der Theologie nicht bewandert: Montaigne und die Theologie* (Tübingen and Basel: Francke Verlag, 2000).

Blair, Ann, *The Theater of Nature: Jean Bodin and Renaissance Science* (Princeton: Princeton University Press, 1997).

Bloom, Harold, ed., *Michel de Montaigne*, Modern Critical Views (New York: Chelsea House, 1987).

Blum, Claude, ed., *Montaigne, "Apologie de Raymond Sebond": De la "Theologia" à la "Théologie."* (Paris: Champion, 1990).

Blumenberg, Hans, *The Legitimacy of the Modern Age*, trans. Robert M. Wallace (Cambridge, MA: MIT Press, 1983).

Boase, Alan, *The Fortunes of Montaigne: A History of the Essays in France, 1580–1669* (London: Methuen, 1935).

Brahami, Frédéric, *Le scepticisme de Montaigne* (Paris: Presses Universitaires de France, 1997).

*Le travail du scepticisme (Montaigne, Bayle, Hume)* (Paris: Presses Universitaires de France, 2001).

and Emmanuel Naya, eds., *Montaigne et l'action*, special issue of the *Bulletin de la Société des Amis de Montaigne*, 8/17–18 (2000).

Briggs, Robin, *Witches and Neighbours: The Social and Cultural Context of European Witchcraft* (London: Fontana, 1996).

Brockliss, Laurence and Colin Jones, *The Medical World of Early Modern France* (Oxford: Oxford University Press, 1997).

Busson, Henri, *Le Rationalisme dans la littérature française de la Renaissance, 1533–1601*, 2nd edn., 1922 (Paris: Vrin, 1957).

Cappelletti, Franco Alberto, *Legge, "coustume," alterità: Lo scetticismo moderno e il diritto* (Naples: Edizioni Scientifiche Italiane, 1989). Publicazioni della Facoltà di Giurisprudenza di Caranzaro, 11.

Carraud, Vincent and Jean-Luc Marion, eds., *Montaigne: scepticisme, métaphysique, théologie* (Paris: Presses Universitaires de France, 2004).

Cave, Terence, *Pré-histoires: Textes troublés au seuil de la modernité* (Geneva: Droz, 1999).

Clark, Stuart, *Thinking with Demons: The Idea of Witchcraft in Early Modern Europe* (Oxford: Oxford University Press, 1997).

Comte-Sponville, André, "Montaigne cynique?," *Revue Internationale de Philosophie*, 181/2 (1992), pp. 234–79.

*"Je ne suis pas philosophe": Montaigne et la philosophie* (Paris: Champion, 1993).

" 'Je ne suis pas philosophe': Montaigne et la philosophie," *Bulletin de la Société des Amis de Montaigne*, 35–6 (1994), pp. 15–27.

Conche, Marcel, *Montaigne et la philosophie*. 2nd edn. (Paris: Presses Universitaires de France, 1993).

*Montaigne ou la conscience heureuse*, 5th edn. (Paris: Presses Universitaires de France, 2002).

Conley, Tom, *The Graphic Unconscious in Early Modern French Writing* (Cambridge: Cambridge University Press, 1992).

"Friendship in a Local Vein: Montaigne's Servitude to La Boétie," *South Atlantic Quarterly*, 97/1 (1998), pp. 65–90.

Coppin, Joseph, *Montaigne traducteur de Raymond Sebond* (Lille: Morel, 1925).

Couturas, Claire, "Repères médiévaux et renaissants vers la *prud'hommie* selon Montaigne," *Réforme, Humanisme, Renaissance*, 56 (June 2003), pp. 41–59.

Cranefield, Paul, "On the Origin of the Phrase 'Nihil est in intellectu quod non prius fuerit in sensu'," *Journal of the History of Medicine*, 25 (1970), pp. 77–80.

Daston, Lorraine, "Can Scientific Objectivity Have a History?" *Alexander von Humboldt Stiftung Mitteilungen*, 75 (2000), pp. 31–40.

Davidson, Donald, *Inquiries into Truth and Interpretation* (Oxford: Oxford University Press, 1984).

Dear, Peter, *Discipline and Experience: The Mathematical Way in the Scientific Revolution* (Chicago and London: University of Chicago Press, 1995).

Defaux, Gérard, ed., *Montaigne: Essays in Reading*, special issue of *Yale French Studies*, 64 (1983), pp. 273–305.

"A propos 'Des Coches' de Montaigne (III, 6): De l'écriture de l'histoire à la représentation du moi," *Montaigne Studies* 6/1–2 (1994), pp. 135–61.

Demonet, Marie-Luce, ed., *Montaigne et la question de l'homme* (Paris: Presses Universitaires de France, 1999).

"Les êtres de raison ou les modes d'être de la littérature," in Eckhard Kessler and Ian Maclean, eds., *Res et Verba in the Renaissance* (Wiesbaden: Harrassowitz, 2002), pp. 177–95.

*A plaisir: Sémiotique et scepticisme dans les "Essais"* (Caen: Paradigme, 2003).

and Alain Legros, eds., *L'écriture du scepticisme chez Montaigne* (Geneva: Droz, 2004).

Desan, Philippe, *L'imaginaire économique de la Renaissance* (Mont-de-Marsan: Editions Interuniversitaires, 1993).

ed., *La Philosophie et Montaigne*, special issue of *Montaigne Studies*, 12 (2000).

ed., *Dictionnaire de Montaigne* (Paris: Champion, 2004).

Desrosiers-Bonin, Diane, *Rabelais et l'humanisme civil* (Geneva: Droz, 1992).

Dewald, Jonathan, *The European Nobility, 1400–1800* (Cambridge: Cambridge University Press, 1996).

Dickason, Olive, *The Myth of the Savage and the Beginnings of French Colonialism in the Americas* (Edmonton: University of Alberta Press, 1997).

Durán Luzio, Juan, "De la immoderación de Hernán Cortés a 'De la moderation' de Michel de Montaigne," *Montaigne Studies*, 6/1–2 (1994).

Duval, Edwin M., "Le Début des *Essais* et la fin d'un livre," *Revue d'Histoire Littéraire de la France*, 88/5 (1988), pp. 896–907.

Eco, Umberto, *A Theory of Semiotics* (Bloomington: University of Indiana Press, 1976).

Frame, Donald, *Montaigne: A Biography* (London: Hamish Hamilton, 1965).

Friedrich, Hugo, *Montaigne*, trans. Dawn Eng, ed. Philippe Desan (Berkeley: University of California Press, 1991).

Fumaroli, Marc, Preface to Michael A. Screech, *Montaigne et la mélancolie* (Paris: Presses Universitaires de France, 1992).

Genicot, Louis, *La Loi* (Brepols: Turnhout, 1977), Typologie des Sources du Moyen Âge Occidental, 22.

Gerbier, Laurent, "Médecine et politique dans l'art machiavélien de la prévision," *Nouvelle Revue du Seizième Siècle*, 21/1 (2003), pp. 25–42.

Gliozzi, Giuliano, *Adamo e il nuovo mondo. La nascità dell'antropologia come ideologia coloniale: dalle genealogie bibliche alle teorie razziali (1500–1700)* (Florence: La Nuova Italia, 1977), trans. Arlette Estève and Pascal Gaberllone, *Adam et le Nouveau Monde. La naissance de l'anthropologie comme idéologie coloniale: Des généalogies bibliques aux théories raciales (1500–1700)* (Lecques: Théétète, 2000).

Goyet, Francis, "La prudence: entre sublime et raison d'Etat," in Isabelle Cogitore and Francis Goyet, eds., *Devenir roi: Essais sur la littérature adressée au Prince* (Grenoble: Ellug, 2001), pp. 163–78.

"Humilité de l'essai? (Réflexions sur Montaigne)," in P. Glaudes, ed., *L'essai: métamorphoses d'un genre* (Toulouse: Presses Universitaires du Mirail, 2002), pp. 201–15.

"La notion éthique d'habitude dans les *Essais*: articuler l'art et la nature," *Modern Language Notes*, 118 (2003), pp. 1070–91.

Gray, Floyd, *Montaigne bilingue: Le latin des "Essais,"* (Paris: Champion, 1991).

Greene, Thomas, *The Light in Troy: Imitation and Discovery in Renaissance Poetry* (New Haven: Yale University Press, 1982).

Guerrier, Olivier, *Quand "les poètes feignent": "Fantasie" et fiction dans les "Essais" de Montaigne* (Paris: Champion, 2003).

Guilhiermoz, Pierre, *Enquêtes et procès: Etude sur la procédure et le fonctionnement du Parlement au XVIe siècle, suivie du style de la Chambre des Enquêtes* (Paris: Alphonse Picard, 1892).

Hacking, Ian, *Why Does Language Matter to Philosophy?* (Cambridge: Cambridge University Press, 1975).

*The Emergence of Probability* (Cambridge: Cambridge University Press, 1995).

Hadot, Pierre, *What is Ancient Philosophy?* trans. Michael Chase (Cambridge, MA: Harvard University Press, 2002).

Hale, J. R., *War and Society in Renaissance Europe 1450–1620* (Baltimore: Johns Hopkins University Press, 1985).

Hampton, Timothy, *Writing from History: The Rhetoric of Exemplarity in Renaissance Literature* (Ithaca: Cornell University Press, 1990).

Hartle, Ann, *Michel de Montaigne: Accidental Philosopher* (Cambridge: Cambridge University Press, 2003).

Hendrick, Philip, *Montaigne et Sebond: L'Art de la traduction* (Paris: Champion, 1996).

Henry, Patrick, ed., *Montaigne and Ethics*, special issue of *Montaigne Studies*, 14 (2002).

Hoffmann, George, *Montaigne's Career* (Oxford: Oxford University Press, 1998).

"Emond Auger et le contexte tridentin de l'essai 'Du repentir,'" *Bulletin de la Société des Amis de Montaigne*, 8/21–2 (2001), pp. 263–75.

"Anatomy of the Mass: Montaigne's 'Cannibals,'" *Publications of the Modern Language Association of America*, 117/2 (March 2002), pp. 207–21.

Huppert, George, *Les bourgeois gentilshommes: An Essay on the Definition of Elites in Renaissance France* (Chicago: University of Chicago Press, 1977).

*The Style of Paris: Renaissance Origins* (Bloomington: Indiana University Press, 1999).

Jeanneret, Michel, *Perpetuum mobile: Métamorphoses des corps et des oeuvres de Vinci à Montaigne* (Paris: Macula, n.d).

Jouanna, Arlette, *Le devoir de révolte: La noblesse française et la gestation de l'état moderne, 1559–1661* (Paris: Fayard, 1989).

*La France du XVIe siècle 1483–1598* (Paris: Presses Universitaires de France, 1996).

Kelley, Donald R., *The Beginning of Ideology: Consciousness and Society in the French Reformation* (Cambridge: Cambridge University Press, 1981).

Langer, Ullrich, *Divine and Poetic Freedom in the Renaissance: Nominalist Theology and Literature in France and Italy* (Princeton: Princeton University Press, 1990).

"Montaigne's Customs," *Montaigne Studies*, 4 (1992), pp. 81–96.

*Perfect Friendship: Studies in Literature and Moral Philosophy from Boccaccio to Corneille* (Geneva: Droz, 1994).

*Vertu du discours, discours de la vertu: Littérature et philosophie morale au XVIe siècle en France* (Geneva: Droz, 1999).

ed., *Au-delà de la* Poétique: *Aristote et la littérature de la Renaissance / Beyond the* Poetics: *Aristotle and Early Modern Literature* (Geneva: Droz, 2002).

Le Gall, Jean-Marie, "Réformer l'Eglise catholique aux XVe–XVIIe siècles: restaurer, rénover, innover?" *Réforme, Humanisme, Renaissance*, 56 (2003), pp. 61–75.

Legros, Alain, "Michaelis Montani annotationes decem: Le *Giraldus* de Montaigne et autres livres annotés de sa main," *Journal de la Renaissance*, 1 (2000), pp. 13–88.

Lévi-Strauss, Claude, *Histoire de lynx* (Paris: Plon, 1992).

Long, A. A., *Hellenistic Philosophy: Stoics, Epicureans, Sceptics* (London: Duckworth, 1974).

Long, A. A. and D. N. Sedley, *The Hellenistic Philosophers*, vol. 1 (Cambridge: Cambridge University Press, 1987).

Lories, Danielle, *Le sens commun et le jugement du* phronimos: *Aristote et les Stoïciens* (Louvain-la-Neuve: Peeters, 1998).

Maclean, Ian, "The Place of Interpretation: Montaigne and Humanist Jurists on Words, Intentions and Meaning," in Graham Castor and Terence Cave, eds., *Neo-Latin and the Vernacular in Renaissance France* (Oxford: Oxford University Press, 1984), pp. 252–72.

*Interpretation and Meaning in the Renaissance: The Case of Law* (Cambridge: Cambridge University Press, 1992).

*Montaigne philosophe* (Paris: Presses Universitaires de France, 1996).

*Logic, Signs and Nature in the Renaissance: The Case of Learned Medicine* (Cambridge: Cambridge University Press, 2001).

McKinley, Mary, *Words in a Corner: Studies in Montaigne's Latin Quotations* (Lexington, KY: French Forum, 1981).

*Les terrains vagues des "Essais"* (Paris: Champion, 1995).

Ménager, Daniel, "La culture héroïque de Montaigne," *Bulletin de la Société des Amis de Montaigne*, 8/9–10 (1998), pp. 39–52.

Merleau-Ponty, Maurice, *Signs*, trans. Richard C. McCleary (Evanston: Northwestern University Press, 1964).

Metschies, Michael, *La citation et l'art de citer dans les "Essais" de Montaigne*, trans. Jules Brody (Paris: Champion, 1997).

Miernowski, Jan, *L'ontologie de la contradiction sceptique: Pour l'étude de la métaphysique des* Essais (Paris: Champion, 1998).

Millet, Olivier, *La Première réception des Essais de Montaigne (1580–1640)* (Paris: Champion, 1995).

Muchembled, Robert, *Sorcières, justice et société aux XVIe et XVIIe siècles* (Paris: Imago, 1987).

Nakam, Géralde, *Les Essais de Montaigne miroir et procès de leur temps. Témoignage historique et création littéraire* (Paris: Nizet, 1984).

*Montaigne: la manière et la matière* (Paris: Klincksieck, 1992).

Naya, Emmanuel, *"La loy de pure obeïssance": Le pyrrhonisme à l'essai chez Montaigne* (Paris: Champion, 2004).

"De la *médiocrité* à la *mollesse*: prudence montaignienne," in Emmanuel Naya, ed., *Polysémie sur la médiocrité au XVIe siècle* (Paris: Presses de l'Ecole Normale Supérieure, forthcoming).

Nehamas, Alexander, *The Art of Living* (Berkeley: University of California Press, 1998).

Neuschel, Kristen B., *Word of Honor: Interpreting Noble Culture in Sixteenth-Century France* (Ithaca: Cornell University Press, 1986).

Oakeshott, Michael, *On Human Conduct* (Oxford: Oxford University Press, 1975).

*Religion, Politics and the Moral Life*, ed. Timothy Fuller (New Haven: Yale University Press, 1993).

O'Brien, John, "The Eye Perplexed. Aristotle and Montaigne on Seeing and Choosing," *Journal of Medieval and Renaissance Studies*, 22/2 (1992), pp. 291–305.

"Reasoning with the Senses: The Humanist Imagination," in Philippe Desan and Ullrich Langer, eds., *Reason, Reasoning, and Literature in the Renaissance*, special issue of the *South Central Review*, 10/2 (1993), pp. 3–19.

O'Brien, John, Malcom Quainton and James J. Supple, eds., *Montaigne et la rhétorique* (Paris: Champion, 1995).

Ostreicht, Gerhart, *Neostoicism and the Early Modern State* (Cambridge: Cambridge University Press, 1982).

Ozment, Steven, *The Age of Reform 1250–1550: An Intellectual and Religious History of Late Medieval and Reformation Europe* (New Haven: Yale University Press, 1980).

Park, Katherine, "Natural Particulars: Medical Epistemology Practice, and the Literature of Healing Springs," in Anthony Grafton and Nancy G. Siraisi, eds., *Natural Particulars: Nature and the Disciplines in Renaissance Europe* (Cambridge, MA: MIT Press, 1999), pp. 347–67.

Penelhum, Terence, *God and Skepticism: A Study in Skepticism and Fideism* (Dordrecht: D. Reidel Publishing Company, 1983).

"Skepticism and Fideism," in Myles Burnyeat, ed., *The Skeptical Tradition* (Berkeley: University of California Press, 1983).

Perrier, Simone, "Le subjectif et l'irréfutable: Montaigne et la peine de mort," *Cahiers Textuel*, 34/44, 2 (1986), pp. 45–54.

Popkin, Richard, *The History of Scepticism from Erasmus to Spinoza* (Berkeley: University of California Press, 1979).

*The History of Scepticism from Savonarola to Bayle* (New York and Oxford: Oxford University Press, 2003).

Quine, W. V., *Word and Object* (Cambridge, MA: M.I.T. Press, 1960).

Quint, David, *Montaigne and the Quality of Mercy: Ethical and Political Themes in the* Essais (Princeton: Princeton University Press, 1998).

Rosolato, Guy, *La relation d'inconnu* (Paris: Gallimard, 1978).

*Eléments de l'interprétation* (Paris: Gallimard, 1986).

Salmon, John H. M., *Society in Crisis: France in the Sixteenth Century* (London: Benn, 1975).

Saunders, Jason L., *Justus Lipsius: The Philosophy of Renaissance Stoicism* (New York: Liberal Arts Press, 1955).

Schmitt, Charles B., "Experience and Experiment: A Comparison of Zabarella's View with Galileo's in *De motu*," *Studies in the Renaissance*, 16 (1969), pp. 80–138.

"The Rediscovery of Ancient Skepticism in Modern Times," in Myles Burnyeat, ed., *The Skeptical Tradition* (Berkeley: University of California Press, 1983), pp. 226–37.

Schmitt, Charles B., and Quentin Skinner, eds., *The Cambridge History of Renaissance Philosophy* (Cambridge: Cambridge University Press, 1988).

Schneewind, J. B., *The Invention of Autonomy* (Cambridge: Cambridge University Press, 1998).

Screech, Michael A., *Montaigne and Melancholy: The Wisdom of the "Essays"* (London: Duckworth, 1983).

ed., *Montaigne's Annotated Copy of Lucretius: A Transcription and Study of the Manuscript, Notes and Pen-Marks* (Geneva: Droz, 1998).

Sedley, David, "The Motivation of Greek Skepticism," in Myles Burnyeat, ed., *The Skeptical Tradition* (Berkeley: University of California Press, 1983), pp. 9–10.

Serres, Michel, *La Naissance de la physique dans le texte de Lucrèce: Fleuves et turbulences* (Paris: Editions de Minuit, 1977).

Shapiro, Barbara J., *Probability and Certainty in Seventeenth-Century England: A Study in the Relationships between Natural Science, Religion, History, Law, and Literature* (Princeton: Princeton University Press, 1983).

Siraisi, Nancy G., *Medieval and Early Renaissance Medicine: An Introduction to Knowledge and Practice* (Chicago: University of Chicago Press, 1990).

Starobinski, Jean, *Montaigne en mouvement* (Paris: Gallimard, 1982).

Supple, James J., *Arms versus Letters: The Military and Literary Ideals in the "Essais" of Montaigne* (Oxford: Oxford University Press, 1984).

Taylor, Charles, *Sources of the Self: The Making of the Modern Identity* (Cambridge, MA: Harvard University Press, 1989).

Thibaudet, Albert, *Montaigne*, ed. Floyd Gray (Paris: Gallimard, 1963).

Tournon, André, *Montaigne: La glose et l'essai* (Lyon: Presses Universitaires, 1983).

"L'argumentation pyrrhonienne: Structures d'essai dans le chapitre 'Des boyteux'," in Françoise Charpentier and Simone Perrier, eds., *Montaigne: Les derniers essais. Cahiers Textuel*, 2 (1986), pp. 73–85.

*Essais de Montaigne: Livre III* (Paris: Atlande, 2003).

Traverso, Edilia, *Montaigne e Aristotele* (Florence: Le Monnier, 1974).

Trinquet, Roger, *La jeunesse de Montaigne: Ses origines familiales, son enfance et ses études* (Paris: Nizet, 1972).

Villey, Pierre, *Les Sources et l'évolution des "Essais" de Montaigne*, 2 vols. (Paris: Hachette, 1933).

Walton, Craig, "Montaigne on the Art of Judgment: The Trial of Montaigne," in Richard A. Watson and James E. Force, eds., *The Sceptical Mode in Modern Philosophy: Essays in Honor of Richard Popkin* (Dordrecht: Martinus Nijhoff Publishers, 1988).

Wilson, N. L., "Substance without Substrata," *Review of Metaphysics*, 12 (1959), pp. 521–39.

Woodruff, Paul, "The Sceptical Side of Plato's Method," *Revue Internationale de Philosophie*, 156–7 (1986), pp. 22–37.

Zeller, E., *The Stoics, Epicureans and Sceptics*, trans. Oswald J. Reichel (London: Longmans, Green, and Co., 1892).

# INDEX

Abel, Günter 25
absolutist political theory 12–13
Academics, Academy (philosophical
  school) 72, 143, 183, 186
accidental, unpremeditated thought
  192, 199
Aenesidemus 183
"Affaire des placards" 10
agnostic 191
Albi 14
alchemy 170
Alciati 97
Alençon, François d' 12
Alexander VI (Pope) 87
Alexander the Great 33, 66, 126,
  128
Algra, Keimpe 225
Almquist, Katherine 97, 114, 115
Amerindians 88, 91
Amyot, Jacques 31, 171
Annas, Julia 72, 227
antiquity (see also classical philosophy)
  4, 6, 74, 126
  Montaigne's relation to 53
  as textual presence in the Essays 54–8
  provides models of conduct 65–9
Antony 22
Arcesilaus 183
Argenterio, Giovanni 166
Aristotle, Aristotelianism 2, 42, 50, 55,
  59, 67, 79, 87, 126, 128, 131, 138,
  139, 143, 144, 145, 146, 148, 152,
  155, 156, 157, 168, 170, 175, 176,
  186, 214, 227
  De anima 161
  Metaphysics 176

Nicomachean Ethics 118, 126, 128,
  129, 130, 135, 138, 139, 140, 156,
  207
Physics 165, 166
Posterior Analytics 163, 165
art (technique) (see also nature) 121
arts (disciplines) and practical
  philosophy 153–7
atheism 29, 44, 51, 191, 200, 202
atoms 173
Attaualpa 88, 89, 90
Aubert, Jacques 163, 178
Aubigné, Agrippa d' 13
Augustine (St.) 63, 204, 212, 216
  City of God 204, 227
Aulotte, Robert 70
Avicenna 170
Aztecs 84, 94

Bacon, Francis 147
Baldus 98, 117
Balsamo, Jean 123
Balzac, Guez de 47
barbarity 78, 84
Barclay, William 13
Barnes, Jonathan 227
Bartlett, Robert 181
Bartolus 98
Belon, Pierre 163, 167, 180
Bentham 220
Béranger, Guillaume 190
Bettoni, Anna 180
Bible 10, 25, 33, 74, 161, 185, 209, 224
Billacois, François 25
Biloghi, Dominique 23
Bippus, Hans-Peter, 226

Blair, Ann 179
Blumenberg, Hans 182
Boaistuau, Pierre 163, 178
Boase, Alan 51, 52
Bodin, Jean 12, 13, 19, 100, 101, 163,
    164, 165, 168, 177, 178, 179, 193
body (see also medicine) 1–2
Boethius 155
Boiceau de la Borderie, Jean 103
Bonnefon 114
book
    as index of good faith 35–6
    ethical aim of 119
    presence of author in 39
Boragina, Piero 50
Bordeaux 5, 9, 14, 22, 23, 56, 97, 99,
    114, 122, 123, 166
Borro, Girolamo 166
Boucher, Jacqueline 23
Boucher, Jean 24
bourgeoisie in the sixteenth century
    15–16
Boutcher, Warren 4
Bouwsma, William J. 23
Brach, Pierre de 42, 51
Braden, Gordon 25
Brague, Rémi 182
Brahami, Frédéric 70, 158, 201, 206
Braun, Georg 94
Brazil 78
Briçonnet, Guillaume 10
Briggs, Robin 71
Brockliss, Laurence 180
Bruès, Guy de 208, 226
Bry, Théodore de 95
Budé, Guillaume 45
Bunel, Pierre 44, 46
Burin, Pierre 167
Busson, Henri 177

Cabral 93
Caduveo Indians 92
Caesar 22, 33, 39, 66, 67, 72, 88, 128
Cahors 23
Caldari Bevilacqua, Franca 50
Calpurnius 87
Calvin, John (see also Calvinism,
    Huguenot, Protestant) 10, 23
Calvinism (see also Calvin, Huguenot,
    Protestant) 10, 48

Camus, Jean-Pierre (bishop) 137
Canephius, Baruch 178
Capuano, Alvise 172
Caribbean 81
Carneades 64, 65, 72, 106, 183, 187
Carpenter, Richard 178
Carthaginians 79
Cartier, Jacques 75
Catherine de' Medici 12, 14, 23
Catholic, Catholic Church 9, 10, 11, 12,
    13, 14, 15, 23, 35, 41, 42, 43, 46, 47,
    48, 93, 123, 133, 134, 137, 141, 186,
    200, 209, 217, 226
Cato the Younger 66, 67, 126, 127, 137,
    217
Catullus 55, 58
causality (see Lucretius, medicine)
Cave, Terence 69, 70
Céard, Jean 138, 140, 177, 180
censorship of the Essays 172
Cesalpino, Andrea 178
Charlemagne 17
Charles V 130
Charles IX 11, 14, 81, 82
Christian theology, Christianity (see
    also faith) 21, 28, 42, 75, 164, 167,
    185, 187, 191, 204, 209, 217, 218,
    223, 224
Chrysippus 193
Chrysostom, St. 226
Cicero 21, 55, 68, 106, 112, 132, 134,
    153, 175, 196, 207, 216
    Academica 184
    [pseudo-] Ad Herennium 118
    De inventione 118, 131
    De natura deorum 173
    De officiis 112
    Orator 137
Clark, Stuart 71
classical philosophy (see also moral
    philosophy)
    Montaigne's relation to 59–65
Cleirac, Etienne 100, 115
Clément, Jacques 12
Clitomachus 72, 186
Collingwood, R. G. 158
Columbus, Christopher 74, 75, 78, 93
Comte-Sponville, André 215, 227, 228
Conche, Marcel 181
Condé, Henri de 11, 12

Conley, Tom 5, 95
conservatism (Montaigne's) 118, 119,
    157, 195
contraries, resolved by time 154
Conti, François de 11
Cook, Harold J. 179
Copernicus 145
Coppin, Joseph 226, 227
Coquille, Guy 102
Cortez, Hernando 84, 85
Cotgrave 138
Couzinet, Marie-Dominique 140
Coutras (battle of) 11, 23
Couturas, Claire 139
cowardice (see "softness")
Cranefield, Paul 159
credulity (Montaigne's) 190,
    192
Crespet, Pierre 164
Crouzet, Denis 24
Cujas, Jacques 97
curiosity cabinet 165
custom (see law)
Cuzco 88

Daston, Lorraine 142
Davidson, Donald 160
Davidson, Nicholas 181
Dear, Peter 159
decision-making, chronology of
    130–1
Defaux, Gérard 95
definition (see law, science)
Demades 144
Democritus 160
Demonet, Marie-Luce 70,
    160
Desan, Philippe 25, 161
Descartes 4, 27, 177, 189
Desrosiers-Bonin, Diane 140
Dewald, Jonathan 24
Dickason, Olive 95
Diderot 81
Diodorus Siculus 55, 172
Diogenes Laertius 55, 60, 208
    Life of Pyrrho 183, 184
director of conscience, Montaigne as
    135
distinguo 150, 154
dogmatic skepticism 42
dogmatism 42, 107, 143, 186

Dorandi, Tiziano 227
Dordogne river 79
Du Bellay, Joachim 124
    Defense and illustration of the French
        language 134, 135
Dubois, Jacques 166, 169, 170, 179
duel 18–19
Du Moulin, Charles 25
Dupèbe, Jean 179
Du Plessis de Mornay, Philippe 41, 42,
    47, 48, 51, 168
Durán Luzio, Juan 94, 95
Du Tilh, Arnaud 116
Du Vair, Guillaume 21, 164, 172
Duval, Edwin M. 180

Eco, Umberto 160
economy in the sixteenth century 16
education, early 218
Eliot, T. S. 204, 206
England 11
Epaminondas 66, 217
Epictetus 21, 208
Epicurus, Epicureans (see also Lucretius)
    3, 7, 51, 60, 72, 160, 171, 186, 196,
    207, 214, 215, 216, 217, 225
equity 6, 105, 112, 156
Erasmus 34
Erler, Michael 227
essay 3, 127, 199
Essays (passages discussed or referred
    to)
    "To the Reader" (prologue) 32, 35, 36,
        74, 92, 123, 137, 160
    I.1 118, 128, 168, 196, 197, 198
    I.6 72
    I.8 56–7, 109, 135
    I.9 151
    I.10 199
    I.11 199
    I.14 218
    I.18 165
    I.20 215
    I.21 109, 161, 166, 192
    I.22 167
    I.23 22, 25, 100, 101, 102, 108, 195,
        218
    I.24 101, 102, 138, 140
    I.25 36, 50, 122, 139
    I.26 25, 45, 50, 59, 70, 72, 123, 158,
        159, 162, 175, 207, 217, 223

*I.27* 203
*I.28* 47, 53–4, 55, 56, 76, 77, 82, 85, 104, 138, 139, 175, 223
*I.30* 77, 84, 94
*I.31* 77–85, 102, 172
*I.32* 84, 228
*I.35* 140
*I.36* 91
*I.37* 66
*I.40* 32
*I.42* 138
*I.43* 100
*I.44* 2, 72
*I.47* 130
*I.48* 132
*I.50* 49, 128, 136, 173, 199
*I.54* 125, 203
*I.56* 70, 217, 224, 226
*II.1* 127, 160, 196, 197, 198
*II.2* 70, 127, 166, 195, 217
*II.3* 61
*II.4* 31
*II.5* 106, 116
*II.6* 171
*II.8* 25, 104, 167
*II.10* 31, 32, 54, 72, 125, 160, 161, 162, 175, 215
*II.11* 25, 67, 71, 72, 126, 131, 139, 171, 172, 195
*II.12* (see also Sebond, natural theology) 1, 2, 6, 28, 29, 30, 32, 40, 41, 42, 43, 45, 48, 51, 59, 60, 61, 62, 64, 65, 67, 70, 71, 72, 76, 90, 99, 101, 102, 104, 107, 118, 120, 132, 138, 139, 140, 143, 146, 155, 156, 157, 158, 159, 160, 161, 162, 163, 165, 166, 167, 170, 171, 173, 174, 176, 183, 184, 185, 186, 187, 188, 189, 190, 191, 192, 193, 194, 196, 200, 201, 202, 203, 204, 208, 213, 214, 216, 218, 221, 223, 224, 225, 228
*II.13* 139
*II.16* 123, 176, 216
*II.17* 34, 103, 158, 159, 160, 171, 195
*II.18* 33, 70, 72, 91, 103, 104, 136, 165
*II.19* 133
*II.25* 169
*II.26* 122, 215
*II.27* 121, 138
*II.28* 72, 85
*II.29* 1, 205, 217
*II.31* 70, 127, 165
*II.32* 193, 228
*II.34* 72
*II.36* 66
*II.37* 31, 33, 96, 132, 160, 166, 169, 170, 171, 172, 218
*III.1* 26, 102, 122, 123, 133, 135, 138, 151, 160, 197–8
*III.2* 111, 112, 126, 134, 135, 138, 139, 158, 159, 173, 217, 219, 223, 224
*III.3* 31, 101, 125, 134, 138, 140, 224
*III.4* 118, 135, 175
*III.5* 31, 57–8, 77, 85, 106, 116, 121, 135, 136, 137, 139, 158, 161, 168, 196, 223, 224
*III.6* 59, 77, 85–90, 94, 101, 102, 134, 159, 171
*III.7* 77, 85, 124
*III.8* 9, 37, 67, 99, 104, 107, 110, 111, 123, 124, 128, 132, 133, 138, 140, 159, 161, 162, 199
*III.9* 1, 22, 32, 35, 70, 76, 94, 102, 104, 109, 111, 113, 119, 133, 135, 137, 138, 139, 158, 161, 173, 194, 195, 215, 217
*III.10* 25, 49, 101, 102, 111, 118, 126, 132, 133, 134, 139, 161, 175, 195
*III.11* 24, 48, 62, 63, 64, 72, 106, 111, 131, 160, 161, 167, 171, 176, 185, 200
*III.12* 16, 21, 22, 32, 49, 50, 59, 64, 65, 66, 67, 68, 69, 72, 94, 99, 120, 121, 138, 140, 160, 163, 170, 219
*III.13* 32, 67, 72, 96, 98, 99, 101, 102, 108, 111, 124, 132, 135, 139, 158, 159, 160, 161, 162, 166, 169, 170, 171, 173, 176, 198
Estienne, Henri 60, 184
ethics (see also moral philosophy) 120, 153, 176
ethics, classical 21, 121
ethnocentrism 83
Euclid 201
excellence (see superiority)
exception 1
exemplarity 219
Eyquem (family) 15
Eyquem, Pierre 34, 43, 44, 45, 46, 47, 49, 52, 185

faith, religious 191, 200, 211
  in dialectic with rationality 201–4
falsity, logical and moral 150–1
familiar 199
fate 173
Febvre, Lucien 93
Fernel, Jean 166
fictional existence 151
fideism (skeptical) 186, 189, 191, 200,
  202
Fioravanti, Leonardo 166
Foix (family) 123
Foix, Diane de 40
Foix, Frédéric de 11, 41
Foix, Jacqueline de 41
Foix, Louis de 123
Foix de Candale, François de 40, 41, 42,
  43, 47, 48, 50, 51, 164
fortune 171, 172
Fotherby, Martin 179
Frame, Donald 51, 140, 158, 166,
  205
François I. 9, 10, 16, 44, 45, 130
Franklin, Julian H. 24
free will 211, 213, 222
Friedrich, Hugo 122, 171
friendship 82, 85, 175
Frisch, Andrea 116
Fuller, Steve 49
Fumaroli, Marc 122, 136, 141

Galen 158, 166, 170, 171, 173, 174
Garonne (river) 22
Gascon 20
Gaukroger, Stephen 182
Geneva 10, 11
Gerbier, Laurent 138
Germany 11
Giocanti 138
Gliozzi, Giuliano 93, 178
Goffart, Walter 93
Gómara, Lopez de 84, 94
good, highest 216, 218, 219, 221
good life (see also moral philosophy)
  207, 208, 214, 215, 217, 224
Goulart, Simon 181
Goyet, Francis 5, 138, 140
Gracian, Baltazar 136
Grammont, Diane de 85
Gray, Floyd 69

Grazoni, Girolamo 172
Greene, Thomas 73
Gregory XIII (Pope) 62
Guerre, Martin 106
Guerre, Pierre 116
Guerrier, Olivier 69
Guicciardini 125
Guise (family) 11, 12
Guyenne (province) 23, 114, 123

Hacking, Ian 160, 181
Hadot, Pierre 182, 227
Hale, J. R. 25
Hampton, Timothy 73
Harrie, Jeanne 51
Hartle, Ann 6
Hendrick, Philip 227
Henri III 11, 12, 13, 19, 134, 172
Henri de Navarre (Henri IV) 11, 13, 14,
  15, 19, 21, 23, 41, 42, 123
Henry VIII (of England) 33, 34, 35, 38
hermeneutic vs. philosophical
  questions 142
"Hermes Trismegistus" 40, 41, 43, 50
Herodotus 55
Hobbes, Thomas 220
Hoffmann, George 6, 23, 49, 93, 123,
  124, 138, 140, 178, 181
Hogenburg 94
Holt, Mack P. 23
Homer 66
"honest" man 125
Horace 55, 56, 57, 66
Hospital, Michel de l' 12
Hotman, François 24, 97
Huguenot (see also Protestant, Calvin,
  Calvinism) 9, 11, 12, 13, 14, 15, 22,
  23, 24, 47
human 223, 224
Hume, David 221, 222, 228
Huppert, George 24, 25, 180
Husserl 27

imperturbability 184, 190, 196, 197,
  198
inconstancy 197, 198
Indies, East 79
Indies, West 87, 91
inflation in the sixteenth century 19
innovation (political or social) 134–5

integrity
  consistency 198
  "prud'hommie" 125
interest and usury in the sixteenth
    century 19
intuition 149
Italy 166

Jacquart, Jean 25
Jeanneret, Michel 70
Jesus Christ 41
Johnson, Thomas 180
Jouanna, Arlette 23, 24, 52
Jones, Colin 180
Joubert, Laurent 166
judgment 4, 5, 121, 127–8, 177, 184,
    190, 194
justice 127
  and personal autonomy 111–13
Justinian (emperor) 97
Juvenal 55, 58

Kant 7, 220–1, 222, 223, 225
Kelley, Donald R. 24
Kent, Dale 50
Kingdon, Robert M. 24
Kraye, Jill 225, 226
Kusukawa, Sachiko 181

La Boétie, Etienne de 6, 13, 47, 48, 53,
    54, 56, 68, 82, 85, 100, 102, 104,
    175
La Croix du Maine 31
Lambin, Denis 164
Langer, Ullrich 70, 94, 182
language, circularity of 149
La Primaudaye, Pierre de 165, 168
La Roche Flavin, Bernard de 114,
    116
Las Casas, Bartolomé de 8, 87
Laudonnière 75
law 5, 144, 145, 153, 154, 157, 222
  and intention 149
  custom 99–102, 218
  definition, legal 154
  judicial practice in Renaissance
      France 102–7
  law in Renaissance France 97–9
  legal inquiry and the Essays 107–11
  Montaigne's critique of 96

natural law (see also nature, laws of)
    167, 218, 219, 220
  Roman law (Corpus iuris civilis) 97,
      98, 99, 112, 115, 161, 217
  "written law" 99–102
Lee, Edward 34
Lefèvre d'Etaples, Jacques 10
Le Gall, Jean-Marie 141
Legros, Alain 179, 180
Lenoble, Robert 177
Leo X (Pope) 34
Lepidus 22
Le Roy, Louis 164
Le Roy Ladurie, Emmanuel 25
Léry, Jean de 13, 80
Le Thiec, Guy 23
Lévi-Strauss, Claude 93, 95
liar paradox 147, 158
liberality (magnificence) 33
liberty (loi) to judge others' opinions
    47–8
Ligue, Catholic 11–12, 13, 23, 102
Limbrick, Elaine 51, 52
Lipsius, Justus 21, 28, 40, 208
Livy 55
Locke, John 228
logic (see also science) 149
  of opposition 149–50
Long, A. A. 205
Lories, Danielle 139
love of God 211, 212
Loyola, Ignatius of 136
Lucan 55, 57, 66
Lucinge, René 164
Lucretius 6, 55, 57, 58, 164
  causality and randomness 171–3
  Montaigne's application of Epicurean
      naturalism 173–7
  Montaigne's edition of 173, 176, 178
Luther, Lutheranism 10, 29, 34, 35, 44,
    47, 48, 185
Lycurgus 80
Lyons 19

Machiavelli, Machiavellianism 5, 12,
    122, 123, 124, 125, 134, 145, 151
  The Prince 134, 135
Maclean, Ian 5, 70, 158, 159, 160, 161,
    162, 171, 181
MacPhail, Eric 182

Magellan 93
*Malcontents* 12
Malestroit 19
management (*mesnagerie*) 133
  domestic management ("economics")
    153, 176
Maniald, Etienne 166
Manilius 66
Marande, Léonard de 139
Marcenaro, Giuseppe 50
Marguerite de Navarre 10
Marguerite de Valois 14, 41, 51
Martial 55, 57, 66
Mattecoulon, Bertrand de 11
Mayenne, Duke of 23
Maximilian (emperor) 40
McKinley, Mary 69
Medici (family) 45
Medici, Cosimo de' 33, 39
medicine, medical practitioners 145,
    163, 166, 172
  and causality, semiology 168–71
mediocrity, middle (see also superiority)
    125, 126, 128
Melanchton, Philip 166
Ménager, Daniel 23, 138, 139, 160
Mercator, Gerard 74
mercifulness 198
Merleau-Ponty 27, 200, 206
Mesmes, Henri de 166
Metschies, Michael 69
Mexico 78
Micard, Claude 51
"Michelade" 14
Millanges, Simon 40, 41
Millet, Olivier 50, 52, 139
Miron des Archiâtres, Marc 172
moderation 185
*monarchomaques* 12, 13
Montesquieu 81
moral perspectivism 173
moral philosophy (see also Sebond) 6–7
  classical moral philosophy 214–17
  Montaigne and 207–25
  Montaigne's response to Sebond's
    moral philosophy 212–14
  versions available in the Renaissance
    207–8
morality, common 219, 220
More, Thomas 34

Moses 41
Moulins, ordinance of 103, 104
Muchembled, Robert 24
Münster, Sebastian 94

Nakam, Géralde 22, 66, 72
Nantes (Edict of) 15
natural reasoning 51, 156, 185
natural theology 143, 163, 168, 200, 202
naturalism (see also Lucretius, medicine
    and causality) 6, 51, 177
  definition of 163–4
nature 185
  as opposed to art 121, 132
  laws of 217–18, 220, 222
Naya, Emmanuel 7, 70, 140
Nehamas, Alexander 207, 227
Nelli a S. Geminiano 116
Nérac 23
Neuschel, Kristen B. 24
Neveux, Hugues 25
New World 4–5, 16, 134, 164, 165, 174
  and self-discovery 75–6
  and nakedness 90–3
Nicholas of Cusa 152, 161
Nietzsche 7, 8
Nîmes 14
Nizolio 140
nobility 121, 127
  definition of 17–18
  Montaigne as nobleman 122–7
non-contradiction, rule of 144

Oakeshott, Michael 199, 205
O'Brien, John 4, 69, 70, 71, 140
Octavius 22
Ortelius, Abraham 74
Ostreicht, Gerhart 25
Otho (emperor) 2
Ovid 55, 131
Ozment, Steven 23

Pacard, Georges 168
Palestine 79
Palissy, Bernard 165, 179
Palinurus 134
Papacy 45
Paracelsus 145, 166
Paré, Ambroise 163, 167
Paris 1, 11, 14, 23, 166

Park, Katherine 180
Pascal 27
Pasquier, Estienne 12, 47,
    180
*patron*, meaning of 32–4
peasants and rural life 20–1
Pelletier, Monique 93
Penelhum, Terence 205
Périgueux 5, 96, 114
Peripatetics 71, 186
Perissin, Jean 14
Persius 55
Peru 78, 89
Peter of Cornwall 172
Phillip II (of Spain) 33
Pichot, Pierre 166
Pizarro 88, 89
Plantin, Christopher 33, 41
Plato 2, 59, 67, 79, 80, 151, 172, 176,
    183, 207
    *Laws* 207
    *Republic* 207
Platter, Felix 166
pleasure 214, 215, 219, 220
Pliny 204
Plutarch 2, 40, 43, 48, 50, 51, 55, 65, 66,
    70, 72, 127, 144, 171, 190, 193, 207,
    215
    as patron-author 31–2
politics 153
politics and morality 124, 151
*Politiques* 12, 21
Pomian, Krzysztof 179
Pompey 22
Pomponazzi 177
Popelinière, Lancelot de la 89, 95
Popkin, R. H. 158, 205
Port Royal (*Logique*) 190
possible worlds 151
Postel, Guillaume 93
post-modern interpretations of
    Montaigne 119, 120, 136
practical, pragmatic philosophy
    (see arts)
Pre-Socratics 60
pride 121
Propertius 55
Protagoras 152
Protestant (see also Huguenot, Calvin,
    Calvinism) 11, 14, 15, 41, 102, 168

prudence 5
    definition of 118
    Montaigne as a "prudent" man
        127–32
    of the Prince 128–9
Ptolemy 74, 93
Pufendorf, Samuel 222
Pyrrho and Pyrrhonism (see also
    skepticism) 1, 3, 5, 42, 43, 59–65,
        66, 67, 70, 72, 99, 104, 106, 107,
        119, 120, 127, 143, 153, 157, 183,
        184, 187, 188, 190, 191, 205, 217
Pyrrhus 78
Pythagoras, Pythagorean 66, 146

Quine, W. V. 160
Quint, David 25, 119, 120, 122, 126,
    127, 136, 137
Quintilian 129, 131
Quito 88

Rabelais 125
Rabot d'Illins, Ennemond 139
Raemond, Florimond de 41, 51
*raison d'Etat* 128
Reformation, Reformers 23, 28, 29, 34,
    42, 185, 186
    and the printed book 34
relativism 218
Renaissance philosophy (see also moral
    philosophy) 2, 5–6, 145
René of Sicily 34
rhetorician, Montaigne as 135, 136
Rigolot, François 51, 52
Rome 88, 124
Rondelet, Guillaume 163, 166
Rosolato, Guy 93
Rouen 81, 82, 84
ruling pattern (*forme maîtresse*) 224

Sales, François de 137
Salmon, J. H. M. 23
Sancerre 13
Saulnier, Verdun-L. 190, 196
Saunders, Jason L. 26
Savoy, Duke of 11
Scaliger, Joseph 40
Scaliger, Julius Caesar 159
Schmitt, Charles B. 159, 205
Schneewind, J. B. 6, 7, 228

Schofield, Malcolm 227
scholastic 147, 148
schools (of philosophy) 215
Schopenhauer 8
science
    certainty of scientific knowledge,
        Montaigne's critique of 145–7
    definition, scientific, Montaigne's
        critique of 147–9
    vs. opinion 145
Scipio Aemilianus 66
Screech, M. A. 49, 141, 205
Sebond, Raymond (see also natural
    theology, Essays II.12) 6, 27, 29, 30,
    31, 41, 42, 44, 45, 46, 49, 52, 143,
    185, 186, 191, 200, 201, 202, 203,
    208, 212, 217, 222, 223, 224, 226,
    227
    history of Sebond's translation 29–30
    moral philosophy in Sebond's book
        209–12
Sedley, D. N. 205
self, self-portraiture, self-diagnosis,
    self-discovery 2–3, 155, 169, 192,
    200
self-interest 220
self-knowledge 190, 198–9
self-love 212
Sellevold, Kirsti 71
Seneca 7, 21, 40, 50, 55, 70, 144, 207,
    214, 215, 216, 217, 223, 227
senses, sense epistemology 146, 188–9
Sepúlveda, Juan Gomez de 87
Serres, Michel 182
Serres, Olivier de 20
Sève, Bernard 138
Sextus Empiricus 3, 47, 60, 62, 71, 106,
    143, 147, 158, 159, 161, 182, 184,
    208
    Adversus mathematicos 184
    Outlines of Pyrrhonism 184, 205
sexuality 224
Shakespeare 163
Shapiro, Barbara J. 181
Simonin, Michel 52
sincerity 142, 151
Siraisi, Nancy G. 182
skepticism (see also Pyrrho, Pyrrhonism)
    6, 66, 72, 127, 143, 152, 153, 163,
    165, 208, 214, 217, 218, 225, 228

in antiquity 183–4
and the Essays 183–204
Montaigne as skeptic 184–9
non-skeptical features of Montaigne's
    thought 189–91
skillfulness, skillful man 125
Socrates 40, 43, 59, 67–9, 126, 127, 183,
    190, 198, 199, 207, 217, 219
"softness" (mollesse, mollitia) 120,
    121
Soissons, Charles de 11
Spain, Spanish 11, 16, 76, 84, 85, 87, 88,
    89, 90, 185
Starobinski, Jean 119, 159, 169
St. Bartholomew's massacre 14, 23,
    167
Stoicism, Stoics 6, 7, 21, 60, 65, 72, 120,
    123, 126, 139, 173, 186, 196, 207,
    208, 214, 215, 217, 218, 225
subjectivism 218, 219, 220
superiority and mediocrity 125–6,
    128
Supple, James J. 24
Switzerland 166
syllogism 147, 158

Tacitus 55
Tahureau, Jacques 208, 226
Taylor, Charles 7
Terence 55
Thales 40
Thevet, André 80, 81
Thibaudet, Albert 93
Thomas, Simon 166
Thomas Aquinas (St.) 30, 122, 130, 131,
    136, 138, 227
Thou, Jacques-Auguste de 172
Timon 183
topics, argumentation by 155–6
Tortorel, Jacques 14
Toulouse 14, 29, 106, 166
Tourette, Alexandre de la 19
Tournon, André 5, 7, 71, 115, 119, 120,
    122, 139, 159
travel 176
Travel Journal (Journal de voyage) of
    Montaigne 50, 54, 166
Traverso, Edilia 70, 157
Trent, Council of 19, 136
Tribonian 97

Trinquet, Roger 23, 96, 179
truth
  definition of 142
  as property of things (*veritas simplex*)
    and of propositions (*veritas
    complex*) 151–3, 157
Tupinamba 78, 80, 81, 84
Turnèbe [Turnebus], Adrien 29, 30, 139,
  227

Ulpian 98
unfamiliar 193
United Provinces 11
universal statements, universality 1, 3,
  150, 156, 218
  general vs. particular 156
University of Montpellier 166
University of Paris 10
University of Toulouse 144

Valet, Antoine 166
Valladolid 87
valor, courage 120, 121, 127
variety of desires, aims and interests
  218, 219, 220, 221
Varro 216, 227
Vasoli, Cesare 225

Vatican library 33, 35, 40
Verrazano, Giovanni da 75
Verstegen, Richard 93
Vian, Nello 50
Villegagnon 75, 78
Villey, Pierre 71, 93, 123, 190, 196, 225,
  226
Virgil 55, 57, 58, 66, 128
virtue 120, 121, 125, 127, 212
  habit (*habitus*) of 131
Voltaire 81
Vuillemin, Jules 182

Wallace, William A. 179
Walton, Craig 205
wars of religion 10–15, 122
White, Nicholas 226
Wilson, N. L. 160
Woodruff, Paul 72
Wolsey (Cardinal) 35

Xenophon 66, 72, 207

Zeller, E. 205
Zeller, Gaston 23
Ziletus 116
Zwinger, Theodor 166